D1139543

The ULTIMATE Book of
COOKING
Hints & Tips

The ULTIMATE Book of
COOKING
Hints & Tips

Christine France

DORLING KINDERSLEY

LONDON • NEW YORK • STUTTGART • MOSCOW

A DORLING KINDERSLEY BOOK

Project Editors Judy Garlick, Jo Richardson
Project Art Editor Sarah Hall
Editor Colette Connolly
Designer Helen Benfield
Series Art Editor Jayne Carter
Managing Editor Stephanie Jackson
Managing Art Editor Nigel Duffield
Senior Managing Editor Krystyna Mayer
Senior Managing Art Editor Lynne Brown
Production Controller Sarah Coltman
DTP Designer Jason Little

First published in Great Britain in 1997
by Dorling Kindersley Limited,
9 Henrietta Street,
London WC2E 8PS

Copyright © 1997
Dorling Kindersley Limited, London

Visit us on the World Wide Web at
http://www.dk.com

All rights reserved. No part of this publication
may be reproduced, stored in a retrieval
system, or transmitted in any form or by any
means, electronic, mechanical, photocopying,
recording, or otherwise, without the prior
permission of the copyright owner.

A CIP catalogue record for this book is available
from the British Library

ISBN 0 7513 0378 X

Reproduced by Chroma Graphics, Singapore
Printed and bound in Italy by Lego

CONTENTS

INTRODUCTION 6

KITCHEN EQUIPMENT 10

PREPARED INGREDIENTS 30

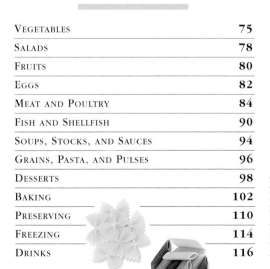

INTRODUCTION

*T*HERE IS NO SECRET RECIPE FOR GOOD COOKING, *but by learning some of the helpful tips and tricks in this book you will be able to prepare and cook food successfully in a well-organized kitchen. Shortcuts and alternative methods of doing ordinary and out-of-the-ordinary kitchen tasks are described, too.*

USING THIS BOOK

EQUIPPING YOUR KITCHEN

Organizing your kitchen well is the first step towards successful cooking. *Kitchen Equipment* describes how best to plan a kitchen and choose, maintain, and obtain the best performance from appliances and cooking utensils. *Prepared Ingredients* tells you how to set up and maintain a useful storecupboard – an essential in any kitchen – and describes the best ways to store dried foods. It lists healthy basics as well as convenience foods, and suggests a range of clever ways to combine the two. This chapter also gives advice on keeping a ready supply of ingredients with which to rustle up a quick, healthy meal at only a moment's notice.

Enriching dried fruits
To learn how to transform a selection of dried fruits into a richly flavoured and luxurious compote, turn to page 36.

Chilling fish
To find out how to select the best fresh fish, chill it quickly, and store it safely, see page 54.

CHOOSING AND PREPARING FRESH FOODS

Good cooking starts with sensible shopping to buy the finest, freshest ingredients, which then need safe storage and careful preparation so that you can extract the very best from them during cooking. *Fresh Ingredients* tells you everything you need to know about choosing, buying, and storing all kinds of fresh foods safely. *Preparing Ingredients* takes you clearly and concisely through all the basic methods of food preparation, and includes numerous simple but effective ideas for adding flavour and variety to enhance a wide range of familiar foods.

COOKING FOR FAMILY AND FRIENDS

Making the very best of good food and enjoying it to the full requires a little basic knowledge of a few simple cooking techniques. *Cooking Methods* describes how to improve the many different methods of cooking, from achieving the best results with grilled or barbecued foods, to preventing the problems associated with baking and preserving. Once you feel confident about using the basic techniques, you can enjoy cooking for friends as well as family. *Entertaining* takes you from the planning and preparation of a wide variety of special occasions – formal and informal – to the cooking and presentation of food.

Garnishing effectively
To discover how to add the finishing touches to dinner-party food by making effective garnishes, turn to page 131.

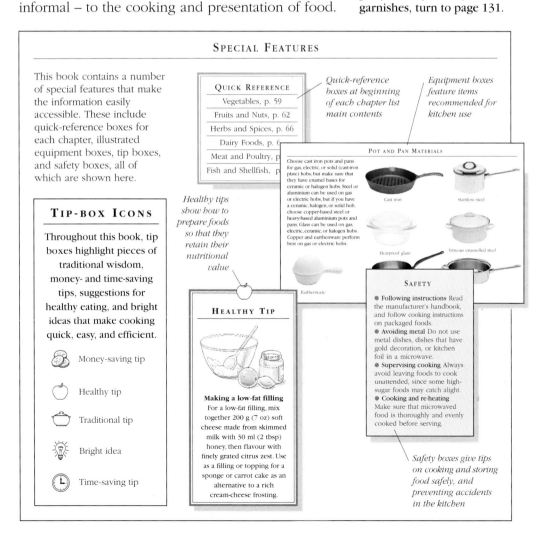

SPECIAL FEATURES

This book contains a number of special features that make the information easily accessible. These include quick-reference boxes for each chapter, illustrated equipment boxes, tip boxes, and safety boxes, all of which are shown here.

QUICK REFERENCE
Vegetables, p. 59
Fruits and Nuts, p. 62
Herbs and Spices, p. 66
Dairy Foods, p. 6
Meat and Poultry, p
Fish and Shellfish, p

Quick-reference boxes at beginning of each chapter list main contents

Equipment boxes feature items recommended for kitchen use

TIP-BOX ICONS

Throughout this book, tip boxes highlight pieces of traditional wisdom, money- and time-saving tips, suggestions for healthy eating, and bright ideas that make cooking quick, easy, and efficient.

Money-saving tip

Healthy tip

Traditional tip

Bright idea

Time-saving tip

Healthy tips show how to prepare foods so that they retain their nutritional value

POT AND PAN MATERIALS

Choose cast iron pots and pans for gas, electric, or solid (cast-iron plate) hobs, but make sure that they have enamel bases for ceramic or halogen hobs. Steel or aluminium can be used on gas or electric hobs, but if you have a ceramic, halogen, or solid hob, choose copper-based steel or heavy-based aluminium pots and pans. Glass can be used on gas, electric, ceramic, or halogen hobs. Copper and earthenware perform best on gas or electric hobs.

Cast iron

Stainless steel

Heatproof glass

Vitreous enamelled steel

Earthenware

HEALTHY TIP

Making a low-fat filling
For a low-fat filling, mix together 200 g (7 oz) soft cheese made from skimmed milk with 30 ml (2 tbsp) honey, then flavour with finely grated citrus zest. Use as a filling or topping for a sponge or carrot cake as an alternative to a rich cream-cheese frosting.

SAFETY

● **Following instructions** Read the manufacturer's handbook, and follow cooking instructions on packaged foods.
● **Avoiding metal** Do not use metal dishes, dishes that have gold decoration, or kitchen foil in a microwave.
● **Supervising cooking** Always avoid leaving foods to cook unattended, since some high-sugar foods may catch alight.
● **Cooking and re-heating** Make sure that microwaved food is thoroughly and evenly cooked before serving.

Safety boxes give tips on cooking and storing food safely, and preventing accidents in the kitchen

Cooking for a Healthy Lifestyle

Making a Safe, Efficient Kitchen

The kitchen is one of the most important rooms in any household, and is often the centre of the home, where meals are not only prepared, cooked, and eaten, but where family and friends often gather together. Bear this in mind, whether you are planning a completely new kitchen or making improvements to an existing one. Start by listing your requirements, and then draw up a plan of the kitchen that would suit your needs. Include labour-saving equipment such as food processors whenever possible to reduce your workload and save time. Ensure that kitchen appliances are running efficiently by checking them regularly. Use a thermometer to check refrigerators and freezers, for example, to ensure that they are working at the correct temperatures for storing food safely.

Using a food processor
If you use a food processor often, invest in an extra bowl so that you can process more than one ingredient at a time without having to repeatedly wash one bowl.

Organizing a storecupboard
To make sure everything is easily accessible in a storecupboard, arrange small jars and regularly used items at the front, and put larger, less-frequently used items at the back or on the higher shelves.

Stocking a Healthy Storecupboard

There is such a wide choice of foods to choose from today that keeping a good supply of healthy foods in stock should not present a problem. Aim to have a few healthy staples to rely on as a basis for all kinds of meals, such as bulgur wheat, wholemeal rice, lentils, or dried pasta shapes. Make use of canned or dried foods for quick meals when time is short, or to cater for an unexpected guest. Rotate the foods in your storecupboard to make sure that each is consumed within its use-by date in order to enjoy the food at its best. Do not forget that the freezer can provide you with a supply of fresh food all year round, and can act as a storecupboard for inexpensive, seasonal gluts of fruits and vegetables. Clearly label and date all packed food before you put it in the freezer so that it is easy to identify. Alternatively, keep a freezer logbook so you have a handy record of all the contents and their details.

GETTING THE MOST FROM FRESH FOODS

Even if you are a novice in the kitchen, once you have mastered a few basic food-preparation techniques and cooking skills, you will find it easy to make a delicious, healthy meal. Start by shopping for the freshest ingredients possible, and look out for seasonal fresh foods that are at the peak of their season, when they will be at their most inexpensive and of the best quality. Choose low-fat cooking methods whenever possible, and cook vegetables lightly to retain flavour and nutrients, using methods such as stir-frying or steaming.

Stir-frying in a wok
Use a wok to keep fat levels low and retain flavour and nutrients in fresh food.

Using pesto as a glaze
Before grilling low-fat meats such as turkey or chicken breast fillets, brush with pesto sauce to keep moist.

ADDING VARIETY TO EVERYDAY MEALS

If you cook every day of the week, it is easy to run out of ideas that are simple, quick, and healthy, but with the wide choice of foods available and a wealth of suggestions for healthy eating to inspire you, you can always find different ways of serving even the most familiar foods. Pep up a plain, roast chicken by tucking a few fresh herbs under the skin, or use flavoured marinades or glazes to keep plain meats moist and add flavour when grilling or barbecuing. Add a topping of crumpled filo pastry to transform simple stewed fruits into a pie in minutes, or introduce texture and extra nutrients to cooked vegetables by scattering them with nuts or seeds before serving.

ENTERTAINING WITHOUT STRESS

Successful entertaining has as much to do with forward planning and creative presentation as culinary skill. The greatest compliment you can pay someone is to invite him or her into your home and offer them food, however simple. Make large celebrations less of a chore by planning in advance. Make lists and timetables to organize the tasks to be done, and you will then be able to relax on the day with your guests. There is no need to cook elaborate dishes; simple finishing touches and creative presentation can make food look special.

Using a mirror tile
The simplest presentation ideas are often the most effective. Use a plain mirror tile instead of a plate for serving canapés with drinks.

KITCHEN EQUIPMENT

A GOOD COOK CAN PRODUCE MEALS with limited equipment, but a well-organized, fully equipped kitchen will improve your efficiency and reduce the time you spend cooking. The kitchen is the most difficult room in the house to plan, so you should take time to consider your requirements. Shop around and see what is available before making decisions about equipment, whether you are choosing major appliances or small utensils.

ORGANIZING A KITCHEN

The number of units and appliances in a kitchen will be dictated largely by space. The quality and layout of kitchen equipment, both of which affect efficiency, are under your control. If you are planning to design a kitchen from scratch, ask the advice of an expert.

PLANNING A KITCHEN
● **Working on paper** When you start to plan your kitchen, draw the walls and doors to scale on squared paper. Make cardboard cut-outs to scale of all kitchen appliances to be fitted in, and experiment with their positions. Draw up several plans before making decisions or spending money.
● **Determining a basic shape** Depending on the space available, plan your kitchen in a U-shape, L-shape, or galley shape. These are the best layouts for moving around efficiently while you work.
● **Keeping surfaces level** Try to plan an unbroken run of worktop, built over and between kitchen appliances, to make efficient use of space and to facilitate cleaning.
● **Anticipating traffic flow** Plan a kitchen so that people passing through do not cross the work area, especially that between the sink and cooker.

PLANNING FOR AN EASY WORK FLOW
● **Minimizing walking** Keep the total distance between the sink, storage area, and cooker to no more than approximately 7 m (23 ft) in order to minimize the amount of walking about you will do while cooking.

● **Placing work surfaces** Link areas between appliances with worktops so that there will be a work surface wherever you need it. This will allow you to prepare and cook food near the appropriate appliances.

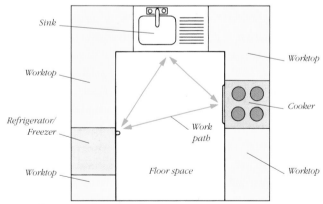

Sink

Worktop

Worktop

Refrigerator/ Freezer

Worktop

Floor space

Worktop

Cooker

Worktop

Work path

Creating a work triangle
If you are planning the design of a kitchen from scratch, try to arrange the positions of appliances so that you create a work path linking the refrigerator, sink, and cooker. This will facilitate an easy flow of work that minimizes inefficient activity in the kitchen.

KITCHEN IMPROVEMENTS

I F YOU ARE PLANNING TO UPDATE OR IMPROVE an existing kitchen, there are many inexpensive adjustments to consider. Change the style of the kitchen by replacing cupboard doors, or improve existing doors with a new paint finish.

WORK SURFACES

Worktops should be fitted at a height that is comfortable to work at. A recommended, standard working height may not be suitable for you. Choose a hard-wearing material that is heat resistant, does not scratch, chip, or stain easily, and is easy to maintain and keep clean.

CREATING SURFACES

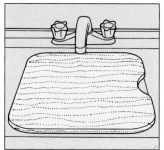

Covering a sink
To create a work surface that you can use if space becomes tight, cut a piece of wood to fit neatly over a sink. When the sink is not in use, put the wood in place.

FITTING FOR EFFICIENCY
● **Positioning worktops** Make sure that there is a surface near the entrance on which to place shopping or garden produce when you enter the kitchen.
● **Fitting insets** Consider having a marble or wooden inset fitted into a worktop for chopping and pastry making. This should extend the whole depth of the worktop to avoid creating dirt traps, and the front edge should match that of the worktop.
● **Avoiding dirt traps** Avoid joins in worktops, since they may trap dirt and become a health risk. Seal unavoidable joins with kitchen sealant.
● **Preventing dripping** Look for a worktop with a ridged front edge to prevent spilled liquids from dripping over the edge.

MAKING PAN RESTS

Using tiles
Make sure that there is always a stable, heatproof surface on which to place hot pans by keeping two sturdy kitchen tiles on the worktop next to the hob.

USING DEAD SPACE
● **Storing in corners** Make use of worktop space in corners for storing small appliances, such as food processors.

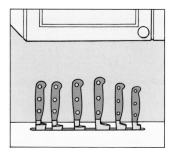

Fitting a knife slot
Store sharp knives in a slot cut into the rear part of the worktop behind a drawer unit. Check carefully before cutting the slot to make sure that the knives will not block the drawer.

LIGHTING WORK SURFACES
● **Using spotlights** Choose flexible spotlights so that you can direct the lighting. Recess them into the ceiling, or place on top of wall cupboards.
● **Avoiding glare** Eliminate glare by positioning diffusers over low-level lights.
● **Reducing heat** Reduce the heat generated in a kitchen by installing fluorescent lights.
● **Locating switches** For flexibility, fit separate switches for different areas, such as an eating area or worktops.

SAVING SPACE
● **Folding items away** In a small kitchen, fit a hinged worktop or a table that will fold away while not in use.

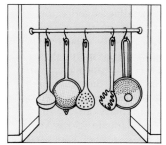

Using a rail
To help keep work surfaces clear, hang regularly used, small utensils from a rail fitted between two wall cupboards, within easy reach of the area where you will need them.

CUPBOARDS AND SHELVES

There is a wide range of kitchen units to choose from today, and they are available in many different styles. Since units last many years, do not be influenced by the latest fashion. If your budget is tight, use plain, whitewood furniture, which is inexpensive and practical.

KEEPING CUPBOARDS CLEAN

Using plastic coving
To prevent dust and dirt from collecting beneath a floor-mounted cupboard, fit coving along the edge of the unit's plinth. Lay flexible flooring, such as vinyl, to cover the coving, and tuck it into the corner where the cupboard meets the plinth.

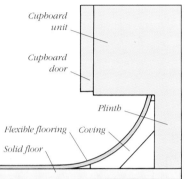

Cupboard unit

Cupboard door

Plinth

Flexible flooring *Coving*

Solid floor

● **Sealing wood** To protect natural wooden units with a hard-wearing, water-repellent finish, coat with polyurethane. Seal hardwood worktops with oil where appropriate, and reapply the seal frequently.

● **Cleaning interiors** Choose cupboards lined with laminated coatings and drawers lined with heavy-duty plastic, so that you will easily be able to wipe up spills and the sticky residues left by food containers.

CHOOSING & SITING CUPBOARDS

● **Siting cupboards** If possible, attach a cupboard to a shaded, outside wall if it is to be used for storing food, since this will be cooler than an internal wall. Fit an airbrick or filter into the wall for ventilation.
● **Checking stability** Ask a builder to check that a wall is structurally sound enough to take the weight of cupboards before fitting wall units. You may find that a partition wall is unable to support the weight.
● **Making a partition** Divide kitchen and dining areas in the same room by installing a peninsular unit. This will provide extra storage space while permitting easy access from one area to another.
● **Selecting cupboard doors** Consider fitting cupboards that have sliding doors or counter-balanced doors that slide up and over. Doors that open outwards can present a hazard.

● **Making a wine store** To adapt a floor cupboard for storing bottles of wine, first remove any existing shelves. Then make an X-shaped shelf for the bottles using two pieces of plywood slotted together to fit the cupboard from corner to corner.

Fitting a plate drainer
Remove the bottom of a wall-mounted cupboard above the sink, and fit a plate-draining rack inside. Wet crockery can then drain into the sink, and you can close the doors to hide it away.

PLANNING STORAGE

● **Adjusting shelves** Choose cupboards with adjustable shelves or racks on runners, so that the heights can be adjusted to suit your needs.
● **Using corner space** Install a corner unit with revolving shelves to make use of an otherwise inaccessible corner.
● **Disposing of waste** Site a flip-top waste bin in a cupboard beneath the sink or in the area where most of the food is prepared, so that waste can be disposed of easily.
● **Using wall space** Use the space beneath wall units to hang a paper-towel holder or utensil rack. This will help to keep work surfaces clear.

KEEPING SHELVES CLEAN

● **Covering with a blind** Fit a fireproof roller blind over shelves built into a recess so that dust and grease do not settle on the shelves' contents.
● **Using open shelves** Dust settles easily on open shelves, so use them for items that are used and washed daily.

SAFETY

● **Choosing units** Choose units with rounded corners and recessed handles. Sharp corners and protruding knobs are likely to cause injury.
● **Placing wall units** Avoid placing kitchen units on a wall above a hob; reaching over a hot burner to gain access to a unit is dangerous.
● **Siting for height** Site wall units so that the top shelves are easily accessible without needing to climb on to a chair or finding a stepladder.

SPACE-SAVING DEVICES

Many domestic kitchens are quite compact, with limited storage space, so creative use of space is essential for the efficient organization of a kitchen. Make use of corners by inserting corner shelves, and hang small items from racks on the wall if you run out of cupboard space.

SAVING CUPBOARD SPACE

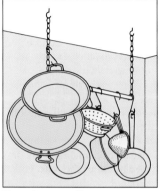

Hanging a rail
Suspend a wooden or metal rail from the kitchen ceiling, and hang pots and pans using butcher's hooks. Do not hang the rail too low, and check the length of chain needed to bring the pots and pans to an accessible height.

FILLING EMPTY SPACES

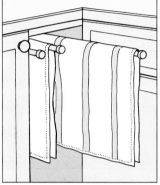

Using gaps between units
Position a pull-out towel rail in a gap between two kitchen units or appliances to keep tea towels tidy and accessible. Alternatively, use gaps between units for storing baking sheets and trays, releasing cupboard space for other items.

BRIGHT IDEA

Using window space
If your kitchen window has an unpleasant view, or no view at all, fit toughened glass shelves across the window. Use them for storing attractive glass jars and bottles, plants, or pots of fresh herbs.

COOKERY BOOKS AND RECIPES

Most cooks have a collection of favourite cookery books, and inevitably these books become well-worn. Buy a cookery book stand, or use the tips below to protect your books while cooking. Also make sure that you keep your favourite recipe cuttings in good condition.

PROTECTING & STORING COOKERY BOOKS

● **Using a polythene bag** To protect the pages of a cookery book, slip the opened book inside a clear polythene bag to prevent it from being splashed during food preparation.
● **Keeping books dry** Attach a narrow wooden shelf with a rim to the wall above a work surface, and use it as a book rest. It will help keep books out of the way of food splashes.
● **Storing books** Place a bookshelf on top of a chest of drawers to create a kitchen dresser in which you can keep your cookery books, display attractive pieces of crockery, and store kitchen equipment.

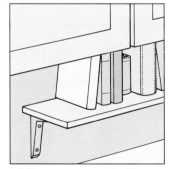

Adding an extra shelf
Fix a narrow shelf between a work surface and wall cupboard to create storage space for cookery books. This will give you quick access to them, and save space on the work surface.

KEEPING CUTTINGS

● **Colour-coding recipes** Store different categories of recipe cutting in differently coloured photograph albums with peel-back plastic pages. Use blue for fish dishes, for example.
● **Using a scrapbook** Paste recipe cuttings into a scrapbook so that you can write notes next to them if necessary.
● **Sticking cuttings down** Store favourite, frequently used recipe cuttings in a decorative way by pasting them on to a board or tray to make a collage. Paint over or spray with waterproof varnish so that any splashes of food or grease can be wiped clean.

COOKING APPLIANCES

COOKERS REQUIRE MAJOR FINANCIAL INVESTMENT and should therefore be chosen with the expectation of long-term use. Everyone has different requirements when selecting a cooker, and there is a huge range from which to choose.

CHOOSING A COOKER

When choosing an oven or a hob, consider your individual cooking needs, bearing in mind the advantages and availability of different fuels, and any space limitations in the kitchen. Look for a design that is attractive and practical, with few dirt traps so that cleaning will be easy.

CHOOSING AN OVEN

When buying an oven, decide which features will be most useful, bearing in mind your lifestyle. Below are some features to consider first.

● **Capacity** Choose a large or a double oven to give you flexibility, especially if you cook for a lot of people.
● **Cleaning** facilities Choose an oven that is self-cleaning, or that has stay-clean features.
● **Auto-timer** Consider an auto-timer to control cooking for you while you are busy.
● **Fan-assistance** To encourage even cooking and reduce cooking times, choose a fan-assisted convection oven that circulates heat evenly.

SELECTING HOB SURFACE & FUEL TYPE

● **Choosing a hob** Select a hob that will be easy to clean. Consider a ceramic hob, which also uses electricity efficiently. When not in use for cooking, the cool, ceramic surface can be used as a work surface for rolling out pastry or dough.

● **Combining fuels** If you are able to combine fuels, choose two gas burners and two electric rings. A mixed hob combines the safety advantages of electricity with the easy heat adjustment of gas burners, and is useful in a power failure.

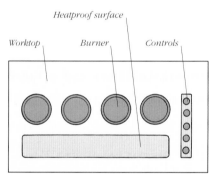

Heatproof surface

Worktop　　*Burner*　　*Controls*

Placing burners

If you are planning a new kitchen, consider setting hob burners or rings into a worktop in a line, rather than a square formation, and set them back from the front edge. Install a heatproof surface for resting hot saucepans in front of the rings.

CONSIDERING DETAILS

● **Catalytic liners** Reduce oven cleaning by choosing an oven with a catalytic oven lining that carbonizes food splashes. Alternatively, select a pyrolytic oven, which has a high-temperature, self-cleaning cycle.
● **Built-in ovens** Choose a built-in oven, which is usually mounted at waist height, for convenient positioning.
● **Eye-level grills** Choose an oven with the grill positioned at eye level if you want to check food frequently during cooking. The grill pan should have a support and stops to prevent it from being pulled out too far.

USING OVEN DOORS

Resting a hot dish

Choose an oven with a door that drops down rather than opens sideways. The door will provide a useful surface on which to rest hot casseroles or baking sheets as they come out of the oven.

CONSIDERING SAFETY

● **Choosing warning lights** Pick a hob with controls that light up and warn you when the burners or rings are hot, even if not glowing.
● **Checking safety** Make sure that, if a gas hob has a glass lid for covering the burners when not in use, the hob has a cut-out switch, and the lid is made of toughened glass.
● **Avoiding accidents** If you have young children, fit a hob guard to deter them from touching hot saucepans. Always turn saucepan handles inwards to prevent children from pulling them off the hob.

USING A COOKER

Whatever type of cooking you do most often, it is a good idea to be aware of your oven's rate of energy consumption, and to check regularly that it is running efficiently. Refer to the manufacturer's handbook for tips on how to make good use of special functions.

CHECKING TEMPERATURE

Using a thermometer
Check the accuracy of your oven regularly by placing an oven thermometer in the centre of the middle shelf. Heat the oven to 180°C (350°F), then compare with the thermometer reading.

COOKING EFFICIENTLY
● **Saving energy** Turn solid electric rings off a few minutes before you finish cooking, since the food will continue to cook on the residual heat.
● **Preheating the oven** Allow at least 10 minutes for an oven to heat to temperature. Arrange the oven shelves before turning on the oven to avoid losing heat or burning yourself.
● **Setting a timer** Avoid opening the oven door, which lowers the oven temperature, to check if food is done. Use a timer to monitor cooking times.
● **Avoiding scratches** Prevent damage to a ceramic hob surface by lifting pans off rather than sliding them across it.

SAVING FUEL

Cooking a complete meal
Use fuel economically by cooking a complete meal in the oven at the same time. Place dishes that need a high temperature at the top of the oven, and other dishes on the lower shelves.

CLEANING A COOKER

Wipe up cooking spills on a hob or inside an oven immediately after they have occurred. Once they harden or burn on to the surface, you will have to use a commercial cleaner to remove them. Always switch off the power before cleaning an electric oven or hob.

CLEANING EFFICIENTLY
● **Reducing cleaning** Stand pies and casseroles on a baking sheet in an oven to catch spills.
● **Wiping a ceramic surface** Wipe up fruit juice, sugar, and acid food spills on a ceramic hob immediately, since they may cause etching or pitting on the smooth ceramic surface.
● **Cleaning shelves** Wash oven shelves in the dishwasher, remove them before the drying cycle, and wipe over with a cloth. Alternatively, place them on an old towel in the bath, and soak in a solution of ammonia and hot water to loosen food deposits.
● **Saving energy** Start a self-cleaning cycle when the oven is still warm to save energy.

REMOVING BURNT FOOD

Using a damp cloth
If food burns on to a hob around a burner, turn the heat off, allow to cool, and cover with a cloth wrung out in a solution of water and washing-up liquid. Leave for two hours, then wipe clean.

MONEY-SAVING TIP

Cleaning chrome trim
To clean rust from chrome trim, rub it with a piece of kitchen foil wrapped around your finger, shiny side out. Buff up the trim with a cloth dipped in rubbing alcohol.

USING A MICROWAVE

Cooking in a microwave is quick, easy, and economical. However many people you cater for, a microwave can be an invaluable addition to the kitchen, saving time and energy. If you have never used a microwave before, you will need to adapt your cooking methods.

CHOOSING A MICROWAVE

Many microwaves have useful features that you should consider before buying.

● **Power** Most full-power ovens use 650–750 watts. The higher the wattage, the shorter the cooking times.
● **Controls** Digital controls will give more accurate timings than dial controls.
● **Turntables** Ensure that the oven has a turntable. If it does not, the food will have to be turned manually.
● **Browning facilities** These will add a rich, golden colour and crispness to food.
● **Cleaning** Look out for self-cleaning interior panels on combination ovens.
● **Compact models** If space in the kitchen is limited, choose a tabletop model.

LEARNING BASIC SKILLS

● **Adapting recipes** To adapt a conventional recipe for the microwave, reduce the cooking time by about two-thirds.
● **Adjusting cooking times** When doubling recipe amounts for the microwave, increase the cooking time by one-quarter to one-third. When halving recipe amounts, reduce the cooking time by approximately one-third.
● **Checking temperature** Use a microwave thermometer to check that food is thoroughly cooked. Ready-made meals should reach 70°C (158°F).
● **Adding colour** To enhance the colour of food cooked in a microwave, top savoury dishes with toasted nuts or a sprinkling of paprika, and top sweet dishes with toasted nuts, brown sugar, or ground spices.

INCREASING CAPACITY

● **Stacking plates** Use plate-stacking rings to cook two portions of food at once, and increase the cooking time by 1½ minutes. Swap the plates around halfway through.

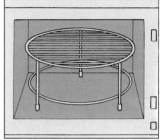

Using shelves
Buy shelves and trivets, both of which are available as microwave accessories, so that you can cook more than one item at a time. Alternatively, choose a microwave fitted with a shelf.

MICROWAVING SAFELY

Follow a few basic guidelines to ensure that you use a microwave safely, choose suitable containers, and cook food thoroughly. Used correctly, a microwave is a versatile appliance, cooking and reheating food in a fraction of the time that it would take in a conventional oven.

COOKING THOROUGHLY

Place narrowest part of food inwards

Arranging food
For safety, make sure food is cooked thoroughly. Distribute it evenly in a dish, and cook wedge-shaped items, such as pears or fish fillets, with the narrow ends pointing to the centre of the dish.

CHOOSING DISHES

Checking heat resistance
To ensure that a dish will not overheat, place it in a microwave with a cup of cold water on High for two minutes. The water should heat up and warm the cup, while the dish should remain cold.

SAFETY

● **Following instructions** Read the manufacturer's handbook, and follow cooking instructions on packaged foods.
● **Avoiding metal** Do not use metal dishes, dishes that have gold decoration, or kitchen foil in a microwave.
● **Supervising cooking** Always avoid leaving foods to cook unattended, since some high-sugar foods may catch alight.
● **Cooking and re-heating** Make sure that microwaved food is thoroughly and evenly cooked before serving.

COLD STORAGE

REFRIGERATORS AND FREEZERS ARE INVALUABLE ITEMS of equipment in the kitchen. Both these appliances ensure that we have a wide choice of safe, fresh food at any time of the year, and can help us to create a varied, healthy diet.

CHOOSING APPLIANCES

When you are selecting a refrigerator or a freezer, consider carefully the needs of your household. Decide on the capacity that you require, taking into account the space available and the foods you store most often, such as garden produce or convenience foods.

ADDING STORAGE

Using baskets
Add extra storage baskets to a chest freezer. They will make it much easier to find and organize the contents of the freezer. Extra storage baskets can usually be ordered from the supplier.

BUYING A FREEZER
● **Assessing capacity** Allow 57 litres (2 cu ft) of freezer space for each person in your household, together with an extra 57 litres (2 cu ft) if you do a lot of entertaining.
● **Fitting the space** If space is tight, choose an upright freezer, which will take up less floor space than a chest freezer.
● **Positioning a freezer** Check that there is enough space to open the freezer door or lid. The door of an upright freezer may need to open through an angle of more than 90° so that the drawers can be pulled out.

CONTROLLING STOCKS

Using drawer markers
If you choose an upright freezer, look for a model that has contents cards on the front of the drawers. These will help you to keep track of items stored. List the foods in each drawer on the attached card.

BUYING A REFRIGERATOR
● **Assessing capacity** Make sure that your refrigerator is large enough. Allow 228 litres (8 cu ft) for the first two people in the household, then another 28 litres (1 cu ft) for each additional person.
● **Reducing workload** For easy maintenance, it is best to choose a frost-free refrigerator or fridge-freezer, since these do not need to be defrosted.
● **Selecting shelves** Make sure that refrigerator shelves are adjustable. A shelf with hinged flaps is useful so that tall bottles can be stored beneath.

LOOKING FOR FEATURES
● **Checking temperature** When choosing a refrigerator or freezer, look for one with a built-in temperature indicator on the outside. This will enable you to check that the appliance is running efficiently without opening the door.
● **Moving easily** If your house has solid floors, choose a refrigerator or freezer with castors, since they will make the appliance reasonably easy to move. Castors may damage soft flooring such as vinyl.
● **Lighting the interior** Check whether a freezer has an interior light, which is especially useful in a chest freezer. If not, keep a battery-operated clip-on light handy so that you can see the contents easily.

INSTALLING APPLIANCES

● **Adjusting height** Make sure that a refrigerator or freezer is stable. Use a spirit level to check whether the appliance is level, and adjust the legs or castors accordingly.
● **Moving easily** To move an appliance without castors, slip an old piece of carpet under the legs to help it slide.
● **Avoiding damp** To allow the air to circulate all around a freezer that is stored in a garage, raise the appliance 5 cm (2 in) off the ground by placing it on blocks.

USING APPLIANCES EFFECTIVELY

To maintain food stored in a refrigerator or freezer in the best condition, you must keep these appliances running efficiently. Regulating the temperature is important, since too high a temperature will cause food to deteriorate, and too low will cause energy to be wasted.

PREVENTING DEPOSITS

● **Wiping bases** When packing items into a refrigerator or a freezer, keep a clean, damp cloth handy to wipe the bases of messy containers. This will prevent food spills from transferring on to the shelves.

Lining with foil
Prevent ice-cube trays or frozen-foods spills from sticking to the base of a freezer or freezer compartment by lining it with a layer of foil. Replace the foil regularly with a clean piece.

**CHECKING
TEMPERATURES**

For safe and efficient running of refrigerators and freezers, check the internal temperature regularly with a thermometer.

● **Refrigerators** Run a refrigerator at 5°C (41°F) or below. The coolest section of the refrigerator should be 1°C (34°F). To check the temperature, place a thermometer in the centre of the top shelf, and leave overnight. In summer, adjust the refrigerator's thermostat.
● **Freezers** Keep a freezer at –18°C (0°F) or below. Check the temperature by placing a thermometer on the top shelf or the upper edge of the top basket, and leave overnight.

REDUCING FUEL USAGE

● **Siting correctly** Place freezers and refrigerators in a cool site away from direct sunlight and appliances that generate heat.

Filling spaces
If possible, keep your freezer full, since it is not energy-efficient to run it half-empty. Fill large spaces with loaves of bread, or use crumpled newspaper to prevent air from circulating.

PREVENTING PROBLEMS

● **Labelling switches** To make sure that a freezer is not turned off by mistake, place tape over the switch, or label the plug with "freezer" in red ink.
● **Avoiding stale smells** To prevent an unpleasant odour from developing while a refrigerator or freezer is in storage, clean and dry it thoroughly, then prop the door open with a block of wood, and secure it in place with strips of masking tape.
● **Moving house** Before moving a refrigerator or freezer, turn it off 24 hours in advance. Clean thoroughly, remove loose parts, and secure the door. Always keep a refrigerator or freezer in an upright position during transportation.

FREEZING EFFICIENTLY

● **Cooling foods** Cool foods completely before storing in a refrigerator or freezer. To cool hot food quickly, sit the base of the container in a sink half-filled with cold water.
● **Limiting amounts** To avoid raising the temperature of a freezer, freeze no more than one-tenth of the appliance's capacity of food at one time.

STORING SUCCESSFULLY

● **Arranging foods** When placing foods in a refrigerator, leave some space around each item so that air can circulate and chill the food evenly.
● **Avoiding "freezer burn"** Always wrap foods tightly before freezing to exclude air. This will prevent moisture from being drawn out of the foods, which results in loss of nutrients and dehydration.

MONEY-SAVING TIP

Checking a door seal
Make sure that the door seals on a refrigerator, freezer compartment, or freezer are working efficiently by closing the door and trapping a piece of paper. If the paper can be pulled out easily, the seal is worn and should be replaced.

CLEANING REFRIGERATORS AND FREEZERS

Regular cleaning of refrigerators and freezers will help to keep them as safe environments in which to store food. In addition to cleaning the insides, look after the outer surfaces, since these are subject to daily wear and tear, and sometimes the damaging effects of steam.

PROTECTING SURFACES

● **Preventing rust** If a freezer or refrigerator is prone to condensation on the outside, protect the outer surface by rubbing it with silicone polish applied with a soft cloth.

● **Using glycerine** After defrosting a freezer, wipe the interior with glycerine. Next time you defrost it, the ice will be easier to remove, eliminating the need for scraping.

● **Cleaning doors** If someone uses felt-tip permanent markers on the refrigerator door, remove the marks by rubbing with lighter fluid applied with a soft cloth. Wash with detergent, rinse and dry.

RETOUCHING SCRATCHES

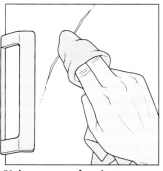

Using enamel paint
Cover a scratch on a refrigerator or freezer door with enamel paint. First, clean with detergent and wipe dry with a clean cloth. Test the colour on an unseen area, and retouch with a fine brush.

CLEANING INTERIORS

● **Wiping spills** Always wipe up spills in the refrigerator as soon as they occur to avoid contamination or odours.

● **Removing odours** Remove lingering smells from the interior of a refrigerator or freezer by wiping with a cloth rinsed in a solution of 15 ml (1 tbsp) bicarbonate of soda to 1 litre (1¾ pints) warm water.

● **Unpacking foods** Remove all foods from a refrigerator or freezer before cleaning or defrosting. Pack ice-creams into a coolbox, and stack chilled or frozen foods closely together, covering them with a blanket or duvet for insulation.

DEFROSTING FREEZERS

The most convenient time to defrost a freezer is when stocks of food are at their lowest, for instance after holiday periods during which supplies are depleted, or in early summer before you stock up with garden produce. Remember to turn off and unplug the freezer before defrosting.

DEALING WITH A BREAKDOWN

If your freezer breaks down, or if there is an unexpected power cut, follow these simple emergency rules:

● **Check the electrics** Make sure that the wiring, plug, or fuse is not at fault before calling out a service engineer.

● **Keep doors closed** Avoid opening the freezer. If it is full, the contents should stay frozen for at least 12 hours.

● **Save food** If the problem is long-term, ask neighbours or friends if they have spare freezer space you can use.

● **Use thawed food** Cook or use up thawed food quickly. Never refreeze food, since this may cause food poisoning.

DEFROSTING EFFICIENTLY

● **Lining with foil** Line the shelves of a freezer with foil when defrosting. Make a hole in the centre of each layer to enable you to funnel water into a bowl underneath.

● **Lining with a towel** Before scraping ice from the sides of a freezer, lay a towel in the bottom to collect ice.

● **Clearing up** If you have a wet-dry vacuum cleaner, use it to suck up ice debris and water during defrosting.

● **Drying thoroughly** Before switching the freezer back on after defrosting, wipe around the inside with a bicarbonate solution, and dry thoroughly with paper towels. Leave for one hour after switching on before replacing contents.

SAVING TIME

● **Adding hot water** To defrost a freezer quickly, place bowls of hot water inside. Scrape off the ice as soon as it loosens.

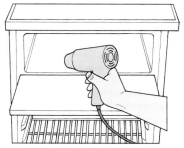

Using a hairdryer
If time is short, blow warm air from a small hairdryer over the ice in a freezer, moving the dryer to avoid overheating one area. Make sure your hands are dry, and keep the dryer moisture-free.

POTS AND PANS

W HEN YOU SET OUT TO BUY POTS AND PANS, you will find a wide range of types and materials from which to choose. Prolong their durability by buying the best quality you can afford, protecting their linings, and cleaning them carefully.

CHOOSING POTS AND PANS

Y our choice of pots and pans will affect the success of your cooking. The material they are made of should be suitable for the type of cooker you have and the kind of cooking you do. Select good-quality pots and pans, and they will give you reliable service for many years.

POT AND PAN MATERIALS

Choose cast iron pots and pans for gas, electric, or solid (cast-iron plate) hobs, but make sure that they have enamel bases for ceramic or halogen hobs. Steel or aluminum can be used on gas or electric hobs, but if you have a ceramic, halogen, or solid hob, choose copper-based steel or heavy-based aluminum pots and pans. Glass can be used on gas, electric, ceramic, or halogen hobs. Copper and earthenware perform best on electric hobs.

Cast iron

Stainless steel

Heatproof glass

Vitreous enameled steel

Earthenware

Copper lined with stainless steel

Aluminum

BUYING POTS & PANS

● **Cast iron** Buy the heaviest gauge of cast iron for the best results. Choose pots and pans with two handles, so that they will be easy to pick up when full. Look for wooden handles, which will remain cool.

● **Copper** Choose copper pots and pans lined with stainless steel. Although expensive, they are more durable than those that are lined with tin.

● **Heatproof glass** Buy heatproof-glass pots and pans for versatility, since they can be used to cook, freeze, reheat, microwave, and serve food.

IMPROVISING SPECIALTY-PURPOSE PANS

Foil will hold asparagus in position

Steaming vegetables
To steam vegetables without a steamer, use a metal sieve and a wide saucepan. Place the sieve just inside the rim, above boiling water. Add the food, and cover.

Cooking asparagus
To make an asparagus steamer, use a deep saucepan and insert a ring of foil. The foil will ensure that the asparagus tips stay above water while they are cooking.

PROTECTING POTS AND PANS

Routine care of pots and pans will ensure that you get the best performance out of them. Whichever materials pots and pans are made of, their surfaces must be protected from damage, which can cause food to stick. Use non-metal tools during cooking to minimize wear and tear.

PREPARING NEW POTS

● **Copper** Immerse new copper pans in boiling water, and leave to soak until cold to remove the lacquer coating.
● **Cast iron** To prevent sticking and protect its surface, season cast iron before use. Brush with vegetable oil. Pour in a little more oil, and place on a low heat for one hour. Cool, and wipe with a paper towel.
● **Enamel** Brush the inner surface of the enamel with oil, then place in a cool oven for one hour. Leave to cool for 12 hours, and wipe clean.

PROTECTING COATINGS

Paper towel protects lining

Caring for non-stick pans
To prevent nonstick linings from becoming damaged by knocks and scratches, place sheets of paper towel between pans when stacking together for storage.

CARING FOR CAST IRON

Preventing rusting
To prevent rusting during storage, dry uncoated cast iron pans well after washing. Rub all surfaces with a paper towel dipped in a little vegetable oil.

CLEANING POTS AND PANS

There are a few basic rules worth following when cleaning pots and pans that will help maintain to their performance during cooking. Techniques for cleaning different materials vary, so it is always advisable to read manufacturers' instructions before cleaning new pots and pans.

REMOVING STAINS

● **Bleaching enamel** To clean a badly stained enameled pan, fill it with a weak solution of about 10 ml (2 tsp) bleach to 600 ml (1 pint) water. Leave to soak for a maximum of two hours to avoid damaging the surface of the enamel.

Brightening aluminum
To remove dark stains from an aluminum pot or pan, fill it with water, add the juice of one lemon, and simmer gently until the aluminum brightens.

CLEANING COPPER

● **Using half a lemon** To brighten up and remove stains from tarnished pots and pans made of copper, dip a cut half of lemon into table salt, then rub it gently over the stained copper surface. Rinse and dry thoroughly before use.

Using a vinegar paste
Make a thick paste from roughly equal parts of vinegar and flour. Dip a soft cloth into the paste, and rub it over the copper until clean. Rinse in hot water, and dry.

PREVENTING PROBLEMS

● **Protecting surfaces** Soak pots and pans in hot, soapy water to remove stuck-on foods. Soak pans coated with sugary substances in cold water.
● **Soaking earthenware** To prevent an earthenware pot from absorbing fat, fill it with boiling water, and let stand one hour before use. The pot will absorb water during soaking, keeping out fat and helping to create steam during cooking.
● **Cleaning handles** Wash wooden pan handles quickly in warm water, since soaking may cause them to crack.
● **Caring for steel** Make sure you wash stainless steel soon after cooking salty food, since salt causes surface pitting.
● **Drying pans** Always dry aluminium or polished steel pans immediately to prevent watermarks from forming.

BAKEWARE

A GOOD, BASIC SELECTION OF BAKEWARE will be useful in any kitchen. Your choice of items will depend on the type of cooking you do. If you bake regularly, it is a good idea to collect a wide selection of tins in different shapes and sizes.

CHOOSING BAKEWARE

Bakeware is usually of a light or medium weight so that it can conduct heat quickly and efficiently. Traditional, uncoated tins are best for baking light sponge cakes, since they result in golden-brown crusts. Non-stick surfaces tend to produce cakes with slightly dark, thick crusts.

BAKING EQUIPMENT

The equipment illustrated below makes up a useful collection of bakeware that would be suitable for most people's needs. Spring-release tins and tins with removable bases allow for the easy removal of moulded foods and facilitate cleaning, especially in the case of deep cake tins and flan tins. Include in your collection some baking sheets that have a rim for baking mixtures that tend to spread, and some that have a rim on three sides only to allow you to slide off delicate items such as pastry easily. Whatever you bake, a large cooling rack is essential for cooling baked items after cooking.

Spring-release cake tin

Ring tin

Large, loose-based flan tin

Individual flan tins

Deep cake tin

Sandwich tins

Loaf tin

Patty tins

Swiss-roll tin

Ovenproof dish

Microwave-proof dish

Baking sheet

Cooling rack

UTENSILS

Each cook will choose a unique range of utensils for the kitchen. However, many utensils can fulfil several functions, and a few well-made, good-quality tools are all that you need. Specialist gadgets are useful, but can be expensive.

CHOOSING KNIVES

The advice to buy the best equipment you can afford applies most especially to the purchase of kitchen knives. A good-quality set will save you time and energy, and should last a lifetime. Start with a selection for everyday cooking, which you can add to in the future.

SELECTING MATERIALS

● **Choosing blades** Make sure that the metal is of good quality. High-carbon stainless steel is expensive, but it is the most practical for cutting all kinds of food. It sharpens easily and does not discolour.
● **Choosing knife handles** Look for wooden knife handles that are sealed with heat-resistant plastic. These handles are hard-wearing and easy to clean.

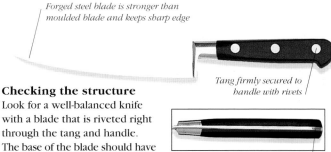

Forged steel blade is stronger than moulded blade and keeps sharp edge

Tang firmly secured to handle with rivets

Checking the structure
Look for a well-balanced knife with a blade that is riveted right through the tang and handle. The base of the blade should have a firm heel or shank to protect fingers and reinforce the blade.

Blade continuous with tang, which extends full length of handle

---

BASIC KITCHEN KNIVES

Follow some basic guidelines when selecting a range of good-quality kitchen knives.

● **Checking balance** Always pick up a knife to feel how well balanced it is. Rest the junction of the handle and blade on the edge of your hand. The handle should fall back gently if the balance is right.
● **Choosing a wide blade** Choose a heavy cook's knife with a wide blade, so that you can use it for crushing garlic as well as slicing other ingredients.
● **Buying heavy knives** When choosing knives for chopping, choose the heaviest that you can handle comfortably, since the heavier the blade, the less force you will need to apply.
● **Following instructions** Always read the manufacturer's instructions to see whether or not knives are suitable for washing in a dishwasher.

Small knife with straight blade

Paring knife

Very sharp, flexible, pointed blade at least 18 cm (7 in) long

Filleting knife

20-cm (8-in) blade with pointed end

Cook's knife

Broad, long, rigid blade for easy carving

Carving knife

Bread knife

Deeply serrated blade for efficient slicing

Safety guard at hilt

Sharpening steel

CARING FOR KNIVES

Having selected the best knives that you can afford, it makes sense to store them safely and maintain them in good condition. The safest way to store knives is to keep them in a knife block or on a magnetic rack. These will help to prevent accidents and protect the blades.

SAFETY

- **Carrying** Always carry knives at your side with the blades pointing downwards.
- **Dropping** If you lose your grip on a knife, allow it to drop to the floor. This is much safer than trying to break its fall, which could result in serious injury.
- **Sharpening** Keep knives sharp, since a blunt knife is more likely to slip and cut you than a sharp one.
- **Washing** Avoid washing knives together with other items, or leaving knives in a washing-up bowl. They may not be visible beneath the soap suds and could therefore be a danger to anyone putting their hands in the water.

PROTECTING POINTS

Hold cork firmly on worktop, and insert knife point carefully

Using corks

If you do not have a knife block or magnetic rack, prevent the fine points of sharp knives from becoming damaged in a cutlery drawer by placing a wine cork securely on each knife tip.

PROTECTING BLADES

- **Choosing a chopping board** Use a polypropylene or a wooden chopping board, since these do not blunt blades.
- **Restricting use** Keep good kitchen knives exclusively for preparing food. Do not use them to cut string or paper.
- **Washing knives** Wash carbon steel knives by hand immediately after use to avoid staining them. Remove any stubborn stains by rubbing the blade with a wet cork dipped in scouring powder.
- **Storing knives** Protect knife blades by using plastic paper binders, which are available from office stationers. Slide a blade into a holder, and push it in as far as it will go.

SHARPENING KNIVES

It takes only a little time and trouble to sharpen knives. If you get into the habit of sharpening them every time you use them, they will perform well for years. If necessary, have your knives sharpened professionally every two or three years if the blades lose their edge.

USING SHARPENERS

- **Soaking in oil** Soak a whetstone in vegetable oil for smooth sharpening.
- **Sharpening regularly** Try to sharpen kitchen knives every time you use them so that they will be maintained in peak condition. Put them once through an electric or manual sharpener, or stroke them three or four times with a steel prior to use.
- **Protecting serrations** Take knives that have serrated edges to a professional knife sharpener, or do not sharpen them at all, since their serrations can be damaged easily during sharpening if extreme care is not taken.

USING ALTERNATIVE METHODS OF SHARPENING

Hold mug firmly by handle, and sharpen away from your hand

Hammer in small tacks to secure paper to wood

Using an upturned mug

If you do not have a steel or a special knife sharpener, use the base of an unglazed earthenware mug. Firmly run the blade across it at a slight angle. Do this several times in the same direction.

Using emery paper

To make a sharpening block, wrap a piece of wood in emery paper, turn the edges underneath, and secure with tacks. Firmly run knives across the surface of the paper to sharpen the blades.

CHOOSING USEFUL UTENSILS

Kitchenware shops are packed with a huge array of useful gadgets for tackling all kinds of kitchen job. Many tools are designed specifically with one task in mind, but some of them are very versatile and can be invaluable tools that may be used for a variety of purposes.

CHOOSING THE BASICS

● **Peeling vegetables** Use a swivel-bladed peeler for peeling vegetables, since it will peel much more thinly than a knife. This tool can also be used for shaving curls of fresh Parmesan cheese, and for making decorative curls from fresh coconut.

● **Lifting delicate foods** Buy a fish slice for lifting foods without breaking them. Use two slices together for moving large, delicate quiches or gateaux on to serving plates. Slide them underneath the item from opposite sides.

● **Removing zest** Use a zester to remove the zest without the pith from citrus fruits.

● **Whisking foods** Choose a balloon whisk – a good all-round whisk – for a variety of tasks, from making meringue to smoothing lumpy sauce.

CHOPPING TOMATOES

Using kitchen scissors
Save money by buying cans of whole rather than chopped tomatoes for cooking. Then chop the whole tomatoes in the opened can by using a pair of sharp kitchen scissors.

USING TOOLS FOR A VARIETY OF PURPOSES

● **Using a canelle knife** Decorate tall tumblers for serving cool summer drinks with long strips of cucumber peel that have been cut lengthways from a cucumber with a canelle knife.

Banding new potatoes
Run a canelle knife quickly around the middle of new potatoes before cooking them whole in their skins. This will prevent the skins from splitting, and improve their appearance.

FINDING ALTERNATIVES

● **Squeezing juice** If you do not have a citrus squeezer, place a halved lemon or lime over the prongs of a fork, and twist to extract the juice.

● **Making a funnel** To fill jars without spills, make a funnel by improvising with an empty, plastic washing-up liquid bottle. Remove the lid, and cut the top part off the bottle at the shoulder. Wash it thoroughly, and dry before use.

● **Cracking nuts** To crack nuts easily without a nutcracker, use a pair of pliers instead.

● **Removing corks** To uncork a bottle of wine without a corkscrew, screw a large metal hook into the cork, place a wooden spoon handle through the hook, and pull the cork out.

● **Using a melon baller** Instead of using a large ice-cream scoop for serving sorbet, use a melon baller to make tiny scoops. Pile these up in serving dishes for an unusual and attractive presentation.

Cleaning an artichoke
Use a melon baller to scrape out the hairy choke from inside a cooked globe artichoke. Pull out the inner leaves to expose the choke, then scrape it out with the edge of the baller.

BRIGHT IDEA

Cleaning a work surface
Use the edge of a fish slice to scrape up pastry or dough that has stuck to a work surface during rolling out. Push the fish slice firmly along the surface so that its edge dislodges any stubborn leftovers. Wipe over the entire area with a damp cloth to remove any remaining flour or pastry crumbs.

Using Other Utensils

A number of other utensils are useful in the kitchen, and a carefully selected assortment of items will help you tackle most everyday tasks confidently and efficiently. As with other kitchen equipment, buy the best you can afford, since the best-quality tools will last the longest.

Using Sieves

Use wooden spoon to press fruit

Puréeing acid fruits
When pressing acid foods such as raspberries to make a purée or remove pips, use a flexible nylon sieve. Metal sieves may react with the acid adversely, and can discolour a purée.

Moulding Dough
● **Measuring thickness** To roll out dough to a precise depth, use pieces of wood or rulers of the required thickness. Place one on either side of the dough, and roll the pin along the wood and over the dough, using the wood as a guide.
● **Moulding shortbread** To shape shortbread without the aid of an expensive wooden mould, press the dough into a fluted metal flan ring placed on a baking sheet.

Using Mixing Bowls
● **Cooking in heatproof bowls** Choose heatproof mixing bowls so that they can be used for cooking food in a microwave or for stirring mixtures over a pan of boiling water if necessary.
● **Preventing bowls slipping** To stop a bowl slipping on a work surface while whisking, place it on a dampened cloth.

Marking Utensils

Paint tip of spoon handle

Colour-coding spoons
To avoid transferring flavours, mark wooden spoon handles with coloured enamel paints so that they can be identified easily. Keep one spoon for stirring onions, one for fruit, and so on.

Using Pastry Brushes
● **Buying coloured brushes** Look in kitchenware shops for pastry brushes with coloured bristles to use for different foods. For example, choose a red-bristled brush for meat.

Position brush in lid so that bristles are just touching base of jar

Making an oil jar
Make sure you always have a brush handy for greasing baking tins by fixing a pastry brush through a hole in the lid of a screw-top jar. Keep a shallow depth of oil inside the jar.

Using Metal Equipment
● **Lining moulds** Line metal moulding tins with clingfilm before filling with acid foods, such as fruit-based jellies. This will prevent a reaction between the acid and the metal, which could spoil the food's flavour and colour.
● **Choosing colanders** When buying a colander, remember that a metal one will be more versatile than a plastic one. It can be placed over a pan as an improvised steamer.
● **Heating scale pans** When weighing sticky foods on scales that have a metal scale pan, warm the scale pan first by rinsing in boiling water; the food will slide off easily.

Handling Meat
● **Using tongs** When turning meat during cooking, use food tongs to lift and then turn it. Piercing with a knife or fork will result in a loss of juices.
● **Basting roasts** Use a syringe-type, bulb-shaped baster to baste roasts during cooking. This will stop you having to lift a heavy tin from the oven to baste the meat with hot fat.

Hold hot skewer with thick oven cloth

Branding foods
To create a decorative, branded effect on grilled poultry, meat, or fish, heat a metal skewer until red hot in a gas flame or on an electric cooker ring, then press it on to the food to mark it.

LOOKING AFTER UTENSILS

If you look after kitchen utensils well, they will give many years of service. Items made from modern materials such as polypropylene are easily maintained, but wooden utensils need to be of good quality, cleaned carefully, and checked regularly for cracks to remain efficient and safe.

SOLVING PROBLEMS

● **Releasing stuck tins** If tins or bowls become stuck inside each other, fill the inner tin with iced water to make it contract, and dip the outer one in hot water to expand it. Pull apart to separate.
● **Removing verdigris** Soak copper utensils for 2–3 hours in a solution of washing soda in warm water. Rub with a soft cloth, rinse, and dry well.
● **Removing tannin** Clean a teapot by filling it with boiling water and adding a handful of domestic borax. Leave overnight, and wash well before use. Clean chromium-plated teapots with a cloth dipped in vinegar and salt.

REMOVING ODOURS

Rubbing with lemon
After using a chopping board for preparing strong-smelling foods such as fish or onions, wash it, then rub the surface with a cut half of lemon. Use a lemon in the same way to remove strong smells from your hands.

CLEANING PRESSES

Bristles clean inside holes

Using a toothbrush
If a garlic press becomes clogged with pulp after use, clean out the holes using a toothbrush. For the best results, clean the garlic press immediately after you have used it, rather than letting the garlic residue dry out.

FINDING ALTERNATIVES

Although a very well-equipped kitchen may be the ideal, it is possible to manage with surprisingly few utensils. If you do certain kinds of cooking only occasionally, improvise with a range of basic items rather than investing in specialist equipment that will be used rarely.

ROLLING PASTRY

● **Dredging flour** To flour a worktop or other surface if you do not have a flour dredger, sprinkle flour through a sieve.

Rolling pastry
Use a straight-sided bottle to roll out pastry if you do not have a rolling pin. To keep the pastry cool and easy to handle, fill an empty bottle with water, and chill before using in this way.

MAKING FUNNELS

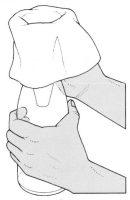

Using a piping bag
To fill a narrow-necked jar or bottle without a funnel, use a piping bag. Place the narrow end of the bag into the neck, then pour in the food or liquid carefully to avoid spills.

INVENTING SUBSTITUTES

● **Making a baking tray** Turn a large roasting tin upside down to make an extra baking tray. Alternatively, use a double thickness of foil, and turn it up at the edges to make a rim.
● **Creating a worktop** If you need a temporary extra work surface in the kitchen, place a chopping board over an open kitchen drawer. Use it only for lightweight jobs such as chopping or slicing.
● **Improvising lids** Make a close-fitting lid for a large casserole or pan by placing a baking sheet over the top of it. Alternatively, fit a piece of crumpled foil inside the top of the pan, and press it against the sides to enclose the steam.

SMALL APPLIANCES

TODAY THERE IS A WIDE CHOICE of electrical kitchen appliances that you can use to save time and energy when carrying out everyday kitchen tasks. Decide which appliances will benefit you most according to the kind of cooking you do.

USING SMALL APPLIANCES

Make maximum use of each appliance by reading the manual before you start to use it. This will tell you which tasks the appliance will tackle and how to get the best performance out of it. Keep regularly used items, such as toasters, close at hand on or near a worktop.

SELECTING APPLIANCES

● **Checking ease of cleaning** Before buying, check that small appliances can be dismantled for cleaning, and whether or not parts are dishwasher-proof.
● **Storing flex** When selecting an appliance for worktop use, such as a toaster, electric kettle, or food processor, look for a model that stores the flex inside the appliance, or one that has a self-retracting flex.
● **Preventing slipping** For safety, buy an electric kettle that is fitted with non-slip feet.
● **Buying a small bowl** If you need to purée small amounts of food for a baby, then look for a food processor with a small bowl that will fit inside the large, main bowl.

USING BLENDERS

Tea towel protects hand from steam

Covering the lid

When puréeing hot foods in a blender, leave them to cool for a few minutes before blending. While blending, hold the lid in place with a folded tea towel in case the steam pushes it off.

USING PROCESSORS

Using an extra bowl

If you use a food processor often for a variety of tasks, it is worth buying an extra bowl and blades so that you can prepare different foods in rapid succession. Spares are available from most suppliers.

SAFETY

● **Disconnecting power supply** Before doing any cleaning, oiling, or maintenance of an electrical appliance, always switch it off first, and unplug it from the electricity supply.
● **Drying hands** Always dry your hands before touching switches or plugging in and unplugging appliances to prevent electrocution.
● **Washing blades** Always wash sharp food-processor or blender blades carefully with a brush. Keep your fingers out of the way of the blade edges. Do not leave blades to soak.

MAINTAINING MIXERS

Use pointed dropper to insert oil into holes

Oiling a mixer

If the beaters of your mixer become stiff and difficult to remove, place a drop of light household oil into each of the holes into which the beaters fit. Insert the beaters, and switch on.

PROCESSING EFFICIENTLY

● **Creating a pulse-switch effect** If your food processor does not have an automatic pulse switch, alternately press the High and Off switches to achieve the same effect.
● **Preventing "walking"** If your food processor "walks" around on the worktop while in use, or if it is noisy, place it on a rubberized or soft plastic mat.
● **Warming working parts** Before mixing or kneading bread dough in a food processor, warm the bowl and blade by rinsing them in hot water before use. This will help the yeast to rise.

CARING FOR SMALL APPLIANCES

Good-quality electrical appliances are built to withstand reasonable domestic use but will benefit from regular care and maintenance. Keep electrical appliances away from hobs to prevent heat damage, and check cables regularly for wear, which could make them dangerous.

PREVENTING WEAR

● **Selecting speed** Use the correct speed on a food processor to avoid straining the motor. Check the manual to find the appropriate setting for the job to be done.
● **Changing speed** If a mixer or food processor motor strains during mixing, switch it on to High, or mix small quantities in separate batches.
● **Correcting faults** If a blender or food processor stops suddenly, switch it off, and check that nothing is jamming the blade. Leave for a few minutes before turning it on, since an overload may have tripped the circuit breaker.

EASING SEALED LIDS

Spray oil inside lid

Using spray oil
Occasionally spray the inside edge of a food-processor lid with spray-on vegetable oil to ease the lid's fit within the rim of the bowl. Avoid spraying the bowl, since this may affect some foods.

STORING APPLIANCES

● **Hanging beaters** Rather than storing mixer beaters in a drawer, hang them on a small hook. This will help prevent them from becoming damaged, and make them easy to find.
● **Storing blades** Store sharp appliance blades in a special rack or box instead of leaving them in a drawer with other utensils. Alternatively, cut slots in a piece of expanded polystyrene from the appliance packaging. Keep blades in slots.
● **Covering appliances** Use a plastic cover to protect a food processor and keep it clean if the appliance is usually stored on a crowded work surface.

CLEANING SMALL APPLIANCES

Kitchen appliances that are in everyday use will benefit from regular cleaning. Read the manufacturer's instruction booklet for special advice before doing this. Always disconnect electrical items from the mains before you clean them, and do not immerse them in water.

REMOVING DEBRIS

● **Using tongs** Keep wooden food tongs or two chopsticks near a toaster to remove foods that have become stuck inside.

Direct air spray into each compartment

Blowing out crumbs
Use a compressed air spray to expel crumbs through the bottom of a toaster. These sprays are available from photographic equipment suppliers. Unplug the toaster before cleaning.

REMOVING DEPOSITS

● **Descaling a kettle** To descale a furred-up electric kettle, cover the element with a solution of equal parts malt vinegar and water. Bring to the boil, and then leave overnight. Rinse thoroughly before use.
● **Clearing clogged filters** Remove mineral deposits from a blocked filter-coffee machine by filling the tank with equal parts distilled vinegar and water. Switch on and brew once, then brew again with clear water before use.
● **Using detergents** To clean a blender goblet easily after use, half-fill it with a solution of washing-up liquid and warm water, then run it for a few seconds to remove food deposits. Rinse, and dry well.

PURIFYING GRINDERS

Using bread
If you have used a coffee grinder or mill for grinding spices, remove all traces of spice odour and flavour that may taint coffee by grinding a few pieces of bread before it is used again.

PREPARED INGREDIENTS

*G*ATHERING TOGETHER A RELIABLE, *varied stock of prepared ingredients is essential to the smooth running of any kitchen. With such a stock, you will have the ingredients to hand to rustle up some ready meals in minutes, without having to shop specifically for them. A well-organized, versatile storecupboard is the key. Include a selection of good convenience foods in your stocks. Used with fresh foods, they have a valuable place in the kitchen.*

STORECUPBOARDS

The most important thing to remember when choosing a cupboard in which to store dry foods is that they need cool, dry, and preferably dark conditions. The best place for them is usually in a cupboard in the coolest part of the kitchen. Alternatively, store dry foods in a walk-in larder.

ORGANIZING STORECUPBOARDS

Large containers, cake tins, and packs
of longlife milk (for emergencies)

Narrow shelf makes
it easy to see what
is stored

Canisters and packs
of dry ingredients
such as flour, sugar,
and dried fruits

Tall bottles behind
smaller ones

Heavy items in
regular use, pickles,
preserves, and small
herb and spice jars

PLANNING STORAGE

● **Siting cupboards** When choosing a position for food cupboards, bear in mind that they should be as cool and dry as possible. A cold outside wall is better than an internal one – ideally at a temperature of about 10°C (50°F).

● **Choosing shelves** Where possible, store foods on narrow shelves, so that you can see and reach items easily. An ideal width of shelf is about 13 cm (5 in).

● **Lining shelves** Before stocking cupboards with food, line the shelves with a wipe-clean surface such as plastic laminate, spongeable shelf-lining paper, or kitchen foil.

Arranging ingredients

Ideally, you should aim to store large, lightweight foods such as cereals on the top shelves. Heavy bottles and cans are easy to remove if stored on lower shelves. Small spice jars should be located at the front of a shelf.

DRY STORAGE

T HE WARM AND OFTEN STEAMY CONDITIONS of many kitchens are not ideal for storing dry ingredients. Careful storage and the appropriate choice of containers can help keep moisture and heat from damaging stored foods.

STORAGE CONTAINERS

T ake a look at the storage facilities already available in your kitchen before buying expensive extra shelving or elaborate storage containers. Economical, space-saving ideas and recycled containers, such as coffee jars, can provide efficient food storage at little cost.

MAKING MAXIMUM USE OF CUPBOARD SPACE

● **Stacking containers** When you are choosing containers for storage where space is limited, make sure that they stack easily. Containers can then be arranged in two layers to make the fullest use of the space between shelves.

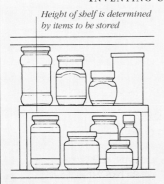

Stuff tube with carrier bags for tidy storage

Storing carrier bags
To store plastic carrier bags for reuse, make a fabric tube about 20 x 50 cm (8 x 20 in), gather the ends, and secure them with elastic. Hang the tube from a hook inside a cupboard door.

Creating hanging space
To keep small packs of herbs, spices, and nuts organized, and to save on shelf space, use a clear polythene shoe-tidy. Hang it from a hook inside a food cupboard door for easy access.

Hanging racks
Keep regularly used small items and condiments on racks hung inside cupboard doors to save on shelf space. Locate the items on butcher's hooks and in clip-on baskets attached to the racks.

REUSING CONTAINERS
● **Recycling screw-top jars** Store dry goods in containers such as coffee jars, which are moisture- and odour-free.
● **Making an airtight seal** To make sure that storage jars are airtight, wrap a strip of masking tape around the lids.
● **Coping without containers** If you do not have any airtight storage containers, place a whole packet of a dry ingredient such as flour into a self-sealing polythene bag.

INVENTING SHELF SPACE

Height of shelf is determined by items to be stored

Making an extra shelf
Make maximum use of deep shelving by adding an extra shelf for storing small items between two existing shelves. A simple, wipe-clean wooden shelf built with two sides about 17 cm (6 in) high will be the most useful. Improvise with a quick, temporary version by resting a narrow length of wood on cans placed at either end of a shelf. Use the extra space for storing small cans and jars.

CLEANING AND LABELLING CONTAINERS

To make the best use of dry ingredients, it is important to store them correctly. Make a note of use-by dates, and always finish the contents of a container before refilling it so that you do not mix old and new ingredients. Wash containers regularly to prevent lingering odours.

CLEANING CONTAINERS

● **Removing odours** To rid a container of lingering odours, fill it with hot water, and add 15 ml (1 tbsp) baking powder. Leave to stand overnight, then rinse and dry before use.

Lid firmly screwed on

Shake well

Loosening debris

Fill a dirty bottle or jar with warm water and a few drops of detergent. Add a 1-cm (½-in) layer of dried beans or rice, then shake to loosen the debris.

LABELLING CONTAINERS

● **Using packet labels** When transferring food from a packet into a storage jar, cut out the name and cooking instructions on the packet, and tape them to the jar.

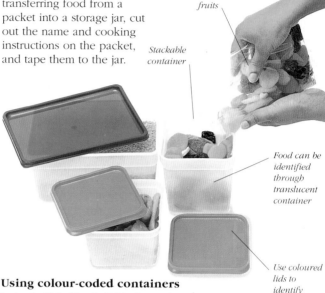

Dried fruits

Stackable container

Food can be identified through translucent container

Use coloured lids to identify contents

Using colour-coded containers

Instead of labelling individual containers, use colour-coded plastic containers to store different types of ingredient. For example, use blue for pulses and green for dried fruits, so that you can identify ingredients at a glance.

OPENING TIGHTLY SEALED JARS AND BOTTLES

Food jars and bottles are often difficult to open when food becomes stuck between the jar or bottle and the lid. To loosen, use a firm grip, tap the lid upside down on a flat surface, or try one of the methods below.

● **Loosening metal lids** Hold a metal lid under hot water to expand the metal. If the jar or bottle has been chilled, start with lukewarm water, and increase the heat gradually to prevent the glass from cracking.
● **Preventing sticky lids** Before resealing a jar or bottle with sticky food, wipe the rim and lid with a paper towel that has been dampened with hot water.

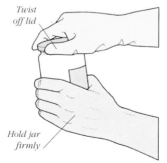

Twist off lid

Hold jar firmly

Loosening a tightly sealed jar

If a jar or bottle lid is difficult to twist open with a normal grip, wear a rubber glove to give you a firm hold on the lid. Or grip with a rubber band, a piece of sandpaper, or a damp cloth.

Lid protected with soft cloth

Apply gentle pressure

Using pliers

To loosen a tight lid on a bottle or jar with a narrow neck, use pliers or a nutcracker, but do not exert too much pressure. Place a cloth over plastic lids to prevent them from being damaged.

STORECUPBOARD STAPLES

N O STORECUPBOARD IS COMPLETE without basic staple ingredients such as pasta, rice, flours, sugars, oils, and flavourings. These items provide the basis for almost every type of cooking, and combine well with fresh ingredients.

DRIED PASTA

T here are more than one hundred different pasta shapes. Most of them are versatile, and are suitable for serving with a wide variety of dishes, but many shapes were designed with a particular sauce or type of food in mind. Dried pasta keeps well in the storecupboard.

CHOOSING AND USING PASTA		
BASIC SHAPES	EXAMPLES	COOKING SUGGESTIONS
LONG, ROUND PASTA Capelli d'angelo Spaghetti	Long, round pasta is available in many thicknesses and includes types such as spaghetti, long macaroni, and buccatini (a thick, hollow spaghetti). Vermicelli (little worms), capellini (fine hair), and capelli d'angelo (angel's hair) are very fine pastas that are traditionally dried and packed in curls that resemble birds' nests.	● Use olive-oil-based sauces such as pesto to keep the strands slippery and separate. ● Use rich tomato, cheese, and meat sauces with spaghetti or buccatini. These are firm pastas that will not be weighed down by the sauce. ● Choose light tomato, butter, or cream sauces for serving with vermicelli-type pastas to keep the delicate strands intact.
LONG, FLAT PASTA Tagliatelle Lasagne	Lasagne is a broad, flat pasta, and may be smooth, ridged, or wavy-edged; lasagnette is a narrow type of lasagne. Tagliatelle and pappardelle are wide, flat pastas; tagliarini, linguine (little tongues), and trenette are narrower versions. Fettuccine, traditionally made with egg, is narrower and thicker than tagliatelle.	● There is no need to precook dried lasagne before using it in a baked lasagne recipe. When substituting dried pasta for fresh pasta, increase the liquid content of the recipe. ● Choose thick, ribbon pastas for egg-based carbonara sauces, since the large surface area helps cook the sauce quickly. ● Toss cooked tagliatelle in a sauce or oil immediately after draining to separate the strands.
SHORT, SHAPED PASTA Penne Farfalle Fusilli	There is a seemingly endless choice of short pasta shapes, the most popular being penne (pens or quills), farfalle (butterflies or bows), fusilli and fusilli bucati (spirals or springs), conchiglie (shells), orichiette (ears), lumache (snails), and ditali (fingers of glove or thimbles). Pastina is a general term for tiny pasta shapes such as farfallini, lumachine, stelline, and ditalini.	● Use penne, fusilli, lumache, and conchiglie with chunky tomato or meat sauces, or with ragù, which will penetrate into the pasta hollows. ● Make a pasta pie from leftover, cooked, short pasta. Layer with a savoury sauce, top with cheese, and bake. ● To make a soup more substantial, sprinkle in a handful of any type of pastina near the end of cooking.

STORING AND USING PASTA

Pasta is available fresh or dried in a variety of shapes, and all types are an excellent source of fibre and carbohydrate. Dried pasta stores well and is a useful standby ingredient for everyday meals and last-minute entertaining. Wholemeal pasta is a particularly healthy option.

STORING PASTA
● **Keeping long pasta** Keep several types of long pasta in one container, but tie each type into a bundle with raffia to avoid mixing them.

USING LEFTOVER PASTA
● **Using up packets** If just a small amount of pasta is left in the packet, cook all the pasta, and use the leftovers in salads, soups, and omelette fillings.

SERVING PASTA SHAPES
● **Encouraging children** Make meals more fun for children by using alphabet or animal shapes, or other pasta shapes in a variety of everyday meals.

Move dryer in circular motion to dry thoroughly

Add farfalle to fusilli

HEALTHY TIP

Using wholemeal pasta
Choose wholemeal pasta for high-fibre, healthy pasta dishes. If you find that wholemeal pasta is too heavy to eat on its own, mix it half-and-half with refined pasta that is the same shape.

Drying a spaghetti tin
Always wash a spaghetti tin or jar with a mild detergent before refilling it. Dry with a cloth, and use a hairdryer to finish drying the inside thoroughly. Then fill with a fresh supply of pasta.

Making a pasta mix
Keep leftover pasta shapes that have similar cooking times together in an airtight container. Farfalle, fusilli, and conchiglie can be mixed together and used in everyday pasta dishes.

TYPES OF ORIENTAL NOODLE

Rice noodles
Rice noodles are made from rice and are available in different thicknesses and shapes. They are usually dried and should be soaked in warm water for 15 minutes before cooking. Use in soups and stir-fries.

Bean-thread noodles
Also called pea starch or cellophane noodles, these are made from mung beans. They are fine and white, and are available dried in neat bundles. Soak for five minutes before adding to soups or braised dishes.

Wheat and egg noodles
These noodles are usually made from wheat or buckwheat flour and egg. Choose flat noodles for use in soups and rounded noodles for stir-fries, or cook them on their own and serve as a side dish with vegetables.

USING NOODLES
● **Bulking out salads** Keep some fine-thread Chinese or Japanese noodles in your storecupboard. Soak in hot water for 5–10 minutes, then drain and toss into salads to make them more substantial.
● **Frying noodles** If you are frying bean-thread noodles, there is no need to soak them first. Just add the noodles straight from the packet to hot oil, and fry until crisp.
● **Substituting in special diets** Many types of noodle, such as rice and bean-thread noodles, are suitable for people on a wheat-free diet. Substitute these noodles in recipes that specify wheat pasta.

CHOOSING AND USING GRAINS

Grains are one of the world's most nutritious staple foods. They are a good source of protein and carbohydrate, and contain valuable minerals. Wholemeal grains are high in fibre. Keep a variety of wholemeal and refined grains in your storecupboard to use in different dishes.

STORING GRAINS

● **Storing white rice** Keep white rice in an airtight container stored in a cool, dark place. Whole, polished rice will store well for about one year if kept at room temperature. Flaked rice will keep for up to six months.

● **Storing wholemeal grains** Store wholemeal grains for a maximum of six months before use. After this time, the oil content of unrefined grain turns rancid from exposure to heat, light, and moisture.

● **Mixing grains** Brown rice and wild rice can be stored and cooked together. They require similar cooking times, and they look interesting when mixed together in risotto- and pilaf-style dishes.

MEASURING & STORING RICE

Pour rice into measured container

Use lid as measuring tool

Marking quantities

Store rice in a clear, straight-sided container that is marked off in 55-g (2-oz) measures. Use the measure as a guide to tip out the correct amount of rice each time you cook some. As a guide, 55 g (2 oz) rice – one portion – fills a volume of 75 ml (2½ fl oz).

Measuring a portion

Containers such as coffee jars can be used to store rice or other types of grain. Choose a container with a lid that holds approximately 55 g (2 oz) of rice, and which will therefore enable you to measure out rice portions quickly for cooking.

COMMON TYPES OF GRAIN

Grains form the basis of many main-course dishes, and can be served as a nutritious side dish. Check the instructions on the packet before cooking.

● **Long-grain rice** This may be brown or white, and it has a slim, long grain.
● **Pudding rice** A short-grain strain of polished rice, this is soft and starchy when cooked.
● **Basmati rice** This is a fine-flavoured, long-grain rice.
● **Glutinous rice** Used mainly in Chinese dishes, this round-grain rice has a sticky texture.
● **Arborio rice** This medium-grain rice absorbs more liquid than other types of rice.
● **Wild rice** This grain is the seed of a wild, aquatic grass.
● **Cracked wheat** A processed wheat, this is also called bulgur.
● **Couscous** This is a processed grain made from semolina.

White long-grain rice

Brown long-grain rice

Pudding rice

Basmati rice

Glutinous rice

Arborio rice

Wild rice

Cracked wheat

Couscous

FLOURS

As long as your storecupboard is clean, dry and cool, storing flours and other grain products should not be a problem. Products that are bought in paper packaging will keep best if they are transferred to clean, dry, airtight containers once they have been opened.

MAKING A SHAKER

Using a screw-top jar
To make a homemade flour shaker, make several holes in the metal lid of a screw-top jar by hammering a nail through it while resting it on a wooden board. Fill the jar with flour.

STORING FLOUR
● **Keeping fresh** Store plain, white flour in a cool, dry place for up to six months; store self-raising flour for up to three months. Wholemeal and brown flours have a higher fat content, so buy small amounts and use within two months.
● **Storing in a cool place** If the temperature is above 24°C (75°F), or if humidity is high, wrap flour in a polythene bag, and chill to prevent infestation and mould.
● **Using chilled flours** If flour has been stored in a cool place, bring it to room temperature before baking to avoid a heavy texture in the finished products.

FLOUR SUBSTITUTES

Each type of flour has different properties. Sometimes one type can be substituted for another.

● **Making self-raising flour** Sift 12.5 ml (2½ tsp) baking powder with 225 g (8 oz) plain flour. Use in the same quantities as ready-made self-raising flour.
● **Adding texture** Grind oats in a food processor, and use the resulting flour to replace up to one third of the wheat flour in bread recipes to provide texture and flavour.
● **Using cornflour** If using cornflour instead of wheatflour as a thickening agent, use half the amount given in the recipe.

DRIED FRUITS AND NUTS

Both dried fruits and nuts are useful for adding texture, flavour, and nutritive value to sweet and savoury dishes. Keep a good selection to hand, but use them up or replace them regularly, since dried fruits can over-dry and harden, and nuts easily become rancid.

BUYING & STORING
● **Tasting before buying** If possible, taste nuts before you buy them to make sure that they are not rancid.
● **Buying nuts in their shells** Buy unshelled nuts, which keep for twice as long as shelled nuts, as long as they are fresh when you buy them.
● **Choosing for freshness** Avoid shelled nuts that are shrivelled or discoloured. If they are in polythene bags, break one nut through the wrapping: if it is fresh it will snap apart rather than bend.
● **Storing at low temperature** Pack large quantities of fresh nuts in sealed bags, and store in the freezer for up to eight months. They will keep in the refrigerator for half that time.

STORING IN ALCOHOL

Cover fruits with brandy

Soaking fruits in brandy
Fill a preserving jar with dried fruits such as prunes, apricots, bananas, and figs, and add brandy or a liqueur to cover. Use the plump, richly flavoured fruits for making luxury desserts.

ADDING VARIETY

Put flaked nuts in airtight container

Using a food processor
Make flaked hazelnuts in a food processor to use as an alternative to flaked almonds. Use whole, unskinned hazelnuts; the fine slicing blade of the processor will flake them finely.

PULSES

Pulses, including beans, peas, and lentils, are an excellent source of proteins, minerals, and carbohydrates. They can be used whole in salads, puréed in soups, or ground for dips. Pulses are inexpensive and store well, but buy in small quantities, since they toughen with age.

STORING UNCOOKED PULSES

● **Using glass jars** Tip packets of pulses into airtight jars for storage, and make a note of soaking and cooking times and purchase dates on the lids.

● **Rotating stock** Use up any old stock of pulses before adding newly bought pulses to a jar. Cooking times may vary between old and new.

STORING COOKED BEANS

● **Refrigerating** If covered, cooked beans will store well in a refrigerator for several days. Alternatively, they can be frozen for up to three months.

Cannellini beans can be mixed with red kidney beans

Making a bean mix
Make up your own colourful mixture of dried beans, and store in a jar ready to add to soups and casseroles. Combine types of bean with the same cooking time.

Lay whole chillies on top of pulses

Deterring insects
To protect pulses from insect damage during storage, put a few dried chillies in the storage jars with them. Replace the lids tightly, and store as usual.

TRADITIONAL TIP

Checking beans
Tip dried beans into a bowl of cold water, and discard any that float to the surface, since this is an indication of insect or mould damage.

VARIETIES OF LENTIL

Lentils are richer in protein than any other pulses except soya beans. Most do not need soaking before cooking.

● **Continental lentils** These are the most common type, flattish in shape, and green or brown in colour. They retain their shape well when cooked.
● **Split orange or red lentils** These quick-cooking lentils are useful for thickening curries or casseroles.
● **Puy lentils** Greenish-grey in colour, these are considered to have the best flavour. They complement smoked meats.
● **Yellow lentils** Also known as yellow dahl, these lentils are often served as a side dish in Indian cooking.

CHECKING & CLEANING
● **Inspecting carefully** Before storage, check pulses and their packaging for signs of insect infestation. Discard any that appear shrivelled, discoloured, or otherwise damaged.

Sift lentils with fingertips

Sifting out grit
Tip pulses on to a shallow tray before use, and sift through them lightly to pick out any traces of grit. Look out for damaged ones at the same time.

USING PULSES
● **Cooking dried peas** If you are short of time, use split dried peas rather than whole ones: split peas do not need to be soaked before cooking.
● **Combining proteins** Mix beans or lentils with cereals such as rice or pasta. These combinations provide a nutritionally complete meal, so they are particularly useful foods in vegetarian diets.
● **Saving time** Cook a larger batch of beans than you need, and freeze half for later use to save time and fuel costs.
● **Baking blind** Save old and stale beans to use for baking blind when you make a pastry case. Store the beans in a separate jar and label clearly, since they will not be edible.

SUGARS AND SWEET FLAVOURINGS

Sugars and sweet flavourings play a very important role in our enjoyment of food. Their appearance, texture, taste, and versatility can be utilized in many ways to enhance cakes and pastries, fruit desserts, and even savoury dishes.

SUGARS

There is no difference in the calorific content of white and brown sugars, but the flavours are very different. Some of the darkest sugars add a particularly rich flavour and colour to both sweet and savoury dishes, and are often specified in recipes for sweets and cakes.

SOFTENING & STORING BROWN SUGAR

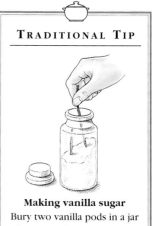

TRADITIONAL TIP

Making vanilla sugar
Bury two vanilla pods in a jar of sugar, and leave for at least one week. Stir occasionally. Use this vanilla-flavoured sugar in sweet dishes.

Softening in a microwave
To soften brown sugar, place in a microwave-proof dish, and add a wedge of apple. Cover tightly, and microwave on High for 30 seconds. Stir well.

Storing brown sugar
Keep brown sugar moist by storing in an airtight container with one or two wedges of apple. Alternatively, use a whole citrus fruit, or a piece of fresh bread.

FLAVOURED SUGAR

Pare citrus zest thinly to remove long strip

Adding a citrus flavour
To add subtle flavour to sweet dishes, desserts, cakes, and biscuits, flavour the sugar used. To impart a citrus flavour to sugar, pare long, thin strips of zest from an orange, lemon, or lime. Bury the strips of zest in a container of sugar, and store for at least three days before using.

● **Making scented sugar** Add two sprigs of fresh lavender or rosemary to a container of sugar, and shake well. Leave for 24 hours, then shake again, before leaving for one week. Use to sweeten milk puddings and fresh fruit desserts.

STORING & USING

● **Preventing lumps** To keep packets of brown sugar from absorbing moisture and forming lumps during storage, place them in a thick plastic bag in a cool, dry place.
● **Making caster sugar** If you run out of caster sugar, make your own from granulated sugar. Place in a food processor with a metal blade, and process for a few seconds for a fine consistency.
● **Keeping flasks fresh** Add a sugar cube or a teaspoonful of white sugar to a dry, empty vacuum flask before storing it away. This will prevent stale smells from developing inside.

HONEY, SYRUPS, JAMS, AND JELLIES

Like most natural products, honey is affected by light and heat and does not respond well to fluctuations in temperature. Manufactured syrups, jams, and jellies are more stable, but they also will deteriorate if exposed to air and heat. Once opened, keep them in a refrigerator.

RESTORING HONEY

Reliquefying in hot water
If clear honey becomes crystallized during storage, reliquefy it by standing the jar in a bowl of hot water for five minutes. Then rotate the jar a couple of times until the honey becomes clear and liquid.

MEASURING HONEY
● **Using a heated spoon** To measure amounts of set honey and syrups easily, use a metal spoon that has been dipped in hot water. Honey and syrup will not stick to a heated spoon.

USING SUBSTITUTES
● **Using blended honey** Choose blended types of honey for cooking, since these have a robust flavour. The delicate flavours of more expensive flower honeys are destroyed by heat during cooking.
● **Substituting syrup** Honey and golden syrup contain 20 per cent water, so reduce the liquid content of recipes when using instead of sugar.

JAMS AND JELLIES

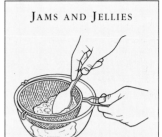

Making an apricot glaze
Gently warm some apricot jam with a squeeze of lemon juice, then rub through a sieve. Store in a screw-top jar in the refrigerator for a ready-made, sweet glaze.

● **Keeping preserves fresh**
Buy preserves that have a minimum of 60 per cent sugar content, which prevents mould.

CHOCOLATE

Chocolate is available in several different forms. In general, the better the quality of the chocolate, the better the flavour will be, since inexpensive chocolate contains fewer cocoa solids and more sugar. Chocolate is damaged by moisture and heat, so store it carefully.

FREEZING CHOCOLATE

Press firmly against grater

Fine curls

Storing grated chocolate
Grate chilled chocolate on a food grater to make fine curls. Store in a polythene bag in the freezer so that you can remove just the amount you need for cooking or decorating.

STORING CHOCOLATE
● **Cooling to keep fresh** Wrap chocolate closely, and store at a low temperature, ideally around 15°C (60°F).
● **Preventing bloom** Seal in flavour and keep out moisture by storing chocolate wrapped in parchment paper, then overwrapped with foil.
● **Storing chocolate chips** Keep chocolate chips in a storage jar, ready to tip into cake mixtures. They are low in cocoa solids so they are less sensitive to temperature than other forms of chocolate.
● **Preventing lumpy cocoa** Cocoa absorbs moisture easily, so store it in a container with a tight lid. Remove any lumps by sieving before using.

BRIGHT IDEA

Enriching meat dishes
Use chocolate to enrich the flavour of spicy meat or game casseroles. Add one square of dark, plain chocolate per portion to chilli con carne, for example, during cooking to enhance its flavour.

HERBS, SPICES, AND SEASONINGS

IT IS REALLY WORTHWHILE HAVING A GOOD SELECTION of dried herbs and spices in stock to add flavour to all kinds of everyday dish. Bear in mind that many dried herbs have a limited storage time and should be used within six months.

DRIED HERBS

Most herbs store successfully in dried form, and there is a wide range of commercially dried herbs to choose from. Freeze-dried herbs retain their colour and are therefore visually more attractive than traditionally dried herbs, but they are usually a little more expensive.

BUYING DRIED HERBS

● **Choosing jars** When buying herbs packed in jars, choose jars that have a good, airtight seal. Herbs retain their flavour best if stored in either screw-top or flip-top jars, both of which are more securely airtight than cork-top jars.
● **Buying whole-leaf herbs** If possible, choose whole-leaf dried herbs such as rosemary or bay. Dried herbs that have been crushed or ground are likely to lose their flavour much more quickly than those whose leaves are left whole.

STORING HERB JARS FOR EASY ACCESS

Place jars on their sides so that contents are clearly visible

Using drawer space
Herbs and spices are best stored in a dark place such as a cool kitchen drawer. Keep small jars flat and tidy; the herbs and spices will be easy to select since you can see the contents or labels of each jar at a glance.

DRYING & STORING HERBS

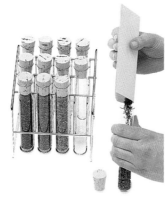

1 When drying herbs such as sage, thyme, or parsley, keep the leaves on the stems until completely dry. Rub the stems gently between your fingertips, crumbling the leaves into a small bowl. Discard the stems, or use to flavour stocks.

2 Tip some of the crumbled leaves into small containers such as test tubes, using a piece of paper to funnel the herbs in easily. Keep the containers in a rack ready to use in cooking. Store any remaining herbs for future use.

STORING DRIED HERBS

● **Keeping light out** Store dried herbs in airtight glass containers, and keep them in as dark a place as possible.
● **Extending storage life** To prolong the lives of dried herbs, wrap them tightly in polythene bags. Keep the herbs in the refrigerator for three months, or freeze for up to six months.
● **Noting storage times** Write the purchase dates of dried herbs on pieces of masking tape, and stick these on to the bases of the containers. Alternatively, use a felt-tip pen to write the dates on the jars.
● **Arranging alphabetically** If you have a large selection of herb containers, arrange them in alphabetical order so that you can find the herbs you need quickly and easily.

SPICES

Spices, like herbs, need careful storage away from light and heat, both of which shorten their shelf lives. Spices keep their flavour best when stored whole, so it is best to grind them as you need them, or to store ground spices in small amounts and use them within a short time.

USEFUL SPICES

Nutmeg

Keep a selection of basic spices in your storecupboard.

● **Black peppercorns** Crush coarsely for spiced coatings.
● **Nutmeg** Always grate fresh nutmeg since the ground spice loses flavour quickly.
● **Cinnamon** Keep cinnamon sticks and the ground spice for versatility in your cooking.
● **Coriander and cumin** These are useful ground spices to add to many ethnic dishes.

PREPARING SPICE MIXES
● **Making cinnamon sugar** Mix 225 g (8 oz) caster sugar with 25 ml (1½ tbsp) cinnamon. Store in a shaker, and sprinkle on to buttered toast.

Making mixed spice
Make up your own favourite mixture of spices, such as sweet mixed spice for baking. Grind together whole cinnamon, nutmeg, and cloves, or allspice with a pinch of ginger. Store the mixture in a small, screw-top jar.

CHOOSING WHOLE SPICES
● **Selecting seeds** Check that whole seeds such as caraway or coriander have a uniform shape and consistent colour, with no stem or chaff content.
● **Checking cardamom** Buy whole cardamom pods that are pale green, plump, and unblemished. The seeds inside should be black or brown, and slightly sticky.
● **Buying cinnamon** Choose slim cinnamon sticks with an even, pale, soft-brown colour.
● **Choosing cloves** Look for whole cloves that are large, plump, and oily, with a warm, reddish-brown colour.
● **Testing pods for freshness** Bend vanilla pods: they should be supple and resilient.

GRINDING WHOLE SPICES

Tip whole spices into grinder

Using a coffee grinder
Grind your own whole spices in an electric coffee grinder to make a spice blend in seconds. Use a pastry brush or paper towel to clean the grinder thoroughly immediately after use, removing any lingering spice flavours.

USING MUSTARDS
● **Mustard powder** Add a little mustard powder, which acts as a preservative, to mayonnaise and other dressings to prolong their shelf lives, and to add a sharp flavour to the dressings.

Making mustard
Crush white and black mustard seeds together, and mix to a paste with wine vinegar. Add honey and flavourings such as chillies to taste. Keep in a screw-top jar.

KEEPING FLAVOURS
● **Using spices quickly** Ground spices lose their flavour and aroma quickly, so buy only a small quantity at a time, and make sure that you use it up within six months.
● **Choosing chillies** Choose red chillies, which are simply ripened green chillies, rather than green chillies if you want a sweeter flavour. Select yellow caribe chillies for a sweet, mild flavour; green jalapeño chillies, which are the most common type, for average strength; and orange habanero chillies for a hot and distinctive fruity flavour.
● **Toasting whole spices** To get the most intense flavour from spices, toast them whole in a heavy-based, dry frying pan. Shake the pan over a fairly high heat for a minute or two, and use immediately, either whole or ground.

OILS, VINEGARS, AND SEASONINGS

Oils are fats that are in liquid form at room temperature. Exposure to light and air can cause them to deteriorate, so keep them in airtight containers in a cool cupboard along with vinegars, salt, and seasonings, all of which require similar storage conditions.

FLAVOURING OILS & VINEGARS

White wine vinegar with fresh herbs

Cider vinegar with honey, lemon, and mint

Olive oil with garlic and lime wedges

Extra virgin olive oil with orange zest and coriander seeds

White wine vinegar with skewered ginger and garlic

Red wine vinegar with cumin, cinnamon, and cloves

Creating unique flavours
Flavoured oils and vinegars are easy to make at home. Immerse clean, freshly picked herbs, spices, fruits, or scented flowers in oil or vinegar in sterilized screw-top or cork-sealed bottles. Refrigerate for about two weeks before using.

INFUSING FLAVOURS
● **Bruising ingredients** Lightly bruise fresh herbs before steeping in vinegar to help release their flavour. Cloves of garlic and shallots also benefit from being lightly crushed.
● **Infusing quickly** To infuse flavours into vinegar quickly, heat the vinegar gently until almost boiling. Pour it on to your chosen flavouring, cool, then seal in bottles.
● **Flavouring with fruits** Use fresh raspberries, strawberries, blackcurrants, or slices of lemon to make delicately flavoured fruit vinegars, which can be used to add mellow flavours to savoury dishes and drinks.
● **Storing fruit vinegars** To keep fruit vinegars for longer than about one week, strain and then discard the fruits before transferring the vinegar into clean bottles.

USING OILS

● **Nut oils** Oils that are made from nuts, such as walnut or hazelnut, have rich, intense flavours, making them ideal for use in salads or flavouring savoury dishes. Once opened, store them in the refrigerator, since they deteriorate quickly.
● **Olive oil** Save the best-quality extra virgin olive oil for lightly cooked dishes and salads, since too much heat will destroy the fine flavour and aroma of the oil.
● **Healthy oils** Use oils labelled monounsaturated, such as olive oil, or polyunsaturated, such as sunflower, corn, and safflower oils, for a healthy diet. These lower blood cholesterol levels, unlike saturated animal fats.

STORING OILS

Storing bottles of oil
To help keep cupboard shelves clean, stand bottles of oil on a tray that can easily be wiped clean. Use a tray that has deep sides, thus reducing the risk of the bottles being knocked over.

TRADITIONAL TIP

Storing free-running salt
To make sure salt stays dry, and therefore runs freely from the salt cellar, add a few grains of rice to the cellar. Replace the rice every few months – not every time you refill the cellar.

CONVENIENCE FOODS

MOST PEOPLE RELY ON CONVENIENCE FOODS from time to time, usually when they are unable to shop for and cook fresh ingredients. Fast food need not necessarily mean junk food, and there is a vast range to choose from.

STOCKING AND USING CONVENIENCE FOODS		
TYPES OF FOOD	EXAMPLES OF FOOD	GENERAL USES
CANNED, SAVOURY FOODS	Keep a supply of whole and chopped plum tomatoes; beans and pulses; vegetables such as sweetcorn and asparagus; tuna; cooked ham; savoury pie fillings; and condensed soups.	● Add chopped tomatoes to casseroles and pizza toppings. ● Fold whisked egg whites into condensed soup for an easy soufflé.
CANNED, SWEET FOODS	Store canned fruits such as pineapple rings and chunks and peach halves or slices; exotic fruits such as lychees and guavas; fruit pie fillings; ready-made custard; and rice pudding.	● Layer fruits and rice pudding in tall glasses. Stir puréed fruits into ready-made custard for a dessert fool. ● Use ready-made fruit pie fillings as quick cheesecake toppings.
DRY FOODS AND PACKET MIXES	Stock sauce and gravy mixes; dried vegetables; instant mash, pasta and rice mixes; instant whisked desserts; dried milk and custard powder; bread, pastry, batter, and cake mixes.	● Enrich instant mash with single cream and mixed dried herbs. ● Transform a simple cake mix by sprinkling with brandy, then filling with cream and canned fruits.
BOTTLED FOODS AND PRESERVES	Keep vegetables in brine; fruits in brandy; ready-made meals such as cassoulet or ratatouille; pesto; olives; sun-dried tomatoes; and antipasto.	● Spread pesto on ciabatta bread; toast to make bruscetta. ● Add ricotta or feta cheese to sun-dried tomatoes for an easy starter.
LONGLIFE FOODS	Stock up with part-baked breads and pastries; ready-made meals and pasta dishes; milk, cream, whipped desserts, and ready-made custard.	● Use part-baked breads and pastries to create a homemade effect. ● Make a dessert by filling a ready-made pastry case with canned fruits.
CHILLED FOODS	Chill ready-made meals; fresh pasta; soups; sweet and savoury sauces; fruit salad; prepared mixed salads and dressings; fresh pastry; pâtés; and dips.	● Add chopped herbs and croûtons to ready-made soups. ● Prepare salads in advance and chill while you prepare the rest of the meal.
FROZEN, SAVOURY FOODS	Freeze vegetables and stir-fry mixes; French fries; cooked rice; pizza bases; prepared fish and shellfish; meat and poultry; pastry, pies, and quiches.	● Fill an omelette with a stir-fry mix. ● Use ready-rolled pastry sheets or sheets of filo pastry to make a quick base for a flan or tart.
FROZEN, SWEET FOODS	Freeze prepared fruits, especially raspberries and seasonal soft-fruit mixes; melon balls; ices, sorbets, and iced desserts; gateaux; and fruit juices.	● Make summer puddings in winter with frozen soft fruits. ● Purée frozen fruits with icing sugar to make an easy coulis.

FRESH INGREDIENTS

*I*F YOU ARE ABLE TO SHOP FOR FOOD *on a daily basis, keeping perishable ingredients fresh is not a problem. For most people, this is not a practical option, and they have to buy large amounts of fresh foods less frequently. Good planning and organization, sensible shopping, and careful storage will ensure that perishable foods remain fresh, flavourful, and safe.*

SHOPPING

Food shopping needs to begin in the kitchen if it is to be successful. Making a detailed list of everything you need can be an ongoing task, and every member of the household can help. Plan several days' menus in advance, and use them as a basis for fresh-food shopping.

BUYING WISELY
● **Making the most of bargains** Look out for seasonal best buys, and plan menus around foods that are in season.
● **Avoiding waste** You should buy only what you can store. Bulk buying is usually a false economy if you cannot use the food while it is fresh.

MAKING LISTS
● **Listing in order** Organize items on your shopping list into groups and, if possible, arrange the groups so that they follow the layout of the supermarket. This will make shopping quick and easy, and you will be less likely to miss items that are on the list.

USING REMINDERS
● **Noting dates** Note use-by dates on perishable foods, and keep these in mind when planning meals and shopping in advance. It may be possible to freeze certain items for a few days to extend their shelf lives, but check the labels on packets for refrigeration details.

MONEY-SAVING TIP

Collecting vouchers
Clip food-discount vouchers together with a large paper-clip, and attach them to a kitchen pinboard. They will then be easy to find when you go shopping.

Keeping a list handy
Keep a current shopping list attached to the refrigerator door with a magnet. Each time an item of food is used up, add it to the list as a reminder to replace your stock of ingredients.

Clipping to a trolley
When you go shopping, take a bulldog clip or a clothes peg with you to attach your shopping list to the trolley so that the list does not get lost. It will also help you to read the list at a glance.

PACKING

The priority on any food shopping trip is to keep the food cool and fresh until you get home. If possible, shop for perishable items last, and avoid leaving them in a warm car. Invest in cool bags with ice-packs if you cannot put food into a refrigerator quickly.

PACKING SHOPPING TO KEEP IT COOL

Keep foods cool with ice cubes

Using a cool bag
If the weather is warm, pack perishable food into an insulated cool bag. Put a tightly closed jar filled with ice cubes or several ice-packs inside the bag.

Lining a shopping basket
Make your own improvised cool bag by insulating an ordinary shopping bag or basket with a layer or two of crumpled newspaper or bubble wrap.

MAKING PACKING EASY
● **Starting with heavy items** When packing at the check-out, always begin by placing heavy items at the bottoms of bags or boxes. Lighter, more delicate items should be placed on top to avoid damage.
● **Keeping a spare bag** Always keep a string bag or folding bag on hand, ready for any extra or unexpected shopping.
● **Keeping foods separate** Pack chilled and frozen foods separately from your other shopping and, if you are travelling by car, load frozen foods last. You can then unload them first, and freeze them immediately.

STORING

Storing food safely is largely a matter of common sense. It is worth following some simple guidelines to avoid health risks. Check use-by dates when buying food, and adhere to them; always keep highly perishable foods cold; and keep raw and cooked foods separate.

STORING FOOD SAFELY
● **Finding the coldest zone** To identify the coldest zone of a refrigerator, check the manufacturer's handbook, since the location varies according to make and type. Frost-free refrigerators have an even temperature throughout.
● **Keeping opened canned foods** Empty the contents of a part-used can of food into a bowl, cover, and refrigerate.
● **Avoiding contamination** Always store raw meats and foods to be defrosted beneath any cooked foods to prevent drips from raw foods from contaminating cooked foods.
● **Removing packaging** Leave foods wrapped unless their packaging recommends that you do otherwise.

ORGANIZING A REFRIGERATOR	
AREA	FOODS TO BE STORED
Cool zone: middle to lower shelves beneath freezer compartment	Milk, yoghurt, fruit juices, hard cheeses, eggs, butter, margarine, low-fat spreads, cooking fats.
Cold zone: shelf below freezer compartment, or bottom shelf of larder refrigerator	Precooked chilled foods, cooked meats, soft cheeses, prepared salads, home-prepared dishes and leftovers; raw meats and fish (at lowest level).
Salad drawers or bins	Vegetables and fruits suitable for low-temperature storage, and salad items such as unwashed lettuce, whole tomatoes, radishes, cucumbers, and celery.
Refrigerator door and compartments	Milk, soft drinks, fruit juices, opened bottles and jars of sauces, preserves, eggs, and salad dressings.

VEGETABLES, FRUITS, AND HERBS

F OR A HEALTHY, WELL-BALANCED DIET, it is essential to include a wide range of vegetables and fruits that are rich in vitamins, minerals, and fibre. Fresh or dried herbs help to add colour and a distinctive flavour to every meal.

CHOOSING VEGETABLES

E ach vegetable has particular indicators of quality, but in general crispness and a bright colour are good signs to look out for. Choose vegetables in season for the best value. Imported produce adds variety and interest to meals but costs more than locally grown vegetables.

CHECKING VEGETABLES FOR QUALITY & FRESHNESS

Press centre gently

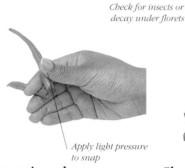
Apply light pressure to snap

Check for insects or decay under florets

Checking a cabbage
Before buying a cabbage, check that the heart is firm by pressing the centre with your thumb. Avoid those that have soft or discoloured outer leaves, and brown or damaged patches.

Snapping a bean
To make sure that French beans are fresh, hold a bean between your forefinger and thumb, and bend it gently. If it is fresh, the bean will snap in two – not bend – under light pressure.

Checking a cauliflower
Always pull back the outer leaves of a cauliflower, and look carefully between the florets to ensure that there are no insects or signs of decay. The florets should be firm and white.

SHOPPING WISELY
● Selecting shape and size When buying vegetables such as Brussels sprouts, choose those of a uniform size and shape so that they cook evenly.
● Testing avocados Test an avocado by cupping it lightly in your hand and squeezing very gently. If it gives slightly, it is ready to eat. Pressing with fingertips will cause bruising.
● Buying garlic Buy plump garlic with tightly packed cloves and dry skin. Avoid any bulbs with soft, shrivelled cloves or green shoots.
● Selecting chillies Choose chilli peppers according to your taste. In general, the smaller the chilli, the hotter it will be.

SALAD AND FRUIT VEGETABLES

Ripening tomatoes
If you need to speed up the ripening of green tomatoes, place them in a paper bag with an apple or a ripe, red tomato. Place the bag in a warm, dark place, and leave it there for a couple of days until the tomatoes ripen and turn red.

● **Lettuces** Choose lettuces that are firm and crisp, with bright, undamaged leaves. Avoid any that have discoloured or yellow outer leaves.
● **Peppers** Red, yellow, and orange peppers have a sweeter flavour than green peppers, and are more suitable for salads.
● **Cucumbers** Select cucumbers that are large, straight, and firm with fresh, shiny skins.
● **Other vegetables** Some vegetables, such as courgettes, cauliflower, and mushrooms, that are usually served cooked, make delicious salad ingredients. Use them raw or cooked to add extra texture to salads.

STORING VEGETABLES

Most vegetables have a limited storage time. Green vegetables should ideally be used within two days, but some root vegetables can be stored for several weeks in a cool, dark, airy place. All vegetables lose nutrients as soon as they are cut, so prepare them just before use.

STORING GARLIC

Garlic should be completely covered with oil

Storing in oil

To store garlic ready for use, peel a whole head of garlic, place the cloves in a jar, and cover with olive oil. The oil will preserve the garlic, and the garlic will flavour the oil, making it delicious for salad dressings. Refrigerate the flavoured oil for up to two weeks.

REVIVING CELERY

Add drops of lemon juice

Iced water

Maintaining crispness

Revive wilted celery sticks by placing them in a bowl of iced water for at least one hour. Add a squeeze of fresh lemon juice to improve the flavour. To revive a whole head of celery, cut a thin slice from the root end, and stand the head in iced water.

BRIGHT IDEA

Making a garlic pot
Keep garlic fresh by allowing air to circulate around it. Instead of buying a purpose-made garlic pot, use an upturned terracotta pot that has a drainage hole in its base. Place the garlic on a small saucer, and cover with the terracotta pot.

COLD STORAGE

Most vegetables can be stored in a cool, dark, well-ventilated place. Vegetables that perish quickly should be stored in the refrigerator. However, low refrigeration temperatures can bring about changes to the flavour and texture of some vegetables, such as potatoes.

- **Mushrooms** Store fresh mushrooms in a paper bag at the bottom of the refrigerator.
- **Cabbage and celery** Keep cabbage and celery in the salad drawer of the refrigerator in order to retain flavour and texture.
- **Tomatoes** Store tomatoes in the refrigerator only if they are ripe. Low temperatures can spoil the ripening process of underripe tomatoes.

STORING ONIONS

- **Saving pieces of onion** Leave the skin, and try to retain the root end on the piece of onion that you wish to keep. Wrap in clingfilm, and store in a refrigerator for up to three days.

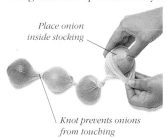

Place onion inside stocking

Knot prevents onions from touching

Stringing onions

Onions and garlic are best stored hung up in strings. Put the onions or garlic bulbs in a nylon stocking. Tie a knot between each onion or garlic bulb, then hang in a dry place.

KEEPING CHILLIES

- **Freezing in freshness** Chillies freeze very successfully and can be used straight from the freezer, without thawing first. Freeze fresh, whole chillies in a polythene bag.

Thread through top of chilli, not stem

Making a garland

String fresh chillies in a garland to dry and store. Using strong cotton or nylon thread and a clean needle, string them, knot the thread ends together, then hang the chillies to air-dry.

SHOPPING FOR FRUITS

Methods of testing ripeness vary from one fruit to another, but plumpness, firmness, and a good fragrance are usually good, general indicators of freshness in most types of fruit. Test for ripeness very carefully before making your choice to avoid bruising delicate fruits.

ENSURING FRESHNESS

● **Grapes** Before buying grapes, shake the bunch gently. The grapes should stay on the stem. If a few fall off, the branch is not fresh.

● **Citrus fruits** Citrus fruits such as lemons, oranges, and grapefruits should feel heavy for their size if they are juicy.

● **Banana skins** The skins of bananas become slightly flecked with brown when ripe. Slightly green, underripe bananas will ripen at room temperature in a few days.

● **Blackberries** These should be plump and glossy, with good colour. If the hulls are still attached, the berries were picked when underripe, and they will lack flavour.

CHECKING FRUITS FOR QUALITY & RIPENESS

Gently press with both thumbs

Pull leaf out from top of pineapple

Checking a melon
To determine whether or not a melon is ripe, hold it firmly in both hands. Lightly press the area immediately around the tip of the melon, at the opposite end to the stem end; the surface should give slightly. A ripe melon will also have a pleasantly sweet scent.

Checking a pineapple
To check whether a whole pineapple is ripe and ready to eat, pull gently at a leaf at the top of the pineapple. If the leaf pulls out easily, the fruit is ripe. Like melons, pineapples have a sweet scent when ripe. Soft, dark patches indicate bruising.

STORING FRUITS

Most fruits should be consumed quickly, when they are at their best and most nutritious. If it is necessary to store fruits, the correct conditions will help preserve their flavours and vitamin content. Remove tight packaging unless the label states otherwise.

COLD STORAGE

Wrapping fruits
To store citrus or hard fruits for longer than one week, wipe each fruit dry, and wrap in newspaper. Pack in a polythene bag or a box, and store in a cool, dry place.

● **Storing long-term** Store pears for up to six months at −0.5°C (30°F). Store in single layers to avoid bruising.

STORING BERRIES

Preventing damage
To keep soft berries at their best, tip them from their punnet into a single layer on a tray lined with paper towels. Discard any damaged or mouldy berries, and cover lightly with more paper towels before chilling.

KEEPING FRUITS

● **Storing grapes** Wrap bunches of grapes loosely in newspaper, and keep them in the dark.

● **Getting the most juice** Citrus fruits will yield the most juice if they are stored at room temperature. If they have been stored in a refrigerator, warm each one in the microwave on High for about five seconds.

● **Freezing bananas** Freeze whole bananas in their skins, wrapped in clingfilm, for up to six months. Eat them while slightly frozen, or mash them and use in baking or drinks.

● **Keeping husks** Leave the husks on cape gooseberries during storage, and they will stay sweet and juicy for weeks.

MAINTAINING A SUPPLY OF HERBS

Herbs make such a wonderful difference to even the simplest everyday dishes that it is worthwhile ensuring that you always have a supply of both fresh and dried versions. Even in winter, you can have a choice of fragrant leaves for both cooking and garnishing.

HARVESTING HERBS

● **Using potted herbs** Herbs in pots bought from a supermarket often have a limited life, but if you use just a few top shoots at a time, they will thrive for longer.
● **Managing growth** Allow herbs to become established before harvesting them regularly, and pick evenly to keep them in good shape.
● **Growing herbs closeby** Grow your herbs on a kitchen window-ledge or by the kitchen door so that they are always within easy reach, even when it is dark or raining.
● **Letting herbs flower** Allow a few herbs, such as borage, rosemary, or chives, to flower, and use as a pretty garnish.

CHOOSING & GROWING HERBS

Oregano has a spicy aroma and enhances tomatoes and meats

Chives have a mild onion flavour

Sage is strongly flavoured and is used in stuffings

Tender flat-leaved parsley can be served whole in salads

Trailing silver thyme has a strong, savoury character

Golden lemon thyme complements fish and chicken well

Growing herbs for cooking

Grow a variety of herbs together on your kitchen window-ledge. Herbs that will grow well together for culinary use are parsley (either curly or flat-leaved), chives, thyme, oregano, and sage.

STORING HERBS

Once herbs are cut, they have a short life, and their aroma and flavour soon diminish. With careful storage, however, herbs can be kept fresh for several days. Tender-leaved herbs such as basil, chervil, and coriander wilt quickly, so they should be used up as soon as possible.

PREPARING DELICATE HERBS FOR STORAGE

Cut stems diagonally

Take care not to crush herbs with bag

1 Before storing delicate herbs, cut the ends off the stems with a sharp knife. Place the herbs in a tall glass of cold water covering at least 2.5 cm (1 in) of the stems. Add a pinch of sugar to the water.

2 Place a polythene bag loosely over the herbs and glass, and secure with a rubber band. Store in a cool place or in the refrigerator. Change the water and recut the stems every one or two days.

REVIVING HERBS

Use plant spray

Reviving limp herbs
To refresh fresh sprigs of delicate herbs that have wilted, place them on paper towels, and moisten them with a fine water spray. Chill briefly in the refrigerator before use.

DAIRY FOODS

Dairy products are highly nutritious foods, but they are often high in fat and should therefore be used in moderate quantities. The refrigerator is the best place for storage, although many dairy products also freeze successfully.

EGGS

Eggs are an excellent source of both protein and vitamins. They are an extremely versatile food and can be boiled, fried, poached, or used to thicken, emulsify, coat, bind, or glaze. Eggs are sensitive to temperature changes and should be warmed to room temperature before use.

MARKING BOILED EGGS

Mark cross on eggshell

Using a pen
Use a food-colouring pen to mark a cross on hard-boiled eggs. The cross will distinguish them from uncooked eggs if stored together.

TESTING EGGS

Salt water

Checking for freshness
Dissolve 30 ml (2 tbsp) salt in 600 ml (1 pint) water. Place the eggs in the water. If an egg sinks, it is fresh; if it floats, it is stale.

BUYING & STORING
● **Checking for cracks** When buying eggs, move each egg gently in the carton to check that none are damaged.
● **Keeping freshness** Store eggs in a carton in the refrigerator to prevent them from losing moisture and absorbing odours through their shells from strongly flavoured foods nearby.
● **Storing correctly** Always store eggs with the pointed end downwards, to centre the yolk and keep the eggs fresh.

CREAM

There are several types of cream, each of which has different properties, depending on the butterfat content. The butterfat content also determines the cream's richness, flavour, and whipping characteristics. The more fat a cream contains, the less likely it is to curdle.

STORING CREAM

Pour cream into ice-cube tray

Freezing in an ice tray
Open-freeze double cream in an ice-cube tray, then turn out the cubes into polythene bags, and store in the freezer. The cubes can be added directly to hot soups, sauces, or casseroles.

USING CREAM
● **Whipping cream** Choose whipping cream rather than double cream when you need softly whipped cream for folding into mousse-type desserts, or for piping. It is not easily overwhipped.
● **Low-fat alternative** Mix a few tablespoonfuls of natural yoghurt or blended cottage cheese into whipped double cream to lighten creamy desserts or cake fillings.
● **Crème fraîche** Use crème fraîche as a substitute for single or soured cream in hot sauces, since it can be heated to boiling without curdling.

BRIGHT IDEA

Making soured cream
To make soured cream, add 5 ml (1 tsp) lemon juice to 150 ml (¼ pint) single cream. Stir, and leave until thickened.

CHEESE

Cheese is a high-protein food and has many culinary uses. It can be used to add flavour to fillings and sauces, and forms the basis of some desserts. Most cheese is eaten uncooked in salads and sandwiches, or as part of a cheese tray, and is best served at room temperature.

STORING SOFT CHEESE

● **Freezing cheese** Only freeze cheese containing more than 45 per cent fat, since cheese with a lower fat content will separate and become granular.

Wrapping in vine leaves
Wrap pieces of soft cheese such as brie in blanched, fresh vine leaves, or in brine-packed leaves that have been rinsed. This will keep the cheese fresh for 3–4 days if stored in the refrigerator.

KEEPING FETA CHEESE

Add sprigs of herbs for flavour

Preserving in oil
Store cubes of feta cheese in a jar. Add sprigs of herbs, garlic cloves, or chillies for flavour. Fill the jar with a good-quality olive oil. Use the oil later for salad dressings or cooking.

TRADITIONAL TIP

Keeping cheese moist
To keep hard cheeses such as mature Cheddar or Parmesan moist during storage, wrap in a clean piece of muslin or cotton cloth that has been dampened with beer. Place in an airtight container, and store in the refrigerator for 1–2 weeks.

BUTTER

Butter is a natural product that is made from cream. It can be salted or unsalted and is a valuable fat for use in baking, since it adds substance and richness of flavour. Butter can be used for light sautéeing or, if mixed with herbs or other ingredients, as a flavouring.

STORING BUTTER

● **Keeping odours out** Always wrap butter well or store it in a closed container, since it easily picks up odours from strongly flavoured foods.
● **Storing at low temperature** Keep unsalted butter in the freezer for up to a maximum of six months. Freeze salted butter for only three months, since changes in flavour can occur at low temperatures.
● **Clarifying butter** To store butter for several weeks, heat it gently until frothing but not coloured. Strain through muslin to remove salt and moisture, then refrigerate.

PREPARING & STORING HERB-FLAVOURED BUTTER

Blending with herbs
Make flavoured butter by stirring chopped fresh herbs or garlic into softened butter. Use a fork to work the herbs in thoroughly. Serve with grilled meats and fish.

Cutting out shapes
To make shaped butter pats, roll out the butter on a sheet of non-stick paper. Use a small pastry cutter to cut out shapes. Store in a container in the refrigerator.

MEAT AND POULTRY

MEAT OF ALL KINDS IS A GOOD SOURCE OF PROTEIN, B vitamins, and iron. Fat, present in varying degrees, is necessary for flavour and tenderness, but avoid eating high-fat cuts of meat regularly if you wish to have a healthy diet.

BUYING

The most important rule to follow when you are buying fresh meat is to buy it from a reputable supplier. You must be able to rely on the butcher to have hung and stored the meat properly, and to advise you correctly about cuts of meat and appropriate cooking methods.

SELECTING MEAT
● **Checking the colour** Beef should be dark red with a slightly brownish tinge and a light marbling of fat. In the case of lamb, the darker the colour, the older the animal.
● **Choosing the right cut** In general, the front part of an animal produces the toughest cuts of meat, suitable for slow cooking. Tender cuts come from the middle, which has the least-used muscles.
● **Buying quality cuts** Tough cuts may be inexpensive, but they take longer to cook than tender cuts, raising fuel costs.

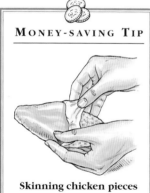

MONEY-SAVING TIP

Skinning chicken pieces
Chicken skin is high in fat, so it should be removed for people on low-fat diets. If you need skinless chicken pieces, buy them with the skins on, and remove them yourself. Pull off the skin using your fingertips.

SERVING QUANTITIES PER PERSON	
CUTS OF MEAT OR POULTRY	QUANTITIES
Steaks without bone, such as beef, lamb, or pork fillet, lean beef sirloin, or pork loin.	125–175 g (4½–6 oz)
Steaks on the bone, such as T-bone steaks or leg-of-lamb steaks.	175–225 g (6–8 oz)
Lamb chops or cutlets on the bone, or boneless lamb noisettes.	2 small or 1 large
Pork loin or chump chops with bone, or pork spare-rib chops with bone.	1 x 175 g (6 oz)
Cuts with a high proportion of bone, such as Chinese-cut pork spare ribs, shin of beef, or oxtail.	400–500 g (14 oz–1 lb 2 oz)
Lean casserole meats, such as diced lamb shoulder, or stir-fry meats such as fillet of pork.	125–150 g (4½–5½ oz)
Roasts on the bone, such as rib of beef, leg or shoulder of lamb, or pork loin.	225–300 g (8–11 oz)
Roasts without bone, such as rib of beef, leg of lamb, or pork loin.	125–175 g (4½–6 oz)
Chicken joints on the bone, such as drumsticks, thighs, wings, or quarters.	2 joints or 1 quarter
Whole roast chicken or turkey on the bone.	350 g (12 oz) oven-ready
Whole roast duck or goose on the bone.	1 kg (2 lb 4 oz) oven-ready
Offal, such as liver, kidneys, or hearts.	100–125 g (3½–4½ oz)

STORING

The correct storage of meat and poultry is vitally important, since they can deteriorate quickly, especially if kept at warm temperatures.

Having bought meat and poultry, refrigerate them as soon as possible. In warm weather, pack them in a cool bag to transport them home.

FREEZING MEAT CUTS

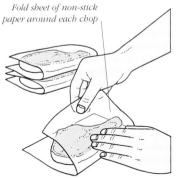

Fold sheet of non-stick paper around each chop

Separating meat pieces
When freezing hamburgers, chops, or steaks, which tend to stick together when frozen, separate them with pieces of non-stick paper or freezer food-wrap. You will then be able to remove the quantity needed without thawing the whole batch.

FREEZING POULTRY

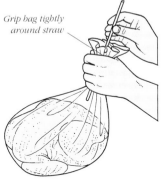

Grip bag tightly around straw

Expelling air
To remove excess air when packing whole poultry ready for freezing, place the bird in a polythene freezer bag, and gather up the opening, leaving a gap of about 5 mm (¼ in). Insert a straw through the gap, and suck out as much air as possible.

SAFETY

● **Keeping raw meats cold** Always put fresh meat and poultry into the refrigerator as soon as you arrive home. Store in covered containers so that the meat cannot drip on to other foods.
● **Preventing contamination** Keep different types of meat separate during storage. Always wash your hands and utensils after handling each type of raw meat, and before preparing other types of meat or food.
● **Using thawed foods** Always use up quickly any thawed meat or poultry, and do not be tempted to refreeze it, since this will increase the risk of food poisoning when the meat is eaten.

THAWING MEAT AND POULTRY

Immerse bird fully in water

Immersing in water
To speed up the thawing of a whole turkey or chicken, leave it in its freezer-proof wrapping, immerse it in a large bowl of cold water, and place in the refrigerator. Change the water at regular intervals until the poultry is completely thawed.

● **Allowing time** Allow plenty of time for meat and poultry to thaw. In a refrigerator, thawing may take several hours, or even two or three days in the case of large joints or whole birds.

● **Preventing drips** Place meat or poultry on a large plate if thawing in a refrigerator. Lay paper towels underneath the meat or poultry to absorb the juices and prevent them from dripping on to other foods.
● **Thawing large birds** Thawing frozen poultry in the refrigerator may not be possible because of the size of the bird. Instead, leave it to thaw in a cool room. Keep the bird in its wrapping, but puncture the seal.
● **Checking for ice** To ensure that whole poultry is completely thawed, feel inside the cavity, and check whether the legs and thigh joints move easily.
● **Using a skewer** To make sure that a large joint of meat is completely thawed, push a skewer through the thickest part of the joint. You should be able to feel with the skewer if there is any ice remaining.

REFRIGERATING MEATS

● **Storing raw meat** Raw meat and poultry should ideally be stored on the bottom shelf of a refrigerator. This will ensure that their juices do not drip on to other foods.
● **Arranging meats** Keep fresh, ready-to-eat foods on the top shelf, and cooked meats on the middle shelf above raw meats.
● **Removing wrappings** If you purchase meat that is wrapped in paper, discard the paper and transfer the meat to a covered dish before storing it in the refrigerator. However, if meat is packed in a sealed tray, you can keep it safely in the tray for storage.
● **Using clingfilm** Place meat or poultry in a deep dish for storing, and cover the dish tightly with clingfilm. Make sure that the clingfilm does not touch the food's surface.

FISH AND SHELLFISH

T HE MOST IMPORTANT THING TO REMEMBER about using fish and shellfish is that they must be totally fresh. They deteriorate quickly, so to enjoy them at their best, buy only what you need, store it with care, and use it as soon as possible.

FISH

F ish is a very important part of a healthy diet. There are so many varieties from which to choose, suitable for all cooking methods, that you will find one that is appropriate for any occasion. If you prefer not to have to bone fish, ask the supplier to fillet it for you.

CHECKING FOR SIGNS OF FRESHNESS

Eyes are clear and bright, not sunken or dull

Scales are intact and shiny

Gills are bright red in colour

Moist, shiny skin is not slimy and has no abrasions

Looking closely for freshness

Look for clear, bright eyes and a moist, shiny skin. The gills, if present, should be bright red, and the scales should be difficult to remove. When pressed with a fingertip, the flesh should spring back easily. The fish should smell fresh and clean.

CHOOSING FISH

● **Round, white fish** Large round fish, such as cod or coley, are usually sold cut into steaks, cutlets, or fillets, with or without the skin.
● **Flat, white fish** Large flat fish, such as halibut or turbot, are sold whole or in fillets or steaks. Small fish such as plaice are sold whole.
● **Oily fish** These include trout, herring, mackerel, and sardines, and are sold whole or in fillets. Oily fish are an important source of vitamins and essential oils that help to prevent coronary disease.

REFRESHING FISH

Immerse fillet completely in iced water

"Crimping" a fillet

If a fish fillet becomes slightly limp on the way home from shopping, revive it in the way that anglers do, by "crimping" it. Add 15 ml (1 tbsp) sea salt to 1 litre (1¾ pints) iced water in a bowl. Soak the fish in the icy salt water for about 15 minutes.

REFRIGERATING FISH

Pack ice cubes closely around sides of fish to chill quickly

Packing with ice

Speed up the chilling of fresh fish in the refrigerator by placing ice cubes or crushed ice around it. Alternatively, fill two polythene bags with ice and seal, then place the fish between them. Make sure that you remove the bags before the ice has melted.

FREEZING FISH

● **Glazing** To keep fish fillets moist in the freezer, first open-freeze the fish until solid, then dip briefly into iced water. A thin covering of ice will form over the fish. Whole fish can be dipped twice in order to produce a thicker ice layer. Then wrap the fish and freeze.
● **Labelling** Always clearly label fish packs before freezing with the date they were frozen. White fish has a storage life of 12 months; oily fish, six months. Cooked fish dishes keep for just three months in the freezer.
● **Refreezing** Check with the supplier that fish has not been previously frozen. It is not advisable to refreeze fish.

SHELLFISH

It is especially important with shellfish to make sure that you buy them from a reputable supplier. Avoid any that may be contaminated or not fresh, since they could cause serious illness. As in the case of fish, shellfish should not be kept for long before preparing and cooking.

BUYING SHELLFISH

● **Mussels and clams** When buying live mussels or clams, choose those with tightly closed shells. Avoid any that will not close if tapped, and those with broken shells, since they may be dead and could therefore cause food poisoning when eaten.

● **Scallops** Buy scallops that are a creamy ivory colour with a bright orange coral. If they are very white, they may have been soaked in water in order to increase their weight.

● **Cockles** When buying cooked cockles, check for sand that may still cover them. This will make them gritty.

● **Lobster** When buying a lobster, choose one that is between 0.5 and 1 kg (1 and 2 lb) in weight. Small lobsters may have too little flesh inside, while very large ones can be coarse and dry.

BUYING CRAB

● **Choosing** If you like the white meat from the claws, buy a male crab. For the rich pink coral from inside the body shell, choose a female.

Hold crab by front claws, and shake gently

Checking the weight

When buying a cooked whole crab, hold it firmly by the claws, and shake it gently. The crab should feel heavy for its size. If it feels light or rattles, it is of poor quality and has water inside.

REFRIGERATING PRAWNS

● **Rinsing** Before storing fresh, raw prawns in the refrigerator, rinse in cold water and drain well. Use within two days.

TRADITIONAL TIP

Cleaning mussels

If you are not sure that mussels have come from clean water, place them in cold water with a handful of oatmeal. Leave for two hours. The mussels will expel dirt as they feed.

STORING OYSTERS

Place curved side of shells downwards in deep tray

Cover with clean tea towel dampened with cold water

Preventing loss of juices

Store live oysters curved-side down to prevent loss of juices. Arrange in an open tray, cover with a damp cloth, and store in the bottom of the refrigerator. Use as quickly as possible, within 24 hours of purchase.

STORING LIVE SHELLFISH

Keep flow of cold water constant

Keeping crayfish alive

If you buy live crayfish, lobsters, or crabs, keep them alive until you are ready to cook them. Place the crayfish in as large and deep a bowl as possible in the sink, and keep the cold tap running continuously into it.

OCTOPUS & SQUID

● **Checking the weight** Avoid buying octopus that is more than 1 kg (2 lb) in weight, since it is likely to be tough.

● **Choosing for freshness** Choose octopus or squid with a good colour, a slippery appearance, and a fresh, salty smell. Avoid any with broken outer skins or those lying in puddles of ink.

● **Saving the ink** If you can, buy squid that has not already been cleaned and still has its ink sac, and clean it at home. Use the ink to add flavour and colour to a sauce.

● **Cleaning** Clean octopus or squid before storing them. Put them in the refrigerator, in a bowl covered with clingfilm.

BAKED FOODS

WHETHER YOU BAKE BREAD AND CAKES YOURSELF, or buy them ready-made, sensible storage will enable you to keep baked foods fresh and appetizing for as long as possible. Bread and most cakes can also be frozen successfully.

BREAD

You may not always be able to buy fresh bread every day, but it is possible to keep bread fresh for several days if you follow a few basic rules. A good circulation of air is necessary to prevent bread from becoming stale or mouldy in storage, or from drying out.

REVIVING STALE LOAVES OF BREAD

Adding garlic butter
Cut a stale French loaf in thick slices almost to the base, then spread garlic butter between the slices. Wrap in foil, and bake in a hot oven for 8–10 minutes.

Steaming in a pan
Place a slightly stale loaf of bread in a colander over a pan holding a small amount of boiling water. Cover with the pan lid until the bread is warmed by the steam.

PREVENTING STALENESS
● **Adding fat** For moist, home-baked bread that will keep well, add 15 g (½ oz) fat to every 500 g (1 lb) flour.
● **Cooling bread** Always cool freshly baked bread before storing because condensation would encourage mould.
● **Allowing air circulation** Stand a bread crock on a triangular wooden pot stand or brick to increase air circulation.
● **Scalding a bread crock** If you always store bread in an earthenware bread crock or metal bin, scald the crock or bin regularly with boiling water to clean out any mould spores, then dry thoroughly.

FREEZING BREAD
● **Separating slices** Before freezing sliced bread, place greaseproof or non-stick paper between the slices so that you can remove them without thawing the whole loaf.
● **Keeping crust** Freeze crusty bread such as French sticks for no longer than 7–10 days, after which time the crust will begin to flake off.
● **Freezing dough** Freeze unrisen bread dough for up to one month and thaw for about six hours at room temperature, allow to rise, and bake.
● **Thawing** Thaw bread loaves and rolls in a warm oven, and they will be crisp and fragrant, like freshly baked bread.

STORING BREAD
Bowl must be big enough to cover loaf completely

Making a bread crock
If you have nowhere to store a loaf of bread, place the loaf on a wooden bread board, and cover with an upturned earthenware bowl. Alternatively, wrap the loaf in a clean, dry tea towel.

BRIGHT IDEA

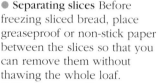

Keeping bread fresh
If you do not have a bread crock or bin, use a cotton drawstring bag to store a loaf of bread. Wash and dry the bag between uses, to prevent mould from developing.

BREADCRUMBS

Breadcrumbs are a valuable storecupboard ingredient, whether in their fresh form or dried for longer storage. Keep both white and wholemeal breadcrumbs for use in stuffings, coatings, or toppings. Breadcrumbs add texture and interest to both sweet and savoury dishes.

PREPARING BREADCRUMBS FOR STORAGE

Bag keeps crumbs tidily in one place

Mix in herbs for savoury breadcrumbs

Making dry breadcrumbs
Dry leftover bread to make into breadcrumbs. Arrange slices on a baking sheet, and bake at 150°C (300°F) or Gas Mark 2 until completely dry and lightly browned. Place in a polythene bag and crush with a rolling pin.

Seasoning breadcrumbs
Add seasonings to fresh or dried breadcrumbs to coat fish and chicken, or to use as toppings for baked and grilled dishes. Stir in crumbled dried herbs, finely grated Parmesan cheese, spices, salt, and pepper to taste.

MAKING & STORING

● **Using a food processor** To make fine, fresh or dried breadcrumbs quickly, drop pieces or slices of fresh bread or toast into the moving blade of a food processor.
● **Making small amounts** If you only need a small amount of breadcrumbs, use a coffee grinder to grind small pieces of bread or toast into crumbs.
● **Freezing crumbs** Keep freshly made breadcrumbs in a polythene freezer bag in the freezer for up to six months.
● **Storing in a jar** Use a screw-top jar to store dried breadcrumbs for about a month. The crumbs must be completely dry before storing.

CAKES AND BUNS

Most people enjoy eating cakes, whether they are simple buns or muffins, or luxurious gateaux. The very many different kinds of cake present a range of storage problems. The longest-keeping cakes are rich fruit cakes and sponges made with honey. Most cakes freeze well.

STORING & USING CAKES

● **Slicing in half** Improve the storage life of a large fruit cake by cutting it in half across the middle, taking slices from the inside of the cake, then sliding the two halves back together. Store in an airtight container.
● **Placing on lid** Store an iced cake on the lid of a cake tin with the inverted tin over it. You can then slice and remove pieces without risking damage.
● **Making trifle** Crumble leftover stale sponge cake in a dish, sprinkle with liqueur, and top with fruit and whipped cream to make a quick, trifle-like dessert.
● **Topping desserts** Make dry cake into crumbs, and sprinkle over desserts and ices.

FREEZING CAKES

Wrap sides of each slice in one piece of paper

Storing gateau slices
When freezing a large cake, cut it into slices before freezing, and interleave each slice with a piece of greaseproof or non-stick paper. Reassemble the cake, and freeze as usual. You can then remove as many slices as you need without thawing first.

REFRESHING BUNS

Moistening muffins
If muffins or small buns have become a little dry in storage, refresh them by brushing with milk and placing them in a warm oven for 6–8 minutes, or until warmed thoroughly. If they are very dry, dip them in milk before placing them in the oven.

PREPARING INGREDIENTS

O *NCE YOU HAVE PLANNED a menu and shopped carefully, you will need to begin preparing the ingredients. All good cooks will agree that sound skills in basic preparation methods are very important, whatever the type of food you are cooking, and whatever the occasion. Learn the correct way to prepare ingredients and you will save time and effort in the kitchen.*

PREPARATION BASICS

The use of good-quality utensils is important even for basic food preparation – not only for the sake of efficiency, but also to make the task more pleasurable. A sharp knife, for example, will make chopping and slicing quick and safe. As your skills improve, try new techniques.

CUTTING UP FOODS

Slicing safely
When slicing vegetables, use your knuckles to guide the knife and prevent it from cutting too close to your fingertips. Keep fingertips tucked in, and slice downwards and forwards.

CHOPPING EFFECTIVELY
● **Chopping finely** To chop food finely, use your knife like a pivot. Hold the tip down, and use a rocking action to chop.
● **Dicing foods** First, square one end of the vegetable or fruit. Cut into slices, stack, and cut lengthways into sticks. Cut crossways for diced pieces.

SLICING THINLY

Cutting julienne strips
To produce extra-thin julienne strips of vegetables, use a vegetable peeler to slice very fine ribbons. Then stack these together, and slice lengthways as thinly as possible.

PREPARING STRIPS
● **Trimming vegetables** Before cutting julienne strips from vegetables such as carrots or cucumber, trim the vegetables into neat, rectangular blocks.
● **Cutting cabbage** To slice cabbage into thin strips, roll each leaf firmly like a Swiss roll. Slice with a sharp knife.

DICING FRUITS

Lemon juice

Preventing discoloration
Sprinkle your chopping board with lemon juice before you dice apples or pears, then squeeze lemon juice on the cut fruits. This will prevent the fruits from browning during preparation.

USING DICED FRUITS
● **Preventing sticking** If the blade of your knife becomes sticky while dicing sugary ingredients, dip it from time to time into a jug of hot water placed near at hand.
● **Using colour** Consider adding diced fruits to a salad for a colourful, "confetti" effect.

VEGETABLES

WHEN PREPARING VEGETABLES FOR COOKING BY ANY METHOD, it is important to retain their colour, flavour, and nutrients. Prepare vegetables just before you need them, since they deteriorate quickly once they are peeled or cut.

GREEN VEGETABLES

Green vegetables, especially those that have delicate leaves, such as spinach, lose vitamins quickly once cut. If possible, tear the leaves rather than cutting or slicing them. Otherwise, use a very sharp knife to ensure that the leaves are damaged as little as possible.

TRIMMING SPINACH

Removing stalks
To remove the stalks from large spinach leaves without cutting, fold each leaf vertically, grasp both sides with one hand, and pull the stalk sharply away from the leaf with the other hand.

TRIMMING BROCCOLI

Using broccoli stalks
To make use of thick broccoli stalks instead of discarding them, trim and slice them horizontally into 5-mm (¼-in) thick slices. Cook them for the same period of time as the tender florets.

PREPARING LEAVES
● **Cleaning leaves** To remove insects and dirt from green-leaved vegetables, wash leaves in a large bowl of cold, salted water before using.
● **Shredding leaves** Stack and tightly roll leaves of spinach, lettuce or cabbage, and slice into coarse shreds to prepare for sautéeing or frying.
● **Using outer leaves** Save the tough outer leaves of a green cabbage for stuffing with a savoury filling. To make the leaves flexible, blanch them in boiling water for one minute, then drain.

BULB VEGETABLES

Bulb vegetables include different varieties of onion, garlic, and leek, all of which are an invaluable source of flavour in savoury dishes. They are also natural antibiotics. Onions and garlic help to lower blood cholesterol levels and therefore protect against heart disease.

AVOIDING ONION TEARS

● **Leaving roots intact** Leave the root end intact when slicing or dicing an onion. This will prevent the release of the strong juices and fumes that cause eyes to water.
● **Using vinegar** Sprinkle a little distilled, white malt vinegar on to the chopping board. This will counteract the effects of the onion juices.
● **Burning a candle** Light a candle nearby when preparing onions to burn off the sulphuric fumes.

CRUSHING GARLIC

Using a garlic press
When using a garlic press, leave the peel on the garlic clove. The soft garlic flesh will still be pushed through the mesh, and the garlic press will be easy to clean out after using.

CLEANING LEEKS

Washing out grit
To make sure you remove all the grit between the leaves of a leek, slit it lengthways, almost to the root end. Hold the leek under running water, fanning out the leaves to wash them thoroughly.

ROOT VEGETABLES

This category includes root vegetables such as carrots and turnips, as well as foods that are really tubers, the swollen roots of plants such as potatoes or yams. Root vegetables are good sources of vitamins and fibre, especially if the skins are not removed prior to cooking.

ADDING INTEREST
● **Keeping the tops** Trim all but 2 cm (¾ in) of the leafy tops from baby carrots and turnips, then cook and serve whole.

Making carrot flowers
Run a canelle knife at close intervals down the length of a peeled carrot to make grooves. Then slice the carrot widthways, producing flower shapes.

PREPARING ROOTS
● **Beetroots** Leave the roots and tops of whole beetroots untrimmed before boiling them, to prevent juices and colour from leaking out.
● **Potatoes** To make crisp chips, rinse chipped potatoes in cold water to remove excess starch. Dry them thoroughly on paper towels before frying.
● **Jerusalem artichokes** To avoid fiddly peeling, boil Jerusalem artichokes whole in their skins. The skins will rub off easily after cooking.
● **Young vegetables** Peel young root vegetables thinly or scrub them, because the peel is high in fibre and the flesh just under it is high in nutrients.

BRIGHT IDEA

Making "hasselbacks"
For really crisp, golden, roast potatoes, make "hasselbacks". Peel the potatoes, then cut thin slices downwards, not quite all the way through. Brush with oil, sprinkle with salt, and bake in a hot oven for 30–40 minutes until crisp and well browned.

SALAD VEGETABLES

Most salads need little preparation apart from the careful cleaning and trimming of all the ingredients to ensure that as many nutrients as possible are retained. To prevent loss of crispness, flavour, and vitamins, avoid preparing salad vegetables too far in advance.

PREPARING LEAVES
● **Tearing lettuce leaves** Always tear lettuce leaves, rather than cutting them with a knife, to preserve the vitamins.
● **Removing the core** To take out the tough core from an iceberg lettuce, bang the lettuce firmly – core downwards – on a worktop. Turn it over, and you should be able to twist and remove the core easily.
● **Drying the leaves** If you do not have a salad spinner, dry washed leaves by rolling them loosely in a clean tea towel. Hold both ends firmly, and shake the towel gently.
● **Refreshing a lettuce** To revive a limp head of lettuce, trim the stem and dip it into iced water for a few minutes.

STRINGING CELERY

Pull peeler blade down ridged outer edge of stem

Using a vegetable peeler
To remove the tough strings quickly from the outer sticks of celery, separate all the celery stems, and lightly stroke a swivel-bladed vegetable peeler down the length of each one.

PREPARING CUCUMBER

Drag edge of melon baller down cucumber

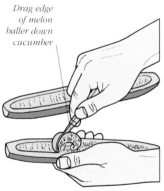

Removing seeds
Use a melon baller to scoop out the seeds from a cucumber before dicing or slicing. Cut the cucumber in half lengthways, and scrape the melon baller down the middle to remove the seeds.

FRUIT VEGETABLES

These include sun-ripened vegetables such as aubergines, sweet peppers, tomatoes, and avocados. With their bright colours and fresh, rich flavours, fruit vegetables play an important role in ensuring that our everyday diet is not only varied, but also appetizing and nutritious.

CUTTING AUBERGINES

● **Scoring** Cut a diamond pattern in the flesh of aubergine halves before grilling or baking, to ensure even cooking throughout.

Removing bitter juices
To reduce the bitterness of an aubergine, lay slices in a colander, and sprinkle with salt. Drain for 30 minutes, rinse, and dry. This also reduces oil absorption.

REMOVING SKINS

● **Blanching** To skin tomatoes, place them in a pan of boiling water. Leave for one minute, then place in cold water. The skins will peel off easily.

Grilling peppers
To skin whole peppers, place on foil, and grill until the skins blacken, turning often. Wrap the foil over so that steam will loosen the skins, then remove them.

TIME-SAVING TIP

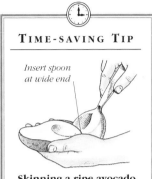

Insert spoon at wide end

Skinning a ripe avocado
Instead of trying to peel a ripe avocado with a knife, cut the avocado in half, and scoop out the flesh from each half in one piece using a large, metal spoon. Keep the spoon close to the skin.

OTHER VEGETABLES

All kinds of vegetables, from all over the world, can be found in supermarkets today. Many do not fit into traditional categories, and some are, strictly speaking, not vegetables at all. Mushrooms are edible fungi, but they can be prepared in similar ways to many vegetables.

CLEANING & TRIMMING

● **Corn on the cob** Use a nylon hairbrush to remove the silk threads from corn cobs without damaging the kernels.
● **Okra** When trimming the stalks from okra, ensure that you do not pierce the central parts and so release the sticky juices from the insides.
● **Chillies** If you need to reduce the strength of chillies for a milder flavour, scrape out the seeds and membranes inside. Wash your hands well or wear rubber gloves while preparing chillies, since they can irritate eyes or skin.
● **Courgettes** If you are grating a courgette for a salad, stir-fry, or stuffing, leave the stem on to give you a grip as you work.

PURÉEING SQUASH

Fibrous tissues catch around blades

Removing fibres
To make a really smooth purée of cooked squash, whisk with an electric mixer. The blades will pick up any fibrous strings during the process, so that you can remove them easily.

MUSHROOMS

Cultivated mushrooms should not be peeled or washed, since this reduces their flavour and vitamin content.

● **Cleaning** Wipe mushrooms gently with soft kitchen paper to remove traces of compost.
● **Keeping colour** To ensure that cultivated mushrooms stay white during cooking, sprinkle with lemon juice.
● **Retaining vitamins** When marinating raw mushrooms, cover closely with clingfilm to prevent loss of vitamins due to contact with the air.
● **Refreshing** To plump up dried mushrooms before use, immerse in boiling water for one minute. Dry before use.

FRUITS AND NUTS

F RUITS AND NUTS REQUIRE A RANGE OF PREPARATION SKILLS so that they can be presented at their best. Whether you are cooking fruits or serving them raw, whenever possible retain the skins and juices since these contain nutrients.

CITRUS FRUITS

C itrus fruits are very versatile and are used in both sweet and savoury dishes. Make use of every part of these fruits, including their zest or peels, juice, and flesh, which can be sliced or cut into segments. Always wash wax-coated fruits before removing the zest or cooking whole.

JUICING CITRUS FRUITS

● **Warming fruits** If citrus fruits have been stored in the refrigerator, they will yield the most juice if allowed to come to room temperature first.

● **Using a microwave** Pierce the skins of the fruits, and heat for 10 seconds on High to increase the juice yielded.

● **Squeezing easily** To make a citrus fruit easy to squeeze, first roll it under the palm of your hand on a work surface.

● **Zesting and juicing** If you need both juice and zest from a citrus fruit, remove the zest before squeezing the fruit.

CUTTING LEMON WEDGES

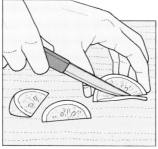

Removing pith
When making lemon wedges for garnishing, slice off the strip of pith running down the ridge of each wedge so that juice squeezes easily, without squirting.

REMOVING SEGMENTS

Cut over bowl

Catching juice
Hold peeled citrus fruits such as oranges or grapefruit over a bowl when removing segments to catch excess juice. Add this juice to fruit salads or drinks.

GARNISHING WITH FRUITS

● **Decorating slices** Before slicing citrus fruits for garnish, score grooves in the peel with a canelle knife which will give the slices rippled edges.

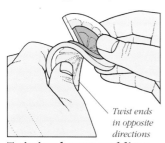

Twist ends in opposite directions

Twisting lemon and lime
Cut thin slices of lemon and lime. Place a lime slice on top of a lemon slice, and cut a slit halfway across the two. Twist the slices into a spiral, making an unusual fruit garnish.

PEELING & ZESTING

● **Removing pith** To peel an orange cleanly, immerse the whole fruit in boiling water for four minutes. Drain and cool, and the pith will come away with the zest.

● **Using a peeler** Pare citrus fruit rind with a potato peeler rather than a knife to avoid peeling the pith as well.

● **Saving zest** If you are squeezing fruit for juice but do not need the zest at the same time, remove it anyway, and freeze for later use.

● **Reusing skins** After squeezing citrus fruit halves, scrape the remaining flesh from inside the skins. Freeze the empty skins, and use as serving bowls for fruit salad, compote, or sorbet.

USING LEFTOVER PEEL

Keep peel in preserving jar, covered with alcohol

Flavouring vodka
Place strips of thinly pared orange, lemon, or lime zest in a preserving jar, and pour vodka over to cover. Mature in a refrigerator for 6–8 months. Add the vodka to drinks, or stir a tablespoonful into desserts such as fruit salad, ice-cream, or chocolate mousse.

STONED FRUITS

Stoned fruits, such as peaches, apricots, and plums, usually need little preparation other than removing the stones. Occasionally, it is necessary to remove the skins to achieve a smooth texture. Fruits that have thick skins, such as mangoes, always need to be peeled.

STONING & PEELING
● **Twisting fruits apart** Find the natural indentation in peaches or nectarines, and cut around each fruit along this line, through to the stone. Then, twist the two halves apart.
● **Stoning plums** Cut around the "waist" of a firm plum, across the indentation, then twist the two halves apart.
● **Blanching and peeling** Remove skins easily from plums or peaches by plunging them into boiling water for one minute, then into ice-cold water until they are cool. Drain, and peel off the skins.

STONING & CUBING A MANGO

1 Remove a thick slice from both sides of the fruit, cutting as close to the stone as possible. Peel the skin and flesh around the stone with a sharp knife, and cube the flesh.

2 Score each thick slice into squares, cutting down to the skin but not through it. Push the skin out into a convex curve so that the cubes can be removed easily.

SOFT FRUITS

Luscious, soft fruits are best served very simply, so preparation is usually minimal. The only essential task is to pick over the fruit thoroughly to remove damaged parts, hulls, and stems, as well as dirt. Always handle soft, ripe berries gently to prevent them from bruising.

PREPARING SOFT FRUITS
● **Washing berries** If delicate berry fruits need to be washed, place them in a colander, and rinse under running water, shaking the colander gently. Tip on to a paper towel to dry.
● **Preparing gooseberries** Use scissors to snip off the tops and tails of gooseberries before cooking or serving.
● **Enhancing flavour** Add a squeeze of lemon juice to berry fruits such as blueberries or strawberries to bring out the flavour. For a special occasion, sprinkle the fruits lightly with rum or brandy.
● **Using overripe fruits** If soft fruits are slightly overripe and not looking their best, mash them lightly with a fork. Serve spooned over vanilla ice-cream, or stir into plain yoghurt to make a quick dessert.

HULLING SOFT FRUITS
● **Removing stems** To hull red- or blackcurrants easily, pull each stem gently through the prongs of a fork, and carefully push off the fruit.

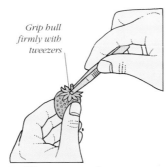

Grip hull firmly with tweezers

Hulling a strawberry
Use flat-ended tweezers to grasp and remove the leafy hull from a fresh strawberry without damaging the fruit. This method will also prevent the juice from staining your fingers.

USING FROZEN FRUITS
● **Keeping shape** To make sure frozen strawberries stay in good shape when thawing, tip them into a serving dish while frozen, thaw slowly in the refrigerator, and serve while still slightly chilled.
● **Decorating from frozen** Decorate desserts with soft fruits such as raspberries or redcurrants straight from the freezer. Leave them to thaw in position for about 30 minutes.
● **Quick-thawing fruits** To thaw frozen fruit quickly without using a microwave, place the fruits in a container in a dish of warm water for 30 minutes.
● **Making sorbet** Whip up an instant sorbet by puréeing frozen raspberries in a food processor with icing sugar to taste. Spoon into chilled glasses, and serve immediately.

OTHER FRESH FRUITS

This section includes many exotic, tropical fruits, some of which may need different methods of preparation from those required for familiar, home-grown fruits. Many tropical fruits are in fact best served simply to show off their vibrant colours and delicate, scented flesh.

PREPARING KIWI FRUIT

Cut large slice off top, then scoop out flesh

Removing flesh
Instead of peeling kiwi fruit, cut a slice from the top, and scoop out the flesh with a teaspoon – as you would when eating a boiled egg. For packed lunches or picnics, slice off the top, and wrap the whole fruit in clingfilm.

CORING PEARS
● **Coring a pear half** Cut a pear in half before removing the core, rather than coring it whole. This makes it easy to see the core, and will ensure that no flesh is wasted.

Scoop core out carefully from base of whole pear

Using a melon baller
If you plan to cook and serve pears whole, remove the cores from the underside of each fruit by scooping out with a small melon baller or the pointed tip of a vegetable peeler. This way, the pears will keep their shape.

SERVING FRUITS SIMPLY
● **Cape gooseberries** To present cape gooseberries with their leafy "capes" on, carefully separate the leaves, and push back away from the fruit. Hold the leaves, and twist firmly to hold in shape.
● **Figs** To serve figs whole, cut a deep cross about two thirds of the way through the fruit from the stem end. Squeeze gently to open out.
● **Papaya** Present papaya simply, like an avocado, as a starter. Cut it in half, and scoop out the seeds with a teaspoon. Serve with a slice of lime. Alternatively, serve slices of papaya sprinkled with lime juice as a starter or dessert.

PREPARING MELON
● **Levelling the base** Before serving a melon half or slice, cut a thin slice from the base of the fruit so that it sits firmly on the serving plate, making the cutting steady and easy.

Conserving juice
When scooping out melon seeds, hold the melon above a sieve placed over a bowl so that none of the juice is wasted. Spoon the melon juice over the melon to serve. Alternatively, add it to fruit salads or drinks.

BRIGHT IDEA

Coring pineapple rings
Remove the hard, central core, and trim the edges of fresh pineapple slices with metal pastry cutters. Use a small, round cutter to stamp out the central core, and a larger one to trim the skin and remove "eyes" from the slice.

TRIMMING & PEELING
● **Star fruit** To remove the brown, damaged edges that can spoil the appearance of a ripe star fruit, run a vegetable peeler quickly down from the point of each ridge before slicing and serving the fruit.
● **Pomegranate** Make slits in the skin of a pomegranate, dividing it into segments. Peel each segment back, and remove with the pith.
● **Dates** If dates have become dull in colour, or if sugar has crystallized on their surfaces, rinse them quickly under hot water. Then dry the dates thoroughly before serving.
● **Tamarillos** Always peel tamarillos thinly before serving, since the peel has an unpleasant, bitter taste.
● **Kiwi fruit** If the skin of a kiwi fruit is difficult to peel, plunge the fruit into boiling water for about 30 seconds, then try peeling it again.

DRIED FRUITS

Dried fruits are a concentrated source of nutrients, with apricots and peaches in particular being rich in iron and Vitamin A. Many are ready to eat, but some need soaking, which provides an opportunity to add flavour by using fruit juice, tea, brandy, or wine.

PREPARING FRUITS
● **Chilling fruits** Chop dried fruits easily by freezing them for one hour before use.
● **Making a breakfast compote** Place dried fruits in a vacuum food flask, and top up with boiling water. Leave overnight, and serve warm for breakfast.
● **Saving time** To speed up soaking, put fruits in a bowl, and cover with water. Cover the bowl, and microwave on High for 90 seconds. Stand for five minutes before use.
● **Using a food processor** Chop dried fruits with a little granulated sugar so that the fruits do not stick to the blades.

SOAKING FRUITS

Plumping up with tea
To plump up dried fruit for adding to cakes or tea breads, soak in tea instead of water. Choose a tea with a distinctive flavour, such as Earl Grey.

CHOPPING FRUITS

Preventing sticking
To chop sticky dried fruits such as apricots without the fruits sticking to the blades, cut with kitchen scissors or a sharp knife dipped previously in hot water.

NUTS

Nuts are a versatile, highly nutritious food, useful in both sweet and savoury dishes. Use fresh, whole nuts, with or without shells, and take the time to crack, chop, blanch, or grind them before adding to a dish, since their flavour is far better than ready-prepared nuts.

USING HAZELNUTS
● **Grinding** Grind whole, fresh hazelnuts in a food processor, and use them as a low-fat alternative to ground almonds.

Removing skins
To remove the fine skins from hazelnuts easily, toast them lightly under a hot grill until they are pale golden, then tip on to a clean tea towel. Fold the towel over the nuts, and rub them firmly. The skins will fall off.

USING FRESH COCONUT
● **Extracting milk** Pierce two of the eyes at one end of a fresh coconut with a skewer, and pour out the milk.

Continue tapping by crack

Opening the shell
Crack a whole, fresh coconut by tapping around the widest part with a small hammer to find the nut's natural fault line. Once a crack appears in the shell, continue turning and tapping the coconut to make a clean break.

SHELLING & BLANCHING
● **Cracking brazil nuts** To make brazil-nut shells easy to crack, place the nuts in the freezer for about six hours, or bake them for 15 minutes at 200°C (400°F) or Gas Mark 6. Cool before cracking.
● **Preventing breakage** To keep nut kernels whole and undamaged, press the middle of each shell gently with a nutcracker, turning the nut so that it cracks evenly.
● **Slitting chestnut skins** Before roasting or toasting whole chestnuts, cut a cross in each skin with a sharp knife to prevent them from exploding.
● **Microwave blanching** To blanch almonds, place them in boiling water, and microwave on High for two minutes. Drain, and peel off the skins.

HERBS AND SPICES

HERBS AND SPICES WILL CONTRIBUTE A WONDERFUL VARIETY OF FLAVOURS to your cooking. Always add herbs and spices to a dish in small amounts, tasting the food after each addition, until you achieve the flavour you desire.

FRESH HERBS

Treat all herbs gently during preparation, since they contain volatile oils that can easily be lost. Soft-leaved herbs, such as basil, coriander, and chervil, are particularly delicate. Most herbs are best added towards the end of cooking to preserve their flavour and colour.

MAXIMIZING FLAVOUR

● **Washing herbs** Shake herbs quickly under cold running water. Dry on a paper towel.
● **Using stems** After using the leaves of fresh herbs such as parsley or dill, chop the stems finely and use to flavour stocks, sauces, and stews.
● **Flavouring with sage** To add a rich, intense flavour to chicken or pork roasts, tuck whole sage leaves just under the skin of the chicken or into small slits cut into the fat of the pork before roasting.
● **Replacing chives** Spring onion tops are similar in flavour and colour to chives. Chop and use as a substitute when chives are not available.

CHOPPING PARSLEY

Scissors cut herbs finely without mess

Using kitchen scissors
To chop parsley easily and quickly, remove the stems, wash and dry the sprigs, and place in a jug or cup. Use a pair of kitchen scissors to snip the parsley inside the jug or cup.

PREPARING MINT

Releasing flavour
To obtain the maximum flavour from fresh mint leaves, bruise them first to release their volatile oils. Place them in a small bowl, and pound gently with the end of a rolling pin. Use immediately.

PREPARING BASIL

Use fingertips to tear gently

Tearing leaves
To avoid losing the flavour and colour too quickly from delicate-leaved herbs such as basil, tear the leaves with your fingers instead of chopping them with a knife. Add to savoury dishes at the end of the cooking period.

MAKING A BOUQUET GARNI

Orange zest

Adding citrus flavour
Introduce a delicate citrus flavour to a bouquet garni by adding a thinly pared strip of orange, lemon, or lime zest to the mixed herbs. Use to flavour soups, sauces, or casseroles.

● **Mixing flavours** Combine sprigs of rosemary, parsley, and thyme with a bay leaf and a stick of celery to flavour red-meat dishes and rich pulse dishes.
● **Flavouring fish** Add delicate herbs such as parsley, chervil, or dill to a bouquet garni for dishes including white fish.
● **Adding tarragon** For a scented flavour in chicken or pork dishes with white-wine or cream sauces, add a sprig of tarragon to the bouquet-garni mix.
● **Using horseradish** Add a bruised root of horseradish to a bouquet garni to flavour stocks or sauces for beef dishes.

DRIED HERBS

Dried herbs are a convenient substitute if fresh herbs are not available. However, they have a much more concentrated flavour than fresh herbs, so you will need to reduce quantities. As a general rule, use about half the amount of dried herbs that you would of fresh.

USING DRIED HERBS

● **Thyme** To remove the leaves of dried thyme from their woody stems, place the sprigs on a clean paper towel, fold over, and rub the herbs vigorously. If using a small amount, rub the herb stems between your fingertips.

● **Bay leaves** Soak dried bay leaves in water for a few minutes before threading on to skewers between cubes of meat, chicken, or fish. The leaves will add flavour to the meat without burning.

● **Stalks** Scatter the stripped, dry stalks of thyme or rosemary on to the coals of a barbecue to give a smoky, herb flavour to the food that is being cooked.

PREPARING ROSEMARY

Stripping leaves
To strip the leaves quickly from the woody stems of rosemary, hold the tip of each sprig in one hand, and strip the leaves off with a finger and thumb, pushing against the direction of growth.

BRIGHT IDEA

Using a tea infuser
If you want to enhance the flavour of a dish without leaving bits of herb behind, put the herbs into a tea infuser, and stir them into the dish at the end of cooking.

SPICES

Most spices can be added directly to dishes during cooking. However, it is well worth spending a little time to crush, bruise, or toast them first to bring out as much flavour as possible. Once ground or bruised, spices should be used immediately to prevent loss of flavour.

SPLITTING VANILLA PODS

Use tip of knife to scrape seeds from inside opened pod

Removing seeds
To obtain a really strong flavour from a vanilla pod, use the tiny, oily seeds rather than infusing the whole pod. To extract the seeds, cut the pod lengthways using a sharp knife. Then add the seeds directly to sweet dishes.

BRUISING ROOT GINGER

Use pan to crush ginger

Using a heavy pan
Bruise a whole piece of peeled, fresh root ginger by placing it on a board and hitting it with the flat base of a heavy pan. If bruised ginger is added to preserves or hot drinks, its flavour will be infused quickly and easily.

CRUSHING & GRINDING

● **Avoiding mess** Crush whole spices by placing them in a small plastic bag and hitting them several times with a rolling pin or a meat mallet.

● **Mixing spices** Mix together 75 per cent black or white peppercorns and 25 per cent whole allspice. Keep in a peppermill ready to grind on to grilled meats or fish. You could also mix black, white, pink, and green peppercorns to spice up plain chicken.

● **Making chilli powder** Roast four dried, red chillies at 200°C (400°F) or Gas Mark 6 for 10 minutes. Remove the stems and seeds, then use a pestle and mortar to grind the chillies into a powder.

DAIRY FOODS

THERE IS AN INCREASING CHOICE OF CERTAIN DAIRY PRODUCTS, such as cheeses, offering a wide range of flavours and low-fat alternatives. Some low-fat products are not stable if cooked, so handle them with care and heat gently.

EGGS

Versatile and nutritious, eggs are the basis of countless sweet and savoury dishes. Whole eggs are used for a range of cooked dishes, whites are used for adding volume and binding, and yolks are used for glazing and enriching. Spare yolks or whites can be stored.

SEPARATING EGGS

Using the eggshell
Crack the shell gently on the edge of a bowl, and carefully pull the two halves apart. Let the white run into the bowl, and tip the yolk several times from one half of the shell to the other.

MAKING MERINGUE

● **Whisking egg whites** If possible, whisk egg whites in a copper bowl, which will produce the greatest volume.
● **Using at room temperature** Remove egg whites from the refrigerator about an hour before needed: they whisk best at room temperature.
● **Keeping whites** Egg whites whisked with sugar will keep their shape for several hours; plain whisked whites must be used directly after whisking.
● **Saving over-whisked whites** To rescue over-beaten egg whites, beat another white separately until frothy, then stir it into the mixture. Whisk again to regain the bulk.

USING WHOLE EGGS

● **Glazing** To make a golden-brown glaze for pastry, bread, or scones, beat an egg with a pinch of salt, and brush over the food before baking.
● **Extending an egg glaze** Make eggs go further for glazing by beating 15 ml (1 tbsp) oil with each whole egg.
● **Making omelettes** When mixing, beat in 15 ml (1 tbsp) of water to every two eggs for a light result. Alternatively, separate the white and whisk until stiff, then fold into the yolks for a soufflé omelette.
● **Scrambling eggs** Beat in a little milk with the eggs to make creamy scrambled eggs.

USING EGG WHITES

Wipe bowl with flesh of lemon

Removing traces of grease
Before whisking egg whites, make sure that your bowl is free of grease by wiping it with the cut surface of a fresh lemon. Alternatively, wipe with a paper towel moistened with vinegar.

REMOVING YOLK TRACES

Use edge of shell to pick up traces of yolk

Using a half-shell
If you get even a trace of yolk in the white after separating an egg, remove it before whisking the white. The best way to do this is by scooping out the yolk with the edge of a halved eggshell.

USING SPARE YOLKS

● **Chilling egg yolks** Place left-over egg yolks in an egg cup. Cover with cold water, and refrigerate for up to two days.
● **Freezing egg yolks** Beat spare yolks with either a pinch of salt for use in savoury dishes, or a pinch of sugar for use in sweet dishes, then label and freeze for up to six months.
● **Enriching dishes** Spare egg yolks are useful for enriching many dishes. Add an extra egg yolk when making omelettes, pancake batters, and baked egg custards.
● **Improving texture** Beat an egg yolk into a hot chocolate sauce or savoury cream sauce for a smooth, glossy texture.

BUTTER AND CHEESE

Butter and cheese are rich sources of fat so are best used in moderation, but both can bring richness and flavour to many dishes. Margarine can be substituted for butter where flavour is not critical, but low-fat spreads are most suitable for spreading, not cooking.

PREPARING BUTTER

● **Softening** Use a microwave to soften butter that has been refrigerated. Put the butter in a microwave-safe dish and cook on Defrost for about 30 seconds for each 100 g (3½ oz).
● **Clarifying** To make a really clear glaze for pâtés or vegetables, clarify butter by melting it with an equal quantity of water. Leave to set, then lift off the cleared butter, leaving the salts and other solids in the water.
● **Making perfect butter curls** Use firm, chilled butter, and dip the butter curler into warm water. Drop the curls into a bowl of iced water, and store in the refrigerator.

SHAVING HARD CHEESES

Using a peeler
Shave thin curls of Parmesan, Pecorino, or other hard cheeses straight from the block with a vegetable peeler. Scatter the curls of cheese over hot pasta dishes, salads, or bruschetta.

MAKING LIGHT PASTRY

Grating butter
To make light shortcrust pastry without rubbing in the butter, chill butter until hard, and grate it into the flour, using a medium grater. Mix evenly with a fork before adding water to bind.

CREAM AND YOGHURT

These foods enrich all kinds of sweet and savoury dishes, and the lighter substitutes for cream make it possible to use dairy produce in almost any diet. Low-fat cream substitutes must be stabilized with cornflour before cooking, so that they can be heated without curdling.

WHIPPING CREAM

● **Checking fat content** To maximize volume when whipping, use cream with a fat content of 38–40 per cent.
● **Increasing volume** Before whipping, chill the whisk and bowl as well as the cream.
● **Adding sugar** Whisk 5 ml (1 tsp) icing sugar into each 150 ml (¼ pint) of cream for a fluffy result that will hold its shape well when piped.
● **Adding flavour** To produce an even texture, always add flavourings such as brandy to cream before whipping.
● **Whisking by hand** Use a balloon or spiral hand whisk, which will allow you to feel subtle texture changes and to avoid over-whipping.

USING EFFECTIVELY

● **Lightening a topping** Mix half natural yoghurt with half whipped cream for a light and healthy dessert topping.
● **Stabilizing** To keep natural yoghurt from curdling in hot dishes, mix 5 ml (1 tsp) cornflour into every 150 ml (¼ pint) yoghurt before heating. Alternatively, add it at the end of cooking, without boiling.
● **Making crème fraîche** Mix together equal quantities of soured and fresh double cream. Cover, and leave at room temperature for two hours or until it thickens.
● **Floating cream** Use double cream with a fat content of at least 48 per cent for floating on to soups or Irish coffee.

BRIGHT IDEA

Making yoghurt at home
Heat 600 ml (1 pint) sterilized milk to 43°C (110°F). Stir in 15 ml (1 tbsp) plain yoghurt and 50 g (1¾ oz) dried, skimmed milk. Pour into a vacuum flask and leave for seven hours, then chill in a bowl until thickened.

MEAT AND POULTRY

C AREFUL PREPARATION OF MEAT AND POULTRY is essential to the success of all types of meat cookery. The skillful use of different cutting methods, marinades, and coatings can make even the most inexpensive cut look and taste delicious.

MAKING GENERAL PREPARATIONS

T here are many ways of preparing meat and poultry to enhance their appearance, flavour, and tenderness. For healthy cooking, trim off excess fat and skin, keeping some fat for flavour and moisture. Retain bones and trimmings to make stock, and freeze for future use.

CUTTING MEAT

● **Slicing for tenderness** Slice meat across, not with, the grain for a tender result.
● **Dicing evenly** When dicing meat for casseroles or curries, make the cubes the same size so that they cook evenly.
● **Trimming kidneys** Use kitchen scissors instead of a knife to cut out and remove the tough cores from kidneys.
● **Cutting stir-fry strips** Freeze meat for 30 minutes before slicing for a stir-fry. This will make it easy to cut thinly.
● **Snipping edges** To prevent the edges of grilled or fried steaks, chops, or bacon from curling, make slits in the fat at 1-cm (½-in) intervals.

COATING POULTRY

Seasoned flour in polythene bag

Shaking in a bag
To coat poultry joints in seasoned flour or spices quickly and cleanly, place the coating mixture in a polythene bag, and add the poultry. Shake the bag until the contents are evenly coated. Remove and cook.

TENDERIZING MEAT

Puréed papaya

Marinating in papaya
To tenderize a tough cut of meat, purée fresh papaya, and spread it over the surface of the meat. Alternatively, pour papaya or pineapple juice over the meat, cover, and refrigerate for three hours. Dry meat before cooking.

PREPARING DUCK

Scoring skin
To prepare duck breast for grilling or frying, score the skin deeply in a diamond pattern. This will help the meat cook evenly, keep its shape, and release excess fat during cooking.

PREPARING OFFAL

● **Soaking liver** For a milder flavour, soak strongly flavoured liver, such as pig's liver, in milk for one hour prior to cooking.
● **Tenderizing liver** To make liver tender, pour tomato juice over it, and leave to soak for three hours before cooking.
● **Cleaning hearts** Wash hearts thoroughly, then soak in lightly salted water for one hour to clean out any blood deposits.
● **Blanching sweetbreads** To keep sweetbreads firm, first blanch them for 20 minutes in salted, boiling water with the juice of half a lemon, then drain, and press between two plates before cooking.

TIME-SAVING TIP

Snipping bacon
To "chop" bacon quickly and easily, use a pair of kitchen scissors. Cut raw bacon slices straight into a pan. Snip cooked bacon over salads.

BONING AND JOINTING

Most of the basic preparation of meat cuts is done before you buy them, but it is worth learning a few simple skills to get the best out of meat and poultry. Boning, jointing, and trussing meat at home saves money, since ready-prepared cuts are the most expensive.

PREPARING LAMB JOINTS
● **Protecting bones** Cover the bone ends of a best end of neck, or rack, of lamb with foil to avoid burning.

Use sharp knife to loosen bone

Loosening bone
For an easy-carving shoulder of lamb, loosen the bladebone from the flesh, but leave it in place. When roasted, the meat will shrink back, and the bone can then be pulled out easily.

SAFETY

Follow these few simple guidelines when handling meat to keep it free from bacterial contamination.

● **Washing hands** Wash before and after handling meat and poultry, and before preparing other foods.
● **Cleaning equipment** To avoid cross-contamination after preparing meat, thoroughly wash knives, surfaces, and cutting boards.
● **Keeping cool** Once meat is prepared and ready to cook, cook it immediately, or cover it with foil and store it in the refrigerator until it is needed.
● **Using stuffings** Always make sure cooked stuffings have cooled completely before using them to stuff raw meat.

TRUSSING POULTRY
● **Tying drumsticks** To truss a whole bird, tie only the drumsticks together, and the bird will keep its shape.

Using dental floss
To truss or sew meat or poultry joints unobtrusively, use some unwaxed dental floss. It is strong enough to hold the shape neatly and firmly, without spoiling the appearance of the dish.

SPATCHCOCKING
● **Pressing flat** To ensure that poultry lies as flat as possible when opened out for cooking, press firmly on the breastbone with the heel of your hand.

Using skewers
To hold a spatchcocked poussin or Cornish hen in shape for cooking, push skewers through the thickest parts of the meat. They will allow the heat to penetrate and ensure thorough cooking.

TRIMMING POULTRY

● **Reducing fat levels** To reduce fat levels in poultry, remove the skin from joints. The skin contains a high proportion of the saturated fat found in poultry.
● **Using paper towels** To remove the skin from a drumstick easily, grasp it with a paper towel, or a clean, dry tea towel. Pull the skin away from the flesh towards the narrow end.
● **Checking the cavity** Before roasting a whole chicken, check inside the cavity, and remove any lumps of fat, which can spoil the flavour and will make the juices fatty.
● **Removing the wishbone** Before roasting poultry, lift the neck skin, and pull out the wishbone. This will make the breast meat easy to carve.

USING POULTRY JOINTS
● **Soaking duck joints** Soak joints of wild duck in cold water for about an hour to remove any excess blood. Dry thoroughly on a paper towel.
● **Jointing whole birds** Buy a whole chicken, and joint it yourself, since this is less expensive than buying ready-cut pieces. Use the trimmings to make a stock for future use.
● **Adding flavours** Remove the skin from poultry joints, and slash the thickest parts of the flesh, before coating in spices or marinades. This will allow the flavours to penetrate fully.
● **Using coatings** Use herb-flavoured, packet stuffing mix as a quick coating for chicken joints. Dip each joint in egg, and then into the stuffing mix before baking or frying.

FISH AND SHELLFISH

Mᴏsᴛ ᴏғ ᴛʜᴇ ᴘʀᴇᴘᴀʀᴀᴛɪᴏɴ ᴏғ ғɪsʜ can be done before it reaches the kitchen. It is worth finding a supplier who will prepare the fish just as you want it. A few basic skills will help you get the best from this nutritious food.

FISH

Fresh fish needs little preparation, and if it is bought already filleted or skinned it can be considered a ready-to-cook convenience food. Frozen fish can usually be used as a substitute for fresh fish. If possible, cook straight from frozen to retain all the juices and

SCALING FISH
● **Rinsing under water** Hold fish under cold water while removing scales, washing them away as you scrape.

Use sharp edge of scallop shell

Using a scallop shell
Remove all the scales from a whole fish with the edge of a scallop shell, scraping firmly down the length of the fish from the tail end towards the head.

REMOVING BONES
● **Boning cooked fish** When flaking fish, check for small bones after cooking, when they can be removed easily.

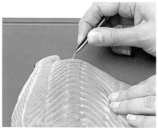

Using tweezers
Use tweezers to pluck out stray bones left in fish fillets after filleting. Press gently with your fingertips to feel for the small bones under the surface.

FILLETING FISH
● **Filleting flat fish** Fillet flat fish without gutting it: there is no danger of the gut being pierced and contaminating the flesh.

Boning mackerel
To bone mackerel, slit open the belly, and place the fish skin-side up. Press firmly with your thumbs down the backbone. Turn over, and lift out the bones.

CLEANING & SKINNING
● **Preventing mess** To scale a whole fish cleanly, place it in a large polythene bag, and scrape off the scales inside it.
● **Using salt** Dip fingertips into salt before skinning fish, to give a better grip. Also, rub salt inside the belly cavity to remove any residues, then rinse well before cooking.
● **Skinning frozen fish** Pull the skin from frozen fillets while still frozen. Use paper towels to help you grip the skin.
● **Removing fishy smells** Rub the cut surface of a lemon over hands, knife, and cutting board after preparing fish to counteract fishy odours.

PREPARING A WHOLE FISH

Trimming the tail
If you are preparing a whole fish, such as salmon or trout, to serve with its tail on, trim the thin edges of the tail with scissors to make a "V" shape. This will prevent the tail from curling up in the heat during cooking.

● **Trimming the fins** Use kitchen scissors to snip the fins off a whole fish before cooking.
● **Cleaning through the gills** To preserve the shape of fish that is to be served whole, remove the stomach contents of the fish through the gill flaps instead of slitting open the belly.
● **Removing the gills** If a fish is to be cooked and served with the head intact, snip out the gills with scissors first, since they can impart a bitter taste.
● **Removing the head** To remove the head from a whole fish, cut following the natural curve behind the gills.

SHELLFISH

Much of the fresh shellfish we eat is sold in the shell and is often live, so preparation must be done at home. Live shellfish, such as oysters, mussels, and clams, are best prepared just before you serve them to ensure maximum freshness and safety, as well as the best flavours.

CLEANING & SERVING

● **Debearding mussels** Remove beards from mussels just before cooking, since they die once the beards are removed.
● **Using crushed ice** Have ready a serving platter with crushed ice when opening oysters, so that the shells can be firmly nestled in and the juices remain in the shells.
● **Chilling shellfish** Put clams or oysters, unopened, in the freezer for 10 minutes before serving; they will open easily.
● **Serving in shells** When buying shelled scallops, ask for the curved shells so that you can use them as serving dishes. Scrub and boil to clean.

CRACKING CRAB CLAWS

Tap claw gently but firmly with hammer

Using a hammer
To crack a crab claw without shattering it, cup it in the palm of your hand, and tap with a small hammer until the shell cracks. Alternatively, crack the claw on a folded tea towel on a board.

OPENING OYSTERS

● **Using the oven** Place oysters in one layer on a baking sheet, and put in a hot oven for 3–4 minutes until they open.

Rest shell in palm to retain juices

Using a can opener
Open oyster shells with the pointed tip of a can opener. Grasp each shell firmly in a cloth, holding the flat side upwards, then insert the opener into the hinge, and push down firmly.

CRUSTACEA

Fresh prawns, lobster, and other crustacea are usually sold in the shell, and a few simple skills are needed to prepare them. Do not be deterred by this preparation, which is speedy and worthwhile. The flavour of fresh crustacea is better than peeled, frozen, or tinned products.

DEVEINING PRAWNS

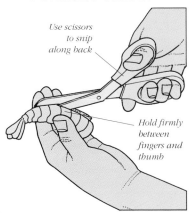

Use scissors to snip along back

Hold firmly between fingers and thumb

Using scissors
To devein large prawns before cooking, cut along the back of each shell. It is easy to see the dark vein running down the back. Lift the vein out carefully, or scrape it out with a knife.

DEALING WITH SHELLS
● **Peeling easily** To peel cooked prawns, grasp the head between finger and thumb, and twist to remove. Pull the legs to one side; as they break away, part of the shell should lift off. You will be able to peel it all off.
● **Cutting shells** Use kitchen scissors or poultry shears to cut lobster shells in half easily.
● **Wiping edges** After cutting lobster or crayfish shells in half for serving, wipe around the edges of the cut shells with a clean, damp cloth to remove small fragments.
● **Serving in shells** To serve lobster attractively in the shell, lift out the tail flesh from each half and replace it, rounded side up, in the opposite half.

USING SHELLS

Use shells to add colour and flavour to stocks, sauces, and other accompaniments.

● **Making fish stock** After boiling lobster and scooping out the meat, return the shell pieces to the cooking liquid, and add a glass of white wine, a few onion slices, and a bouquet garni. Simmer for 20 minutes, then strain.
● **Making a fish sauce** Grind lobster shells in a food processor until smooth. Cook in a little butter, then add white wine and cream to make a rich sauce for white fish.
● **Making prawn butter** Purée equal amounts of prawn shells and butter with a little lemon juice in a food processor.

COOKING METHODS

THE MAIN REASON for cooking food is to make it palatable and easily digestible. Different cooking methods have varying effects on foods, and it is important that you choose a suitable cooking method for each type of food. Rapid boiling, for instance, helps to retain the colour and texture of fresh vegetables, but tough cuts of meat need slow simmering to make them tender. Cooking methods may be combined, as in braising, in which quick frying and slow stewing brown and tenderize meat.

HEALTHY COOKING

The way in which food is cooked plays an important role in determining the food's nutritional contribution to our diet. Whenever possible, choose low-fat cooking methods, or cook with fats that are low in saturates, and use methods of cooking that retain nutrients.

STIR-FRYING
● **Adding in stages** When stir-frying mixtures of vegetables, place each vegetable in the pan separately to maintain the heat. Add the slowest-cooking first and the fastest-cooking last.

BOILING
● **Reusing cooking liquids** Refrigerate liquids that have been used for boiling food, since these contain flavour and nutrients. Add to gravies, sauces, soups, or stocks.

STEAMING
● **Cutting same-sized pieces** To ensure that pieces of food cook evenly and within the same period of time when steaming, cut them all to approximately the same size.

Stir constantly to seal food

Wrap paper securely around food

Sealing food quickly
Use less oil or fat for stir-frying than you would normally use for shallow frying, so that the surface of the food seals quickly. Add just enough oil to the pan to coat the food lightly.

Conserving nutrients
To preserve the vitamins when boiling vegetables, bring the water to a rolling boil before adding the vegetables to the pan. Bring back to the boil quickly, and keep the heat high until done.

Making a parcel
Retain the nutritious, tasty juices from steamed foods by wrapping food in parcels of greaseproof parchment before placing in a steamer. Pour the juices over the food to serve, or add to a sauce.

VEGETABLES

Most vegetables retain their colour, texture, and flavour best if they are cooked quickly and lightly. Many different cooking methods can be used. Vegetables taste best if served as soon as possible after they have been cooked.

POTATOES

Potatoes are very versatile and respond well to most cooking methods. To a great extent the variety of potato determines which cooking method you use. For instance, floury-textured potatoes are good for baking, roasting, and mashing, while waxy types are best boiled.

ENSURING SUCCESS

● **Jacket potatoes** To speed up the baking of jacket potatoes, push metal skewers through their centres to conduct the heat. Alternatively, parboil for 15 minutes before baking.
● **Mashed potatoes** Add a little hot milk (not cold) to mashed potatoes to give them a really fluffy texture. Warm the milk in a microwave for speed.
● **Boiled potatoes** Prevent old-crop potatoes from blackening by adding a squeeze of lemon juice or a teaspoonful of vinegar to the cooking liquid.

CRISPING POTATOES

Roughing up the surfaces
For crisp roast potatoes, cut the potatoes into chunks, parboil, and drain. Shake the covered pan to roughen the surfaces of the potatoes, then roast as usual.

KEEPING MASH HOT

Preventing soggy mash
Use a clean tea towel to cover mashed potatoes and keep them hot before serving. The towel will absorb excess moisture, keeping the mash fluffy and dry.

GREEN VEGETABLES

Most green vegetables are rich in Vitamin C, and they should be cooked quickly in the minimum of liquid to retain this very important nutrient. If you boil greens, keep the cooking water and add to gravies or soups. Alternatively, use water-free methods such as stir-frying.

COOKING CABBAGE

Steaming wedges
Instead of shredding cabbage, cut it into slim, portion-sized wedges, and steam the wedges until just tender. The wedges will retain more nutrients than shredded cabbage and look decorative.

COOKING ASPARAGUS

Add water to create steam

Using a microwave
Arrange asparagus spears in a wide, shallow dish with their pointed tips to the centre. Add 45 ml (3 tbsp) water, cover, and cook on High for about 12–14 minutes per 500 g (1 lb 2 oz).

IMPROVING GREENS

● **Cabbage** Braise cabbage in a little stock instead of water. Shred finely, and cook with just enough stock to moisten, shaking the pan often.
● **Spinach** To remove any excess moisture from cooked spinach, tip into a colander, and press with a potato masher, or press between two plates.
● **Chinese cabbage** Shred the coarse outer leaves of Chinese cabbage, and stir-fry. Save the tender leaves for salads.
● **Brussels sprouts** Cut crosses through the stems of Brussels sprouts for even cooking.

ENHANCING FLAVOUR

Most vegetables are best cooked lightly to retain their flavour, colour, and texture. By experimenting with different cooking methods and adding ingredients such as herbs, it is possible to add interest to, and enhance the flavour of, even the most ordinary vegetable.

USING ONIONS
● **Frying onions** To obtain a sweet, caramelized flavour, fry onions slowly in butter with a pinch of salt until they are a rich, golden-brown colour.

Add juice to other ingredients

Adding onion juice
To add the flavour of onion to savoury dishes without including sliced or diced onion pieces, squeeze half an onion on a lemon squeezer to extract the juice. Add the liquid to the dish.

USING FRUIT JUICES
● **Sprinkling lemon juice** Fresh lemon juice will pep up the flavour of most vegetables. Use it instead of adding salt for people on low-salt diets.

Pour in orange juice to moisten carrots

Flavouring carrots
Add a rich, sweet flavour to plain carrots by cooking in orange juice instead of water. Braise small, whole, new carrots until tender with just the juice of an orange and a knob of butter.

ADDING SPICES
● **Spicing leeks** Add a spicy pungency to leeks by gently sautéeing them until soft in a little butter with a pinch of ground coriander and cumin.

Sprinkle with freshly grated nutmeg

Using nutmeg
Sprinkle freshly grated nutmeg over cooked spinach, parsnips, or potatoes just before serving. The heat of the vegetables will bring out the full, warm, spicy aroma and flavour of the spice.

MAXIMIZING FLAVOUR

● **Brussels sprouts** Instead of boiling Brussels sprouts, shred them finely, and stir-fry lightly in a little olive oil to retain flavour and crispness.
● **Beetroot** Wrap beetroot in foil, and bake instead of boiling to preserve flavour and colour. Trim the tops of the beetroot, and wrap in buttered foil. Bake in a moderate oven for 1–2 hours.
● **Peas and mangetout** Add a sprig of fresh mint when boiling peas or mangetout.
● **Tomatoes** Add a pinch of sugar to cooked tomatoes and homemade tomato sauce.

USING LEFTOVERS
● **Grilling with cheese** Arrange vegetables in one layer in a flameproof dish. Cover with thin slices of Gruyère, and grill.
● **Making bubble and squeak** Mix mashed potatoes with grated onion and cabbage, then shallow-fry until golden.
● **Making fritters** Dip broccoli or cauliflower florets in batter. Then deep-fry in hot oil until they are a golden colour.
● **Tossing salads** Dice cooked, mixed vegetables, and toss with mayonnaise and lemon juice. Serve cold as a salad.
● **Making soup** Purée cooked vegetables with leftover gravy, stock, or milk to taste.

TIME-SAVING TIP

Making vegetable parcels
Wrap prepared vegetables in buttered foil, and cook in the oven in a roasting tin with roast meat for the final 30–40 minutes of cooking time. Add sprigs of fresh herbs to the parcels, and season with salt and pepper. Seal the parcels firmly to keep in the flavours.

ADDING VARIETY

Vegetables are versatile ingredients that will contribute significantly to a healthy diet, but if they are always cooked in the same way they lose their appeal. Be creative by combining vegetables with other ingredients in unusual ways and using different cooking methods.

VARYING PRESENTATION

Draw peeler along length of vegetable

Making vegetable ribbons
To serve carrots and courgettes in an unusual way, and to cook them quickly, slice them into thin ribbons by using a vegetable peeler instead of a knife. Steam or stir-fry the ribbons for 2–3 minutes or until they are tender.

COOKING CREATIVELY

● **Making "confetti"** Use the coarse shredder blade of a food processor to shred evenly vegetables such as carrots, peppers, courgettes, or celeriac. Cook together in a quick "confetti" stir-fry.
● **Adding bacon** Transform cooked French beans or runner beans into a dinner-party dish by tossing with crushed garlic, golden-fried, diced, smoked bacon, and a chopped tomato.
● **Puréeing aubergines** Serve aubergines as a purée. Bake them whole in their skins for about 45 minutes in a moderate oven, or until tender. Scoop out the flesh, mash with a fork, and add salt, pepper, and olive oil to taste.

ADDING TEXTURE

Sunflower seeds

Sprinkling with seeds
To add an interesting texture to plain, cooked vegetables and increase their nutritive value, sprinkle with a few lightly toasted sunflower, pumpkin, or sesame seeds, or add chopped nuts just before cooking.

CORRECTING MISTAKES

If you have overcooked vegetables, there is no need to discard them, since they can usually be revived, or presented in a different way in order to disguise the mistake. You may even find that the end result is preferable to what you had originally intended.

PURÉEING VEGETABLES

Add double or single cream to taste

Mixing with cream
Rescue boiled carrots, spinach, or peas that have overcooked by serving them as a rich, creamy purée. Tip the vegetables into a food processor, and purée until just smooth. Add a few tablespoonfuls of cream to taste.

REVIVING MASH

Rescuing soggy mash
If potatoes intended for mashing are overcooked or they have collapsed, whisk an egg white until stiff, and fold it carefully into the mashed potatoes. Pile the mixture into a dish, and bake in a hot oven until fluffy and golden.

RESCUING DISASTERS

● **Counteracting salt** Rescue oversalted vegetables by pouring boiling water over them. If they are still too salty, stir them gently in a few tablespoonfuls of cream.
● **Reducing toughness** If mushrooms have become tough and dried out, add a few tablespoonfuls of red wine. Leave to soak for 10 minutes, then bring to the boil. Stir in a little cream.
● **Making soufflés** Mash overcooked cauliflower or broccoli, and mix in a can of condensed soup and three egg yolks. Fold in three whisked whites. Bake in ramekins in a hot oven for 20 minutes.

SALADS

S ALADS FORM AN ESSENTIAL PART OF OUR DIET, whether they are simple side dishes
or substantial main courses. Fresh, nutritious ingredients, served raw or
lightly cooked, make a colourful, attractive dish to stimulate the appetite.

USING BASIC INGREDIENTS

B e creative with salad ingredients, and use
fresh flavours, colours, and textures to the
full. Use a variety of leaves to make the most of

a simple, green salad, or create interesting main
courses by combining lots of salad ingredients.
Match ingredients with dressings to your taste.

DRAINING SALADS

Using a saucer
Place an upturned saucer in
the bottom of a salad bowl
before adding the salad. Excess
water and dressing will gather
underneath the saucer, keeping
the salad leaves crisp.

SPROUTING BEANS

Soaking beans in a jar
Sprout mung beans or other
whole beans for use in salads.
Put them in a large jar, and soak
overnight. Drain, cover the jar
with muslin, and rinse twice a
day until the beans sprout.

MAKING RICE MOULDS

*Turn out
compacted
rice carefully*

Moulding rice
Toss cooked rice in a dressing,
then pack firmly into coffee or
teacups, or into a ring cake tin.
Invert the cups on to a serving
dish, and turn out for attractively
shaped rice salad moulds.

PRESENTING LEAVES
● **Using whole leaves** Use
crisp, whole lettuce leaves,
such as cos or iceberg, as
natural serving dishes.
● **Cutting wedges** To produce
interesting shapes and texture
in a green salad, thinly slice an
iceberg lettuce into wedges.
● **Lifting out a core** To remove
the central core from an
iceberg lettuce while keeping
the leaves whole, slam the
lettuce firmly, stem end down,
on to a worktop. The core
should then be loose enough
to be lifted out by hand.
● **Removing bitterness** To avoid
a bitter flavour in chicory, cut
out the core at the stem end.

IMPROVING INGREDIENTS
● **Cucumber** Before adding a
sliced cucumber to salad,
sprinkle the pieces with salt,
and leave to drain for about
20 minutes to remove excess
moisture. Rinse and dry.
● **Onions** To prevent the
strong flavour of onions from
dominating a salad, leave
them to soak in cold water
for one hour before use.
● **Tomatoes** Add interest to
a tomato salad by mixing
beef, sun-dried, and cherry
tomatoes. Sprinkle with a
good olive oil as a dressing.
● **Celery** Keep leftover celery
fresh for reuse by trimming
and standing in chilled water.

**FLAVOURING
WARM SALADS**

● **Adding vinegar** Sprinkle
warm salad ingredients with
a few drops of an aged
vinegar, such as balsamic or
sherry vinegar. The warmth
of the salad will bring out the
full flavour of the vinegar.
● **Using sesame oil** Give an
Oriental flavour to a warm
salad by adding a teaspoon
of sesame oil to the dressing.
● **Cooking shallots** Simmer
finely chopped shallots slowly
in a few tablespoonfuls of red
wine vinegar until soft. Toss
them into a potato or bean
salad for a warm, rich flavour.

ADDING VARIETY

Combine common and unusual ingredients to make imaginative and appetizing salads. Mix crunchy ingredients, such as croûtons and seeds, with soft textures, such as fresh and dried fruits. Contrast sharp flavours with mild ones, and use herbs to add a distinctive flavour.

ENHANCING SALADS
● **Adding anchovies** Stir a few finely chopped canned anchovies into a potato salad.
● **Using herbs** Scatter generous amounts of fresh, chopped herbs, such as parsley, chervil, or chives, into a plain, green salad, or add rocket for a peppery bite.
● **Adding texture** To add a crunchy texture to a simple salad, stir in a handful of toasted sunflower or sesame seeds, flaked almonds, or even salted peanuts, just before serving the salad.
● **Shaving Parmesan** Scatter curled shavings of Parmesan cheese on to a plain salad.

MAKING MIXED SALADS

Layering ingredients
Pour a dressing into a straight-sided bowl, and place layers of colourful, mixed salad vegetables into it. Turn the filled bowl out on to a serving dish for a ready-dressed salad.

ADDING GARNISHES

Use cutter to stamp shapes from bread

Making croûtons
To add a crunchy garnish to a simple salad, use croûtons. Cut shapes from sliced bread with a small cutter. Gently fry the shapes in oil until golden, toss in parsley, and add to the salad.

MAKING DRESSINGS

A well-balanced, freshly made dressing can add a subtle or a distinctive flavour to a salad. Classic recipes, such as vinaigrette, are a good starting point, but imaginative dressings can be created using flavoured vinegars and oils, fruit juices, herbs, spices, seeds, and zests.

COMBINING INGREDIENTS
● **Dressing warm ingredients** Dress rice or pasta salads while they are still slightly warm so that they absorb the flavours of the dressing.
● **Adding nut oils** Enhance salad dressings by using nut oils, such as walnut or hazelnut, for a rich flavour.
● **Lowering fat** Use natural yoghurt or milk, instead of oil, as a basis for a low-fat dressing.
● **Sweetening dressings** If you find vinegar-based dressings too sharp, substitute apple or orange juice for the vinegar, or add a teaspoonful of honey.
● **Adding cheese** Use ripe Stilton or Roquefort for a blue-cheese dressing. Mash cheese with a fork, and stir into single cream or mayonnaise.

MAKING VINAIGRETTE

Using a screw-top jar
To make vinaigrette quickly, pour vinegar, or lemon juice, and oil into a straight-sided, screw-top jar. Use three parts oil to one part vinegar, or four or five parts oil to one part lemon juice. Shake the jar to mix the ingredients.

BRIGHT IDEA

Using a mustard jar
When a mustard jar is almost empty, leave the last scrapings in the jar, and use it to make a salad dressing. Measure the other ingredients into the jar, and shake well. The remaining mustard will flavour the dressing.

FRUITS

SOME FRUITS – EVEN SOFT SUMMER FRUITS – tend to be more palatable cooked than uncooked, but most require only light cooking to bring out their flavour. Gentle poaching, grilling, or baking will maintain flavour, colour, and shape.

BAKING FRUITS

Fruits can be baked just as they are, as in the case of baked apples, or wrapped in pastry parcels to cook gently and retain the flavour. Always prepare fruits just before baking, since most of them soon start to brown and lose vitamins when they are exposed to the air.

ADDING FLAVOUR

● **Sprinkling spice** Mix 60 g (2¼ oz) muscovado sugar with 5 ml (1 tsp) ground cinnamon, and sprinkle over fruit for a sweet and spicy glaze.
● **Adding chocolate** Bake bananas until their skins turn black, then slit down one side, and spoon in melted chocolate. Eat this delicious dessert straight from the skins.
● **Baking peaches** To bring out the flavour of slightly underripe peaches, bake them in their skins, whole or in halves, in a hot oven for approximately 20 minutes. Slip off the skins of the fruits before serving.

BAKING WHOLE APPLES

Score lines vertically from top to bottom

Scoring skins
Use a canelle knife to score the skins of whole, cored apples before baking, so that the fruits cook without splitting. Sprinkle lemon juice on the exposed flesh to prevent browning.

BAKING WHOLE ORANGES

Gather foil, then twist to secure

Wrapping in foil
Remove the peel and pith from oranges, and slice into rings. Reassemble on foil squares, and add a knob of butter and a dash of liqueur. Wrap in foil and bake in a hot oven for 10 minutes.

QUICK APPLE FILLINGS

To bake apples with a tasty filling, remove the cores but leave them unpeeled. Pack the hollowed centres with a filling before baking.

● **Using almond paste** Chop almond paste and dried apricots, and pack into the centres of cored apples. Sprinkle with lemon juice.
● **Crumbling biscuits** Lightly crush macaroon biscuits or ginger nut biscuits, and mix with chopped almonds or walnuts. Spoon into apples.
● **Stuffing with nuts and dates** Make a stuffing for apples from chopped dates and walnuts. Spoon over maple syrup before baking.

MAKING PIE FILLINGS

Mix cornflour thoroughly with fruits

Thickening juices
To thicken juices in fruit pie fillings, toss the prepared fruits in a little cornflour. If sugar is to be added, mix it with the cornflour before adding to the fruits to distribute it evenly.

WRAPPING FRUITS

● **Wrapping pears in pastry** Cut long, thin strips of puff or shortcrust pastry, and spiral around peeled pears, leaving the stems exposed. Brush with milk, and bake in a hot oven until the pastry is golden.
● **Topping apples** Bake whole apples until almost tender, peel off the skins from the top halves, spread stiff meringue over the peeled parts, then bake in a hot oven until the meringue is golden.
● **Making filo parcels** Halve and stone plums or apricots, then put a blanched almond in each cavity. Put halves back together, and wrap in filo pastry. Brush with oil, and bake in a moderate oven until golden.

POACHING FRUITS

Fruits can be poached by cooking gently in syrup until they are just tender. Cook on a low heat to retain flavour and prevent the fruits from breaking up. To make a purée, poach fruits until soft, and beat with a wooden spoon or prepare in a food processor until smooth.

ENHANCING FLAVOURS
● **Counteracting acidity**
Reduce the acidity of rhubarb and improve its flavour by poaching it in orange juice or sprinkling it with ginger.
● **Using lemonade** Poach apple slices in leftover lemonade and white wine.
● **Adding tea** Use a scented tea such as Earl Grey for poaching dried fruits to make an exotic fruit compote. Add a few cardamom pods or star anise for a rich, spicy flavour.
● **Oven-poaching fruits** Allow the flavour of fruits to develop to their full intensity by poaching them in a tightly lidded dish in a cool oven for approximately one hour.

POACHING APRICOTS

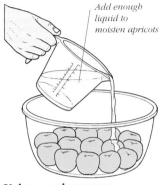

Add enough liquid to moisten apricots

Using a microwave
Pour water or fruit liqueur and lemon juice over the apricots. Cover, and cook on High for 4-5 minutes, turning halfway through. Slip off the skins, and serve apricots in the juices.

SERVING POACHED PEARS

Slice up to, but not through, stem end

Slicing into a fan
Poach whole pears, peeled but with stems on, in wine or sugar syrup until tender. Drain and cut into very thin slices, almost through to the stem end. Press lightly to fan out the slices.

GRILLING AND BARBECUING FRUITS

Grilling fruits is an excellent way of bringing out their sweet, ripe flavours – and almost any fruits can be cooked using this method. The dying heat from a barbecue after cooking the main course is ideal for grilling fruits brushed with spicy glazes or wrapped in foil parcels.

GRILLING PEACH HALVES
● **Adding lemon juice** Sprinkle fresh peach halves with lemon juice before grilling to prevent the flesh from browning.

Adding a topping
Top fresh or canned peach halves with a spoonful of ricotta or mascarpone cheese, sprinkle with a sweet spice such as cinnamon, allspice, or anise, and grill until the cheese bubbles.

BARBECUING PINEAPPLE
● **Glazing** Brush pineapple pieces with a mixture of equal amounts of melted butter, rum, and demerara sugar. Then grill.

Skewering wedges
Cut a pineapple lengthways into quarters, remove the core, and cut between the skin and the flesh, leaving the flesh in position. Slice the flesh, secure with skewers, and barbecue.

GRILLING FRUITS
● **Using skewers** Thread strawberries on to bamboo skewers, brush with melted butter, and sprinkle with icing sugar before grilling.
● **Marinating fruits** Soak peach or apricot halves in brandy for 30 minutes before grilling.
● **Making exotic kebabs** Mix chunks of exotic fruits such as mangoes, kiwi fruits, guavas, and kumquats on skewers, brush with butter, then grill.
● **Using rum butter** Use leftover rum or brandy butter as a glaze for grilled fruits.
● **Serving with sweet toasts** Grill slices of fruit with slices of buttered brioche or currant bread, and serve together, sprinkled with cinnamon.

EGGS

Eggs are a versatile cooking ingredient that can be used to thicken, aerate, enrich, bind, coat, or glaze sweet and savoury foods. They can be enjoyed as a complete food in themselves, whether fried, boiled, poached, or baked.

FRYING EGGS

Fried eggs need not be unhealthy, especially if you choose a light, unsaturated oil for frying. If your frying pan is of good quality or has a non-stick surface, you will need only a minimal amount of oil. To remove excess fat, drain eggs on a paper towel before serving.

COOKING OMELETTES

Carefully fold one-third of omelette over filling

Enclosing a filling
To turn out a filled omelette, fold over one side to the middle using a spatula. Tip the frying pan, and slide the omelette down, then flip the other side over neatly to enclose the filling.

SHAPING FRIED EGGS

Tip egg into cutter

Using biscuit cutters
Heat shaped cutters in a frying pan with oil. Tip an egg into each cutter, holding the cutter if necessary with a spatula, and fry. Run a knife around the inside of the cutter to remove the egg.

HEALTHY TIP

Reducing fat
To "fry" an egg without fat, place a heatproof plate over a pan of boiling water. When the plate is very hot, break an egg on to it. The egg should set in about eight minutes.

PREVENTING EGGS FROM STICKING
- **Using a clean pan** Start with a clean pan when frying eggs. If the pan has been used to cook other foods, such as bacon, the eggs may stick.
- **Choosing oil** Use a good-quality, light oil for frying eggs, such as sunflower or corn oil. Heat the oil, and cook the eggs over a moderate heat.

SCRAMBLING EGGS

- **Lightening** For scrambled eggs that are light and fluffy, beat in a little carbonated mineral water just before cooking.
- **Enriching** Add a dash of sherry to the beaten egg mixture before cooking to give a rich flavour to scrambled eggs.
- **Extending** To make scrambled eggs go further, add 15 ml (1 tbsp) fresh brown or white breadcrumbs to each egg.
- **Adding extras** Stir finely sliced strips of smoked salmon or smoked ham into scrambled eggs as they cook. Alternatively, add finely chopped chervil or chives for a fresh, herby flavour.
- **Making sandwich fillings** If you are short of time to hard-boil eggs for sandwich fillings, scramble the eggs instead, then cool, and mix with mayonnaise and seasoning to taste.

USING A MICROWAVE
- **Frying on a browning dish** Preheat a browning dish according to the manufacturer's instructions, and lightly brush the surface with oil. Break an egg on to the browning dish; the heat will brown the base of the egg. Prick the yolk with a cocktail stick to prevent it from bursting, and cover with a paper towel. Cook on High for about one minute.
- **Allowing standing time** When cooking scrambled eggs in a microwave, remove them just before they set. Stir, and leave to stand for one minute. The eggs will finish cooking in the residual heat and have an even, creamy consistency.

BOILING AND POACHING EGGS

Boiling and poaching are quick and simple methods of cooking eggs, requiring no extra fat. With careful timing, it is easy to cook eggs to perfection. Eggs should be at room temperature prior to boiling to avoid cracking, so remove them from the refrigerator 30 minutes before cooking.

PREVENTING PROBLEMS

● **Preventing black rings** To prevent dark rings from forming around the yolks of hard-boiled eggs, drain them as soon as they are cooked. Crack the shells, and run under cold water to cool quickly.

● **Adding vinegar** If eggshells crack during boiling, add a tablespoonful of vinegar to the water to set the white.

POACHING EGGS

● **Using fresh eggs** Use very fresh eggs for poaching so that the whites will cling to the yolks. Keep the water at a low simmer during cooking for a smooth, soft-textured result.

BOILING EGGS

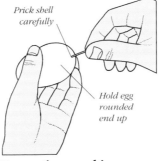

Prick shell carefully

Hold egg rounded end up

Preventing cracking

Before boiling eggs, prick the rounded end with a pin to allow the expanding air to escape during cooking and thus reduce the risk of cracking. Lower into cold water, and bring to the boil.

MARBLING BOILED EGGS

Using teabags

Boil eggs for two minutes, remove each one, and tap with a spoon to crack the shell. Return to the pan with six teabags, simmer for one minute, then cool. Remove shells, and eggs will be marbled.

BAKING EGGS

Eggs can be baked simply in ramekins with nothing more than salt and pepper, or used in more elaborate baked dishes such as soufflés and set custards. A moderate oven temperature, which will prevent egg whites from becoming tough, is best for most baked egg recipes.

MAKING SOUFFLÉS

Cut just inside edge

Creating a "top-hat" effect

When making a hot soufflé, use a sharp knife to cut the mixture around the edge just inside the dish before cooking. This will encourage the mixture to rise evenly, creating a "top-hat" effect when the soufflé is cooked.

BAKING IN POTATOES

Sprinkle cheese on top of egg

Scooping out the flesh

Bake a large jacket potato until tender, and cut a slice from the top. Scoop out the flesh from the centre, and break an egg into it. Season with salt and pepper, cover with cheese, and continue baking until the egg is set.

PREPARING SOUFFLÉS

● **Preparing ahead** To prepare a hot soufflé in advance, make up the mixture, and spoon it into a dish ready for baking. Cover with clingfilm, and chill for two hours before baking.

● **Ensuring even rising** To dislodge any large air pockets in a soufflé mixture, give the dish a sharp tap on a worktop before putting it into the oven.

● **Adding breadcrumbs** For a good rise and a crisp, golden crust, sprinkle a greased soufflé dish with fine breadcrumbs before adding the mixture.

● **Making soufflé tomatoes** For an unusual starter, slice the tops from beef tomatoes, and scoop out the centres. Fill each with cheese soufflé mixture. Bake in a hot oven until risen.

MEAT AND POULTRY

WHEN CHOOSING A COOKING METHOD FOR MEAT OR POULTRY, consider the cut you have chosen. If you use the appropriate cooking method, it is possible to make even the toughest cuts of meat and poultry tender and flavourful.

FLAVOURING MEAT AND POULTRY

Even for everyday meals, it is worth making the most of meat dishes by adding extra flavour with coatings, glazes, or tasty stuffings. In many cases, an accompaniment that adds flavour, such as stuffing or a sauce served with roast meat, helps make the meat go further.

USING COATINGS
● **Sprinkling with spices** Brush poultry skin with oil, and sprinkle with curry spices to give a rich, spicy, crisp skin.
● **Making a glaze** Mix equal quantities of Worcestershire sauce and tomato purée to make a spicy glaze. Brush the mixture over beef, lamb steaks, chops, or chicken joints before grilling.
● **Coating with crumbs** Toss fresh breadcrumbs in olive oil. Add plenty of fresh, chopped herbs, and cover the meat skin with the mixture for the last 30 minutes of roasting.

FLAVOURING HAM
● **Studding with cloves** To give a spicy flavour and an attractive finish to roast ham, score the fat surface, and press a clove into each cut.

Glazing with mustard
For a quick, flavourful glaze for roast ham or bacon, mix equal amounts of powdered mustard and brown sugar. Sprinkle the mixture over the fat surface for the final 30 minutes of cooking.

FLAVOURING CHICKEN

Adding lemon slices
To add flavour and keep a whole chicken moist during roasting, gently lift the breast skin, and tuck slices of lemon or orange underneath. Brush with oil, season, and place in a hot oven. Use unwaxed lemons if possible.

FLAVOURING PORK
● **Adding herbs** Before tying up a joint of boned pork for roasting, tuck a handful of fresh sage leaves inside it for a rich flavour. Roast as usual.

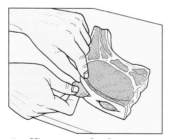

Stuffing a pork chop
To add flavour and interest to a plain pork chop, cut small slits along the fat edge, and open them out to make pockets. Tuck dried apricots or prunes inside, then grill, fry, or bake the chop.

ADDING STUFFING
● **Using mango** To give an exotic flavour to a whole turkey or chicken, and to moisten the flesh, tuck pieces of diced mango into the neck end. The fruit will cook to a purée, sweetening the poultry juices.
● **Flavouring packet stuffing** Mix a few chopped nuts, some dried fruits, or grated Parmesan cheese into packet stuffing mixes to add flavour.
● **Serving separately** Press excess stuffing into oiled ramekin dishes, bake for 20–25 minutes, and turn out to serve with the meat.

FLAVOURING RED MEAT
● **Adding garlic** To flavour lamb, cut deep slits in the surface with a knife, and tuck a sliver of garlic into each slit. This will infuse a subtle flavour to the meat as it cooks.
● **Marinating meat** Immerse lamb or beef steaks in a marinade of olive oil, garlic, red or white wine, and herbs. Keep in the refrigerator for 4–5 days, then grill lightly.
● **Spreading with juniper** For a rich flavour, crush juniper berries to a paste with a little red wine. Spread over the surface of venison steaks or joints before cooking.
● **Drawing out flavour** Season meat with salt just before cooking, since salt draws out the juices from meat.

STEWING MEAT AND POULTRY

Stewing is a slow, gentle cooking method, usually in a covered pan, and with cooking liquids partially covering the food. This method is especially suitable for tough cuts of meat, such as shin of beef, which can become tender and juicy after long cooking in a stew.

THICKENING STEWS

It is best to thicken at the end of cooking, since thickened stews tend to stick and burn during cooking. If a stew contains too much liquid, reduce or thicken it by one of the following methods.

● **Reducing liquid** Reduce liquid by boiling it rapidly without a lid until the correct consistency is reached.
● **Using cornflour** Blend some cornflour with enough stock, water, or wine to make a thin paste, then stir it into the hot juices. Bring to the boil, and stir for about two minutes.
● **Adding breadcrumbs** To thicken stews and casseroles quickly, stir in a few spoonfuls of fresh, white breadcrumbs.

ENHANCING STEWS

● **Replacing water** Use wine, tea, or beer in stews instead of water for a rich flavour, and to tenderize tough meat.
● **Adding beetroot** Add a slice or two of beetroot to meat stews and casseroles to deepen the colour of the sauce to a rich, golden brown.
● **Using herbs** Add tender herbs such as parsley or basil to stews and casseroles at the end of the cooking period, so that the flavours are not lost during the long cooking.
● **Adjusting saltiness** To save an over-salted stew, peel a potato, and cut it into chunks. Add it to the pan, simmer until soft, then remove. Alternatively, dilute the stew with cream or a can of tomatoes.

TRADITIONAL TIP

Cooking lamb in coffee
Instead of using stock or water for a lamb stew or casserole, try the traditional method of adding black coffee. The flavour of coffee complements lamb surprisingly well, and makes the juices rich and dark.

BRAISING MEAT AND POULTRY

Braising is a slow, gentle method of cooking that often uses a bed of vegetables and little or no added liquid. Braising is suitable for tough, mature, or dry cuts of meat and poultry. Pot-roasting is a similar method by which whole joints are braised with a little liquid.

USING VEGETABLES

Place meat on top of vegetables

Increasing flavour
Braise meat on a bed of vegetables such as onions, celery, leeks, or carrots, which may be precooked if preferred. Brown the meat to retain flavour and give it colour before adding to the vegetables.

RETAINING JUICES

Cut paper to size of pot

Covering with paper
Press a buttered round of non-stick or greaseproof paper on to the meat before covering the pot with a lid. This will concentrate the cooking juices and help to prevent the food from steaming.

PREPARING MEAT

● **Browning meat** When browning meat prior to braising, fry a few pieces at a time, so that they cook quickly and the juices are sealed in.
● **Marinating game** Marinate mature game birds in red wine before braising to ensure tenderness and flavour. Braise on a bed of celery or lentils.
● **Adding paprika** Sprinkle a little paprika over meat for simple braising to add colour to the finished dish.
● **Using pork rind** Place a meat joint for pot roasting on a piece of pork rind, which will add flavour and prevent the meat from sticking to the pan.

GRILLING AND BARBECUING

Both grilling and barbecuing are quick, simple, and healthy methods of cooking that are suitable for most meat, fish, vegetables, and fruits. In each case, seal in the juices by cooking initially at a high heat. Then lower the heat to ensure that the food cooks thoroughly.

MAKING A HINGED WIRE RACK FOR BARBECUING

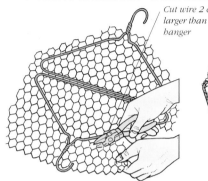

Cut wire 2 cm (¾ in) larger than hanger

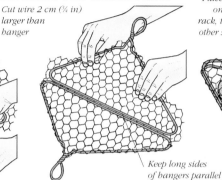

Keep long sides of hangers parallel

Place food on one side of rack, then fold other side over

1 Make a hinged wire rack to turn delicate foods on a barbecue. Lay two wire coat hangers over a square piece of flexible, lightweight chicken wire. Trim the wire to shape.

2 Push the curved hanger handles firmly inwards to form round handles. Fold the edges of the wire over the outer edges of the hangers, tucking in any sharp points.

3 Fold the hangers together at the join. Use the rack for cooking both sides of delicate foods, such as fish and hamburgers, which tend to collapse if turned with tongs.

USING BAMBOO SKEWERS
● **Preventing burning** To grill or barbecue foods on bamboo skewers, first soak the skewers in water for about 20 minutes. This will prevent them from burning during cooking.

ADDING WOODCHIPS
● **Soaking** To extend the lives of hickory or oak wood chips, soak them in water for a few minutes. Then scatter the woodchips on to the coals to add aroma to the barbecue.

PREVENTING STICKING
● **Oiling a grill** Brush a barbecue grill with oil to prevent foods from sticking to it. Heat the grill to a high temperature before you place any food on it for cooking.

GRILLING SUCCESSFULLY
● **Using foil** Line an oven grillpan with a layer of foil, shiny-side up, to reflect heat back on to food while it cooks. This will also make it easy to clean the pan after cooking.
● **Preheating a grill** Always preheat a grill for at least five minutes before cooking.
● **Absorbing fat** When grilling fatty meat, place a few pieces of stale bread in the bottom of the grillpan to absorb fat spills.
● **Turning meat** Use tongs, instead of a fork, for turning meat to prevent the loss of juices due to piercing.
● **Grilling low-fat foods** Brush low-fat foods, such as chicken, with oil to keep them moist.

TURNING FRANKFURTERS

Thread frankfurters from end to end

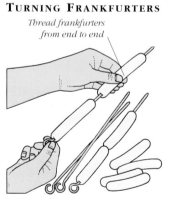

Using skewers
Thread frankfurters or sausages on to flat, metal skewers to make it easy to turn them on a barbecue or grill. The skewers also conduct heat, which helps to reduce the cooking time.

SAFETY

● **Siting a barbecue** Position a barbecue on a sheltered, level surface, away from trees and buildings.
● **Supervising children** Keep children away from the fire.
● **Controlling fire** Keep a bucket of sand and a water spray to hand, in case of fire.
● **Using special tools** Use long-handled barbecue tools for turning and basting foods.
● **Keeping food cool** Keep perishable foods covered and place them in the refrigerator until just before cooking.
● **Ensuring thorough cooking** Make sure that all meat, especially pork, sausages, and poultry, is well cooked.

FRYING AND SAUTÉEING

Frying and sautéeing are quick methods of cooking that seal in food juices effectively. Control the heat carefully to cook foods evenly and prevent overheating. Delicate foods, such as fish fillets, may need to be coated before frying to give them a little extra protection from the heat.

CHECKING TEMPERATURE

Testing with bread
If you do not have a thermometer to check oil temperature, drop a piece of bread into the oil. When the bread browns, usually in about a minute, the oil is hot enough to add food for frying.

REUSING OIL

Paper towel retains food debris

Straining impurities
Before reusing oil leftover from frying, filter out any food debris left in it. Line a sieve with an absorbent paper towel, hold the sieve over a bowl, and then pour the oil through it.

HEALTHY TIP

Brush pan with oil to prevent sticking

Using a ridged frying pan
To "dry" fry fatty foods such as bacon or sausages, use a heavy frying pan with a ridged base. The ridges hold the food above its own fatty juices, which can be poured off when cooking is finished.

COATING & BROWNING FRIED FOODS

● **Drying food** Dry food thoroughly by patting it with a paper towel before dipping it into batter for frying. This will help the batter to cling to the food, coating it evenly.

● **Mixing butter and oil** To obtain a golden colour when shallow-frying, use a mixture of half butter and half oil. The butter browns easily, and the oil prevents it from burning.

PREVENTING PROBLEMS

● **Controlling smells** Wear a shower cap when frying if you want to prevent smells from getting into your hair. After you have finished frying, remove the pan from the heat, and cover. Leave to cool.
● **Avoiding spitting** Always dry food thoroughly to remove surface moisture before adding it to hot oil. If the oil starts to spit, cover the pan with an upturned metal colander or a wire-mesh pan guard.

USING A WOK EFFECTIVELY

Clip-on draining rack

Deep-frying in a wok
Use a wok for deep-frying foods, since the shape will allow you to use less oil than with conventional frying methods. If the wok has a curved base, use a wok stand to steady it.

● **Testing heat** To test whether a wok is hot enough before adding oil, hold the palm of your hand a few inches above the surface of the bottom of the pan until you feel the heat rising from it. Alternatively, wait until a wisp of smoke rises from the bottom of the empty wok.
● **Shaking the wok** When stir-frying food in a wok, keep shaking the pan and stirring the food constantly over a high heat. This will ensure that the food cooks evenly and quickly using the minimum of fat.
● **Using chopsticks** Use long, wooden chopsticks to turn food being cooked in a wok, since they will not overheat.

SAFETY

● **Paying attention** Always stay by a pan of fried food while it is cooking.
● **Controlling temperature** Check the temperature of oil with a thermometer, and keep it just below smoking point.
● **Preventing fire** If fat catches fire, turn off the heat, and cover the pan. Do not use water to put out the fire.

ROASTING POULTRY

Poultry needs to be cooked thoroughly to kill all harmful bacteria. Chicken is ready when the juices run clear, not pink, when the flesh is pierced through the thickest part. Duck and pigeon are suitable for serving slightly less well-cooked, with just a touch of pink in the flesh.

ROASTING SUCCESSFULLY

● **Using the cavity** Tuck a bunch of herbs, a lemon, or a whole onion inside the cavity of a chicken or turkey before roasting. The flavour will penetrate the meat, and will make tasty juices for gravy.

● **Resting poultry** Allow poultry to rest for about 20 minutes after roasting. This will make it easy to carve. Turn off the oven and leave the bird inside, or remove and cover with foil.

● **Using roasting bags** Cook poultry in a roasting bag to eliminate the need for basting. If you want to crisp up the skin, open the bag for the final 20 minutes of cooking.

● **Using a microwave** If you "roast" poultry in a microwave that does not have a browning facility, sprinkle the bird with paprika to add colour.

COVERING WITH BACON

● **Using bacon rind** Keep the breast of birds such as turkey, pheasant, or pigeon moist and tender by laying bacon rind or streaky bacon over the breast.

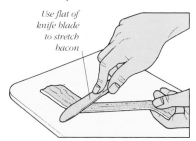
Use flat of knife blade to stretch bacon

Maintaining shape

To retain the shape of small birds, wrap streaky bacon around them. Stretch each rasher first by pressing firmly along its length with a round-bladed knife to elongate it. Then wrap around the bird.

ROASTING TURKEY

● **Maintaining moisture** Roast a turkey breast-downwards for the first hour of cooking to keep it moist. Then turn the turkey over to finish cooking.

Place turkey on celery

Laying on a bed of celery

Before placing turkey in a roasting tin, cover the base of the tin with celery sticks, which act like a roasting rack. The vegetables will add flavour to the meat juices for a delicious gravy.

ROASTING DUCK

● **Crisping skin** For crisp duck skin, prick the skin all over with a fork, sprinkle with salt, and roast on a rack to lift the bird above the fatty juices.

Protecting wings

To prevent the wing ends of a duck from overcooking before the rest of the bird has finished cooking, wrap them in foil before roasting. Remove the foil for the final 30 minutes of cooking to allow the wings to brown.

ROASTING CHICKEN

● **Browning skin** To boost the golden-brown colour of a roast chicken, add a pinch of ground turmeric to the oil or butter that you use for basting.

Flavouring with wine

Pour about 150 ml (¼ pint) red or dry white wine into a large, clean, empty food can. Sit a chicken on the can, then stand in a roasting tray. The wine will flavour meat juices that collect in the can.

TRADITIONAL TIP

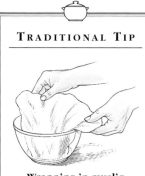

Wrapping in muslin

Instead of covering a large chicken or turkey with foil for roasting, dip a double layer of muslin into melted butter or oil, and lay it over the bird's skin. The muslin will allow the skin to brown and become crisp during cooking without trapping in steam, as a covering of foil would do.

ROASTING MEAT

For a successful meat roast, it is important to place it in a hot oven at the start of cooking to seal in the tasty juices. Reduce the heat once the meat starts to brown. Remove chilled meat from the refrigerator 20 minutes before roasting, so that it comes to room temperature.

ROASTING FATTY MEAT

Rub powder into surface

Using dry mustard
When roasting a cut of beef or pork with a high fat content, cover the surface with dry mustard powder. This will counteract the fattiness, and add flavour to the gravy.

CHECKING TEMPERATURE

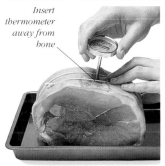

Insert thermometer away from bone

Using a thermometer
Insert a meat thermometer into the thickest part of the meat, avoiding the bone. Bone conducts heat more quickly than flesh so may give a false reading. Leave the thermometer in during cooking.

CRISPING PORK RIND

● **Scoring the rind** Ask your butcher to score pork rind deeply at regular intervals. Alternatively, do this at home with a sharp knife.
● **Salting the rind** Brush scored pork rind with oil, and sprinkle with salt for crisp, golden crackling.
● **Scalding the rind** Pour boiling water over the rind just before roasting the meat.
● **Cooking the rind separately** Using a sharp knife, remove the skin of the pork together with an even layer of fat. Cut it into strips, and sprinkle with salt. Roast with the joint until crisp.

PREPARING ACCOMPANIMENTS

Roast meat and poultry are often associated with standard accompaniments – roast pork is usually accompanied by apple, for example. There are no set rules, however, and trimmings can be varied to suit your taste, and to add extra colour and texture to dishes as desired.

SAVING TIME

● **Thickening gravy** To thicken quickly, whisk in 15–30 ml (1–2 tbsp) instant potato mix.
● **Blending mint sauce** Place a handful of fresh mint leaves in a blender with 30 ml (2 tbsp) caster sugar and 30 ml (2 tbsp) boiling water. Blend until chopped, then add wine vinegar to taste.
● **Grilling bacon rolls** If you are serving rolled-up bacon with roast poultry, thread the rolls on to skewers to make them easy to turn, and cook quickly under a hot grill.
● **Microwaving cranberries** Cook 250 g (9 oz) cranberries in 300 ml (½ pint) water on High until boiling, then for five minutes more, until the berries burst. Sweeten to taste.

IMPROVING GRAVY

Skim surface with paper towel

Skimming off fat
To remove a layer of fat from meat or poultry gravy, drag a piece of absorbent paper towel lightly across the surface of the liquid. Repeat, if necessary, to remove any traces of fat that are left before serving the gravy.

ADDING EXTRAS

● **Flavouring gravy** Stir a generous dash of brandy or port into plain gravy to pep up the flavour for serving with a special roast. Boil for two minutes before serving.
● **Making stuffing balls** When stuffing a joint of meat or poultry, make more stuffing than you need. Roll the extra into balls, and place in the juices around the roast for the last 20 minutes of cooking.
● **Glazing a roast** Just before serving, brush the surface of a roast with warmed redcurrant or cranberry jelly to give it an attractive, sweet-tasting glaze.
● **Spicing batter** To spice up savoury batter puddings, add 15 ml (1 tbsp) Worcestershire sauce to the mixture.

FISH AND SHELLFISH

FISH COOKS SIMPLY AND QUICKLY, and in its many forms, it can be cooked by most methods. Whole fish cooked on the bone has the finest flavour. Filleted fish is versatile enough to be fried, poached, grilled, or even barbecued.

ADDING FLAVOUR

Most types of fresh fish need little flavour enhancement, but it is a good idea to use different flavours to stimulate appetite and add variety. With a simple squeeze of lemon and a sprinkling of herbs, or with more unusual marinades or glazes, fish can take on new flavour.

FLAVOURING OIL

Sliced ginger

Root ginger

Adding fresh ginger
Before shallow-frying or stir-frying fish, add a few thin slices of fresh root ginger to the oil for extra flavour. Stir over a moderate heat for 3–4 minutes, then remove, and cook the fish.

MARINATING RAW FISH
● **Choosing a marinade** Use an oil-based marinade for white fish to moisten and add flavour. Use an acid marinade, based on citrus juice or vinegar, for oily fish to offset its richness.
● **Using yoghurt** Spread a yoghurt-based marinade, such as a tandoori mixture, over fish that is to be grilled. This will seal in the juices and produce a spicy, low-fat crust.
● "Cooking" in a marinade Cut about 500 g (1 lb 2 oz) fresh, white fish into thin strips, and add the juice of four limes or lemons. Chop and stir in an onion, a chilli, and a clove of garlic. Chill for 3–4 hours. The marinade will "cook" the fish, and it will be ready to eat cold.

FLAVOURING FISH

Dribble marinade over warm fish

Seasoning with marinade
Slash the flesh of small, whole fish at intervals before you grill or fry them, but flavour with marinade after cooking. Use white wine and herbs or spices. Leave until cold before serving.

FLAVOURING OILY FISH
● **Using mustard** Spread herring or mackerel fillets with a thin layer of mustard. Then roll the fish in oatmeal or rolled oats before frying.

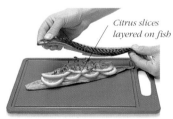

Citrus slices layered on fish

Sandwiching fillets
Add flavour to fillets of mackerel or herring by sandwiching the fillets together with lemon, lime, or orange slices and thyme sprigs. Bake in the oven, or tie firmly with string and grill.

USING COATINGS
● **Mixing with herbs** Instead of coating white fish fillets in plain breadcrumbs, stir in a few crumbled dried herbs, curry spices, or crushed, dried chillies.
● **Using coconut** Dip pieces of monkfish or other white, firm fish in lightly beaten egg. Then toss the pieces in grated, fresh coconut before frying. This will give the fish an unusual, nut-flavoured covering.
● **Adding sesame** For extra flavour, add 5 ml (1 tsp) sesame oil to the egg you use for coating fish. Stir sesame seeds into breadcrumbs to add flavour and texture to a coating.

FLAVOURING WITH HERBS
● **Adding herbs** Tuck sprigs of fresh herbs into the cavity of a whole fish before cooking, so that the flavour of the herbs penetrates the flesh of the fish.

Baking with fennel
Bake whole fish such as sea bass on a bed of sliced fennel stalks, which will add a subtle flavour. Arrange the fennel in an even layer in a buttered ovenproof dish, then lay the fish over it.

GRILLING AND BARBECUING

Most whole fish, particularly oily fish, cook well on a barbecue or grill and need little more than an occasional brushing with oil to prevent them from drying out or sticking. Delicate fish fillets and steaks need careful basting and turning, or wrapping in foil.

GRILLING SUCCESSFULLY
● **Making kebabs** When making fish kebabs, add other quick-cooking ingredients, such as mushrooms or cherry tomatoes, which will cook in the same amount of time as the fish.
● **Slashing flesh** When cooking a whole fish or thick fillets, slash the thickest parts of the flesh to help the heat penetrate evenly, and speed up grilling.
● **Turning fish** Place a layer of oiled foil over the grill rack so that the fish will turn easily without sticking. Alternatively, grill fish steaks on a preheated baking sheet, so that there is no need to turn them.
● **Preventing sticking** Preheat the grill rack to a high heat before cooking to seal in juices and prevent sticking.

GRILLING FISH FILLETS
● **Positioning fish** To prevent damage to the flesh, brush fish skin and grill rack with oil, and place fish skin-side down.

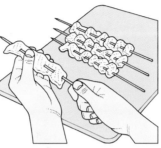

Using skewers
Thread small fish fillets on to wooden skewers for easy turning on a barbecue, and to prevent the fish from breaking up. Soak the skewers in water before use to prevent them from burning.

GRILLING SHELLFISH
● **Keeping moist** Wrap shelled mussels or scallops in streaky bacon to keep moist. Thread on to skewers, and grill.

Butter prevents oysters from drying out

Grilling fresh oysters
Place fresh oysters in the deep halves of their shells on a grillpan. Top each with a spoonful of herb- or garlic-flavoured butter, and scatter with breadcrumbs. Cook under a hot grill until bubbling.

ROASTING AND BAKING

Roasting fish at a high temperature seals in flavours and produces tender, moist flesh. Baking in foil or paper parcels prevents the fish from drying out and allows it to cook in its own juices, which can be added to a sauce or simply poured over the fish before serving.

COOKING FISH IN PARCELS

Buttered parchment

1 Bake small, whole fish or fish fillets in parcels. Cut a heart-shaped piece of non-stick baking parchment to enclose the fish. Butter the centre, and place the fish on one side. Add any flavourings.

Follow shape, tucking in ends with fingertips

2 Fold the other side of the paper over the fish, and tuck and fold along the edge, starting from the rounded end. Finish at the pointed end with a double fold to secure the parcel. Bake on a baking sheet.

PRESERVING FLAVOUR
● **Wrapping in foil** When baking a whole fish such as salmon, wrap it loosely in foil so that the fish stews in its own juices, keeping it moist.
● **Making crispy skin** Baste the skin of sea bass or trout with butter, and season. Roast at a high temperature – about 230°C (450°F) or Gas Mark 8.
● **Baking in salt** Place a whole fish on a layer of rock salt. Completely cover it with salt to seal in the juices, then sprinkle with water. Bake at 200°C (400°F) or Gas Mark 6 until the salt is hard and dry, then break it with a hammer, discard the salt and skin, and serve.

FRYING

Frying is traditionally a popular method of cooking fish, and need not greatly increase the fat content of your diet. If you heat the oil before adding the fish, however, an outer crust will form instantly and hardly any fat will be absorbed, leaving the flesh tender and moist.

WORKING WITH OIL

● **Choosing oil** Use good quality, clean oil for frying fish, since delicate fish flavours can be spoiled by strongly flavoured or tainted oil. Lightly flavoured oils, such as corn or sunflower, are ideal.
● **Heating the oil** For a crisp coating, make sure that the oil is hot enough before frying fish. For deep-frying, the temperature of the oil should be 190°C (375°F).
● **Frying from frozen** To deep-fry fish from frozen, heat the oil to approximately 180°C (350°F) which will allow the inside of the fish to cook before the coating browns.

FRYING SHELLFISH

● **Leaving tails** When peeling prawns for frying, remove the heads, legs, and skins, but leave the tails on. Use the tail to hold a prawn when dipping it into the coating mixture.

FRYING KING PRAWNS

Roll prawn in seasoned cornflour

Coating in cornflour

Prepare king prawns for frying by dusting gently with seasoned cornflour, then dipping in lightly beaten egg white. The cooked prawns will have a light, crisp coating, and remain juicy inside.

MAKING BATTER

Adding beer

To make a light, crisp batter for coating fish, substitute beer for the liquid, or add a tablespoonful of brandy. Alternatively, lighten the batter by folding a whisked egg white into the mixture just before coating and frying the fish.

ADDING EXTRA FLAVOUR

● **Combining oils** When shallow-frying fish fillets, add a subtle, Oriental flavour by mixing 15 ml (1 tbsp) sesame oil with a lightly flavoured oil, such as sunflower, before cooking.

COATING & WRAPPING

● **Mussels** Dip mussels in a light batter, and deep-fry in hot oil for about 30 seconds
● **Fish fillets** When coating delicate fish fillets, dip first in flour, then in beaten egg. Coat evenly with fine breadcrumbs to seal in flavour and prevent the fish from breaking up.
● **Whole fish** To coat small, whole fish, such as whitebait or sardines, in seasoned flour, place the flour and fish in a polythene bag, then shake well to coat evenly.
● **Peeled prawns** For a light, crisp, golden coating, wrap peeled prawns in thin strips of filo pastry, enclosing all but the tail, before frying.

PREPARING SQUID

Diamond pattern will look attractive after cooking

Scoring flesh

Before frying the pouch flesh of squid, score its smooth surface lightly with a sharp knife, making a diamond pattern. This method of scoring the flesh will help the heat to penetrate the flesh evenly during cooking.

PREVENTING SPITTING

● **Using a colander** If fish begins to spit during frying, place an upturned colander over the pan. This will prevent the spits from escaping, but at the same time let steam out.

STIR-FRYING

● **Choosing seafood** Choose a firm-textured, meaty piece of seafood for stir-frying, such as monkfish or squid. Soft-textured seafood breaks up.
● **Using delicate fish** To stir-fry delicate fish, such as cod, coat the pieces in cornflour before cooking. Shake the pan instead of stirring it to keep the fish pieces whole.
● **Cooking small batches** To keep the heat high enough to seal in the juices, stir-fry a small quantity of fish at a time.
● **Keeping pieces separate** Toss pieces of squid in a little sesame oil before stir-frying to help keep them separate.

POACHING FISH

Poaching is a classic method of cooking fish and also one of the most healthy, since the fish is cooked in liquid with no fat added. Poaching is most suitable for cooking whole fish, such as salmon, and delicate white fish fillets that require gentle, even cooking.

POACHING PERFECTLY

● **Handling fish gently** To poach a delicate fish, place it in warm liquid that just covers it. Slowly bring the liquid up to barely simmering.

● **Serving fish cold** To cook a whole fish or fish fillets to be served cold, bring the liquid up to simmering, and cook gently for one minute. Turn off the heat, and allow the residual heat to cook the fish.

● **Using stock** Give your guests slotted spoons to poach fish at table in a richly flavoured stock. Mongolian- or Chinese-style steamers or a fondue set can be used to cook the fish. Serve the stock as a soup.

COOKING LARGE, WHOLE FISH

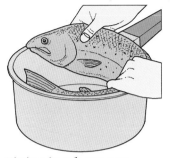

Fitting in a large pan
If you do not have a fish kettle in which to cook a large, whole fish, accommodate the fish in a large saucepan by curling it gently to fit inside the pan, with its backbone facing upwards. Serve on a round platter.

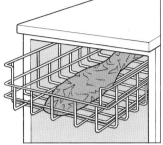

Using a dishwasher
Double-wrap a salmon or any other very large fish in foil, and seal thoroughly. Place it on the upper rack of an empty dishwasher. Run a main wash at 65°C (150°F), without prewash or dry. Remove, and cool in the foil.

STEAMING FISH

Steaming is a healthy method of cooking, suitable for fish fillets or thin steaks. The main rule is that the fish should not touch the water. You do not need a steamer, but if you steam fish often, it is useful to have a steaming compartment that fits over a saucepan.

COMBINING FOODS

Cooking over potatoes
When steaming fish, make economical use of energy by placing the fish in a steamer over a pan of boiling potatoes. Cover and simmer for 10-15 minutes, depending on thickness.

STEAMING SUCCESSFULLY

● **Steaming large fish** To steam a large, whole fish that will not fit into a steamer, pour a shallow depth of water into a deep roasting tin. Place the fish, covered tightly with foil, on a rack in the tin above the water level, and simmer on the cooker top for five minutes per 450 g (1 lb) weight.

● **Using individual baskets** Use Chinese-style steamer baskets, which stack easily, to steam and then to serve individual portions of fish.

● **Topping up liquid** Always keep a kettle of water close to boiling point while you are steaming foods, so that when topping up the liquid in the steamer, the added water will not lower the temperature.

BRIGHT IDEA

Cooking on a plate
Place small fish fillets or steaks between two heatproof plates, and cook over a pan of rapidly boiling water. The fish will cook evenly and quickly in its juices. Pour the juices over the fish to serve.

SOUPS, STOCKS, AND SAUCES

MAKING YOUR OWN SOUPS, STOCKS, AND SAUCES is rewarding, since you can make nutritious and inexpensive dishes that are far superior to anything you could buy, using simple, fresh ingredients and a few basic cooking skills.

MAKING SOUPS AND STOCKS

The basis of a good, home-made soup is a well-flavoured stock. Stock cubes save time, but it is relatively easy and inexpensive to make your own stock using the bones from a roast or leftover vegetables. There is an infinite variety of soups that you can create in your kitchen.

MAKING SOUPS

● **Sweating vegetables** Before adding stock, cook vegetables first by "sweating" in a tightly covered pan with a little butter. Add a few tablespoonfuls of wine or dry sherry for extra flavour. Cook on a low heat for one hour, shaking now and then to prevent sticking.

● **Using lettuce leaves** Instead of discarding the large, tough outer leaves of a lettuce, shred them like cabbage, and cook in a stock. Purée when soft, and stir in a little cream.

● **Using leftovers** Make a quick vichyssoise with cooked potatoes. Fry an onion or a leek until soft, then purée it with the potato and vegetable stock. Add cream to taste.

PURÉEING VEGETABLES

Press vegetables through sieve

Using a ladle

To purée cooked vegetables by hand for adding to soups, tip them into a large sieve over a bowl, and squash them with a ladle. This is quicker than using a wooden spoon for pressing, and requires less effort.

THICKENING SOUPS

Stir in a small amount at a time

Using a beurre manié

To thicken a soup quickly and easily, mix together equal amounts of butter and plain flour to a thick paste. Drop small spoonfuls of the mixture into the hot soup, and stir over the heat until sufficiently thickened.

ADDING VARIETY

● **Using spices** Stir mild curry paste into carrot or parsnip soup to add a warm flavour.

● **Adding texture** Before puréeing vegetables for a soup, keep a ladleful of the cooked, chopped vegetables to add texture to the finished soup.

● **Crumbling cheese** Liven up creamed or canned soups by stirring in some crumbled blue cheese before serving.

● **Making pistou** Crush three garlic cloves with 30 ml (2 tbsp) pine nuts, a handful of basil, and 30 ml (2 tbsp) olive oil. Stir the mixture into vegetable soups to taste.

USING STOCKS

Ice cubes   *Fat*

Stock

Removing fat

To remove fat from the surface of stock effectively, add a few ice cubes. When the fat has set around the ice, lift it off.

● **Cooking on low heat** To make a really rich, clear stock, simmer it slowly over a very low heat. Boiling a stock tends to give a cloudy appearance.

● **Reducing stock** To reduce a cooked stock, reduce it first by boiling it in an uncovered pan until it is very thick and syrupy. The stock will then set to a jelly when cooled, and this will keep longer than a liquid.

● **Using leftovers** Add leftover vegetables, trimmings, or peelings to stock for flavour. Do not use potatoes, since they will make the stock cloudy.

MAKING EGG-BASED SAUCES

Sauces incorporating eggs are made either by creating a thick emulsion, as in mayonnaise or hollandaise, or by gentle cooking, as in the case of custard or cream sauce. Egg-based sauces take longer to make than many other sauces, but their rich, creamy textures are unmatched.

CORRECTING FAULTS

● **Adding ice** If you overheat hollandaise sauce, and it is just starting to curdle, stir in an ice cube to cool it quickly.
● **Re-whisking hollandaise** To smooth a curdled hollandaise sauce, add it drop by drop to a spoonful of vinegar in a clean bowl, whisking hard until the sauce re-thickens.
● **Using egg yolk** If mayonnaise separates, beat a fresh egg yolk in a clean bowl, and whisk in the mayonnaise drop by drop until the mixture thickens.
● **Adding cornflour** If a custard sauce begins to curdle, plunge the base of the pan into cold water, then rub the sauce through a sieve. Whisk a teaspoonful of cornflour into the sauce, and reheat gently without boiling until thickened.

MAKING MAYONNAISE

● **Reducing fat** For a white, low-fat mayonnaise, use whole eggs instead of just the yolks, or mix the mayonnaise with plain yoghurt in equal parts.

Add leaves to colour mayonnaise

Using a blender
Put all the mayonnaise ingredients except the oil into a blender. Run the machine, and add the oil in a thin stream until the sauce thickens. Then add any extra ingredients, such as watercress.

MAKING HOLLANDAISE

● **Using a microwave** Heat 100 g (3½ oz) butter in a large jug on High, and whisk in two egg yolks and flavourings. Cook on Medium for one minute.

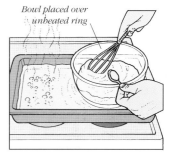

Bowl placed over unheated ring

Avoiding curdling
To make hollandaise sauce without a double boiler, prepare it in a bowl placed in a roasting tin containing simmering water. Make sure that the bowl is not directly above the heat source.

MAKING OTHER SAUCES

There are numerous different types of sauce in addition to custard and the emulsions produced by traditional sauce-making methods. Flour-thickened mixtures are useful, and sauces made from simple purées, salsas, and cream reductions provide interesting alternatives.

MAKING SALSAS

Salsas are an essential part of Mexican cuisine, adding powerful flavours and rich colours to simple meals.

● **Saving time** Place chillies, garlic, onions, tomatoes, and deseeded peppers in a food processor. Pulse until finely chopped for a *salsa cruda*.
● **Mixing fruits** Combine finely-chopped fresh mango, pawpaw, and chillies to serve with grilled fish or chicken.
● **Creating mild flavours** To reduce the strong flavours of raw garlic and onions, simmer for 5–8 minutes before use.

WORKING WITH SAUCES

● **Adding cornflour** To thicken a smooth sauce easily, blend 5 ml (1 tsp) cornflour into 10 ml (2 tsp) cold water, add to the sauce, and stir over a moderate heat until thickened.
● **Correcting lumpy sauces** If a sauce or gravy has become lumpy, pour it into a food processor, and process until smooth. Alternatively, press the sauce through a sieve.
● **Making purées** Use smooth purées of vegetables such as peppers for colourful, simple, low-fat sauces. Grill the peppers to remove the skins, then purée in a processor.

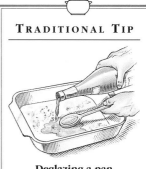

TRADITIONAL TIP

Deglazing a pan
Add wine, stock, or cream to the concentrated juices or sediment left in a roasting tin after cooking meat or poultry. Bring to the boil, and stir well.

GRAINS, PASTA, AND PULSES

T HE WIDE VARIETY OF GRAINS, PASTA, AND PULSES now available from all over the world presents many choices for healthy meals that are easy to prepare. They form the basis of substantial main dishes and delicious side dishes.

GRAINS

G rains are usually boiled or steamed, either on their own or combined with a variety of other ingredients in dishes such as pilafs or risottos. Whole grains take longer to cook than processed white grains, but most varieties of grain will cook within about 30 minutes.

REMOVING STARCH

Rinsing basmati rice
Basmati rice needs to be rinsed thoroughly to keep the grains separate. Place it in a bowl of cold water, and swirl the rice around by hand. Drain, and repeat until the water is clear.

COOLING COOKED RICE

Using a wooden spoon
To cool cooked rice quickly for use in salads, drain through a sieve, and place over a bowl. Prod the rice at intervals with a wooden spoon handle to release the steam and heat.

STEAMING COUSCOUS

Lining a colander
If you do not have a couscous steamer, line a metal sieve with a piece of muslin, and place it over a pan of boiling water. Tip the couscous into the sieve, and cover. Steam until tender.

TRADITIONAL TIP

Making a stomach settler
As a cure for an upset stomach, boil white rice without having rinsed it first, and strain off the starchy cooking liquid. Allow it to cool, then give it to the patient to drink.

COOKING PERFECT RICE
● **Pre-soaking rice** Reduce the cooking time of rice and other grains by soaking them first in cold water for 30 minutes.
● **Cooking on a low heat** When cooking glutinous rice, use a large pan, and simmer on the lowest heat possible. Keep the lid on during cooking, and leave to stand for 10 minutes after draining.
● **Using a microwave** Place 250 g (9 oz) white rice in a large bowl with 450 ml (16 fl oz) boiling water. Cook on High for nine minutes. Cook brown rice for about 15–20 minutes.
● **Forking rice** Fluff up cooked rice by separating the grains with a fork before serving.

ADDING VARIETY
● **Cooking in stock** Add extra flavour to plain, boiled grains by cooking them in a rich meat, chicken, or vegetable stock rather than water.
● **Colouring rice** If you do not have saffron for colouring rice and risottos, stir in a pinch of turmeric after cooking.
● **Using coconut milk** Simmer long-grain rice in coconut milk to accompany oriental dishes. Use about 400 ml (14 fl oz) coconut milk to 200 g (7 oz) rice, and cook until the liquid is absorbed.
● **Using pesto** Replace the butter or olive oil in cooked polenta with a roughly equal quantity of red or green pesto.

PASTA

There are only a few simple rules to follow when cooking fresh or dried pasta. Cook it lightly, in plenty of rapidly boiling water, until it is *al dente* – which translates literally as "to the tooth". This means the pasta is tender to the bite, but still offers a slight resistance in the centre.

COOKING LONG PASTA

Feed pasta in as it softens

Feeding into a pan

To fit long spaghetti into a small pan of boiling water, hold it in a bunch, and put one end into the water. As the ends of the pieces soften, bend the pasta slightly, and feed in the rest gradually.

COOKING STUFFED PASTA

Skimmer will not split pasta

Using a skimmer

To lift cooked, filled pasta such as ravioli out of water without damaging or bursting it, use a flat, metal skimmer or a flat, slotted, draining spoon. Toss in oil or sauce to prevent sticking.

COLOURING PASTA

To add colour and flavour when making pasta dough, mix in additional ingredients.

- **Tomato** Add 10 ml (2 tsp) tomato paste per egg to the beaten eggs, and stir well.
- **Spinach** Thaw 50 g (1¾ oz) frozen, chopped spinach per egg. Squeeze well before adding to the beaten eggs.
- **Saffron** For rich, golden pasta, add a pinch of ground saffron to the flour.
- **Beetroot** Stir 15 ml (1 tbsp) cooked, puréed beetroot per egg to the pasta dough.

PULSES

Peas, beans, and lentils are a valuable source of protein and are versatile enough to be used in all kinds of dishes, including casseroles, pâtés, dahls, and salads. Dried beans take some time to cook, but the cooking is simple, and they are less expensive than canned varieties.

COOKING TIMES

Most pulses need to be soaked in cold water for at least 4–8 hours. Alternatively, soak in boiling water for about one hour. The following cooking times are a rough guide only; recommended times may vary from one type to another, so always check carefully.

- Split lentils: 15–20 minutes.
- Whole lentils, aduki beans, mung beans, split peas: 25–30 minutes.
- Black-eyed beans, lima beans, peas: 45 minutes.
- Black beans, borlotti beans, cannellini beans, red kidney beans, ful medames beans: about one hour.
- Pinto beans, chick-peas, butter beans: 1¼ hours.
- Broad beans, butter beans, haricot beans: 1½ hours.

COOKING BEANS

- **Seasoning** Season beans towards the end of their cooking time, since salt can prevent them from softening.
- **Cooling** If you are cooking beans to serve cold, cool them in their cooking water rather than dry in a colander. This will stop their skins from splitting.
- **Pressure cooking** If you are using a pressure cooker, cook beans on High for a third of their normal cooking time.

SAFETY

Ensure that you boil dried red kidney beans, borlotti beans, aduki beans, and black beans vigorously for 10 minutes to destroy the harmful toxins that cause stomach upsets. Simmer gently until tender.

PREPARING SNACKS

- **Making a dip** Mash cooked, drained butter beans well with a fork. Add crushed garlic, chilli paste, and olive oil to make a rich, spicy dip. Serve with vegetable sticks.

Flour seasoned with ground pepper

Making chick-pea nibbles

Mix cooked or drained canned chick-peas with seasoned, wholemeal flour and crushed garlic. Fry in a little butter and oil on a high heat until crisp and golden. Serve with drinks.

DESSERTS

A HOT OR COLD DESSERT rounds off a meal nicely. Whatever level of skill you possess, and however much time you have to prepare, it is always possible to make a delicious dessert that will bring the meal to a satisfying end.

BAKING PIES AND TARTS

There is no more memorable way of enjoying an abundance of ripe fruits in season than by baking them in a golden, homemade pastry case. Alternatively, dairy produce or storecupboard ingredients can be used to produce a quick, convenient filling for a delicious dessert.

PREPARING FILLINGS

● **Dicing cheese** Add small cubes of a tangy, mature cheese to complement a sweet apple filling in a pie.
● **Creating a quick filling** Make a quick, festive dessert by mixing fresh, seedless grapes with a few spoonfuls of ready-made mincemeat. Spoon into a pastry case, and bake until hot. Serve with fresh cream.
● **Glazing fruits** To glaze and sweeten fresh fruits for a colourful tart or pie filling, warm a few spoonfuls of redcurrant or cranberry jelly with a squeeze of lemon or orange juice in a pan. Toss the fruits in the glaze to coat.

MAKING TOPPINGS

Pinch filo into ruffles

Using filo pastry

Instead of laying sheets of filo or pastry flat on top of a fruit filling, crumple them slightly to give a "chiffon" effect. Brush with butter, and bake as usual, then sprinkle with icing sugar.

FRUIT TART TOPPINGS

● **Marshmallows** Arrange marshmallows to cover the fruits. Grill until golden.
● **Marzipan** Cut marzipan into dice, and scatter over the tart. Bake or grill until golden.
● **Almond crumble** Mix equal amounts of ground almonds, demerara sugar, and flaked almonds, then sprinkle the mixture over the fruits before baking to form a golden crust.
● **Meringue** Whisk one egg white until stiff, then whisk in 55 g (2 oz) caster sugar. Pipe a meringue lattice over the fruits, and bake for a delicious, decorative topping.

MONEY-SAVING TIP

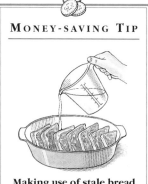

Making use of stale bread

Spread slices of stale bread with butter and marmalade or jam, and layer in an ovenproof dish. Add two eggs beaten in 300 ml (½ pint) milk. Bake in a moderate oven.

ADDING EXTRA FLAVOUR

Distribute coconut evenly

Sprinkling coconut

To add extra flavour to a fruit tart or pie, sprinkle a layer of dessicated coconut over the base before adding the filling. This will also help to prevent the base from becoming soggy.

ADDING VARIETY

● **Baking upside-down tarts** Use a cake tin to make an upside-down fruit tart. Butter and sugar the base, add the fruits, and top with rolled-out pastry. Bake until golden.
● **Making sweet pizza** Roll out puff pastry or bread dough, and top with slices of fruits such as apples, pears, or plums. Sprinkle with brown sugar and spices, dot with butter, and bake in a hot oven until bubbling and golden.
● **Latticing filo strips** Cut filo pastry into long strips with scissors to make a quick lattice for a pie or tart. Use two sheets together, brushed with butter, for the best effect.

MAKING OTHER HOT DESSERTS

Hot desserts are warming and satisfying, and they can be very versatile. Whip up lemon pancakes for an informal occasion, or try flambéed crêpes suzettes for a dinner party. Add variety to milk puddings by stirring in dried fruits, spices, an essence such as vanilla, or citrus-fruit zest.

USING BATTER

● **Adding cocoa** To make delicious, chocolate-flavoured pancakes, replace 10 ml (2 tsp) of the quantity of flour used in the recipe with cocoa powder.

● **Baking batter pudding** To make a fruit batter pudding, pour Yorkshire pudding batter over sugared fruit slices in a heated, greased cake tin. Bake in a hot oven until golden.

● **Making a light batter** For a crisp, light fritter batter, separate the eggs, and mix the yolks with the flour. Whisk the egg whites until stiff, and fold into the mixture. Use the batter to coat sliced apple, pineapple, or banana.

● **Deep-frying pancakes** Place a spoonful of fruit in the centres of cooked pancakes. Fold the pancakes into squares, dip in batter, and deep-fry until golden. Dust with sugar, and serve with fruit sauce.

USING WAFFLE BATTER

Making beignets
Use waffle batter for making beignets as an alternative to waffles. Carefully drop spoonfuls of the batter into hot oil, and fry until puffy and golden. Serve the beignets topped with maple syrup or vanilla sugar.

FLAVOURING MILK

Citrus zester

Adding lemon zest
To lift the flavour of a plain milk pudding such as rice or semolina, use a citrus zester to grate a few strips of lemon zest over the pudding, and stir to mix in evenly before cooking. Orange zest can also be used.

ADDING VARIETY TO STEAMED PUDDINGS

● **Adding breadcrumbs** For a light, steamed sponge or suet pudding, replace 30 ml (2 tbsp) of the flour with fresh, fine white or brown breadcrumbs.

● **Decorating with fruits** Line a buttered pudding basin with orange slices before filling with sponge mix. Cook, then turn out for an attractive finish.

FINISHING SOUFFLÉS

Caramelizing the top
Give a hot, sweet soufflé a golden, caramelized finish on top by sprinkling with icing sugar at the end of cooking. Sprinkle quickly, and bake for 4–5 minutes to brown.

USING A MICROWAVE

● **Cooking sponge puddings** Place a piece of greaseproof or non-stick paper over a sponge pudding when cooking in a microwave to keep the pudding moist and ensure even cooking. Remove the pudding from the microwave when the centre is still slightly moist. Leave to stand, and residual heat will finish off the cooking.

● **Cooking milk puddings** Use a very large, deep container to cook milk puddings in a microwave, since the milk will rise dramatically up the sides.

● **Setting meringue** Cook meringue toppings on desserts in a microwave to save time. Scatter toasted nuts over the surface if it is too pale.

QUICK DESSERTS

● **Filling croissants** Cut open warmed croissants, and fill with hot, stewed plums, then scatter with flaked almonds.

● **Pan-frying bananas** Peel and thickly slice some bananas, and sauté in a little butter and brown sugar for two minutes. Sprinkle with orange juice and a dash of rum.

● **Grilling soft fruits** Sprinkle kirsch over frozen, mixed soft fruits in a flameproof dish. Top with mascarpone cheese and brown sugar, and grill until hot and bubbling.

● **Making fruit compotes** Warm a mixture of canned fruits, their juices, grated lemon zest, and cinnamon in a pan. Serve with cream.

COLD DESSERTS

There are several types of cold dessert, from fresh, light fruit salads, fools, and mousses to rich, creamy egg custards, cheesecakes, and filled meringues. They all have the advantage that they can be made in advance, leaving you free to prepare and serve preceding courses.

PREVENTING PROBLEMS
● **Preventing skin** Lay a piece of non-stick paper over milk puddings and custards as they cool, to prevent a skin from forming on the surface.
● **Slicing meringue** Prevent a soft meringue dessert from sticking when being sliced, either by buttering the knife blade first, or by dipping the knife into boiling water.
● **Adding sparkle** Pep up the flavour of an over-sweetened or plain fruit salad by adding a splash of sparkling wine just before the dessert is served.
● **Making crème caramel** Rinse the dish being used in hot water before pouring very hot caramel into it. This will help prevent the dish from cracking.

FINISHING CRÈME BRÛLÉE

Spray water evenly over surface of sugar topping

Caramelizing sugar
For a perfect, golden caramel topping on crème brûlée, sprinkle the set custard with a thick layer of caster sugar, and spray with a fine water spray. Caramelize under a very hot grill.

MAKING PAVLOVAS

Shape meringue on plate

Preventing breakage
Spoon the meringue mixture for a pavlova on to a ceramic, ovenproof pizza plate so that it can be baked and served in the same dish. You will thus avoid cracking it while transferring it.

GELATINE-SET DESSERTS

Gelatine is the most common setting agent used in cookery. It is available in either powdered or leaf form, both of which should be thoroughly dissolved in hot water before use. Agar-agar, a vegetarian setting agent made from seaweed, is used in the same way.

USING GELATINE
● **Dissolving gelatine** Always add gelatine to hot liquid to dissolve. Do not add the liquid to the gelatine.
● **Preparing fruits** Cook fresh pineapple or kiwi fruit before using in gelatine-set desserts; this destroys the enzyme that prevents gelatine from setting.
● **Eating outdoors** If serving a dessert outdoors in warm weather, slightly increase the amount of gelatine used. Add an extra 5 ml (1 tsp) gelatine for every gelatine sachet.
● **Turning out set desserts** Wet a mould for a thin gelatine mixture such as jelly to make turning out easy. Lightly oil a mould for a thick mixture.

DECORATING JELLIES
Fruits will be held in place when jelly is set

Layering with fruits
Set fruits in a jelly by swirling a little unset jelly mixture into the mould. Arrange the fruits around the base or sides. Chill, or dip in iced water, to set. Continue layering until the mould is full.

SERVING SET DESSERTS
● **Retaining flavour** Remove a gelatine-set mixture from the refrigerator 15 minutes before serving, since overchilling will reduce the flavour of a dessert.
● **Using water** Before turning out a jelly on to a serving plate, rinse the plate in cold water. You will then be able to slide the jelly into position.
● **Turning out a mould** To turn out set mixtures, dip the mould briefly in hot water. Put a plate over the mould, upturn it, and shake to dislodge the dessert.
● **Serving frozen** A cold soufflé that has not set can be served frozen. Put it in the freezer until firm, remove the paper collar, and serve.

CHOCOLATE DESSERTS

When using chocolate in either hot or cold desserts, buy the best you can afford. The better the quality, the better the chocolate flavour your dessert will have. Use cocoa to add a chocolate flavour to cooked mixtures, but remember to include some sugar to taste.

SHAPING CURLS

Cool marble board

Using a zester
Make decorative chocolate curls using a citrus zester. Spread melted chocolate evenly over a cool surface, and leave until just set. Pull the zester across the surface to remove small curls.

MAKING EDIBLE LEAVES

Paint chocolate over leaf with small, soft brush

Imprinting leaves
Select clean, unblemished rose or other non-poisonous leaves. Brush melted chocolate evenly over the front of each leaf. Leave to set, then gently peel off the leaf to reveal its imprint.

USING CHOCOLATE

● **Melting chocolate** To melt chocolate without a double boiler, use a heatproof bowl over hot, not boiling, water.
● **Making curls** Add bought chocolate cake covering to melted chocolate to make it pliable when shaping curls.
● **Adding gloss** Add a rich gloss to a chocolate sauce or a chocolate topping by stirring in a knob of unsalted butter.
● **Substituting cocoa** If you run out of cooking chocolate, use 45 ml (3 tbsp) of cocoa and 15 ml (1 tbsp) of butter for every 25 g (1 oz) needed.
● **Replacing alcohol** Replace the alcohol in a chocolate dessert with the same amount of black coffee, if preferred.

ICE-CREAMS AND SORBETS

Ice-creams are based on simple mixtures and can be produced easily with or without an ice-cream maker. Creamy ice-cream mixtures based on double cream and egg custards are very successful made by hand, but sorbets and yoghurt ices benefit from machine churning.

MAKING ICES

● **Flavouring ices** Slightly over-flavour or over-sweeten sorbet and ice-cream mixtures, since freezing masks flavours.
● **Using gelatine** To make a firm, scoopable sorbet, add a little dissolved gelatine to the mixture before freezing.
● **Sweetening with honey** For a soft texture, use honey rather than sugar to sweeten ices.
● **Making ices by hand** Whisk handmade ices at regular intervals while freezing to break up ice crystals and produce a smooth texture.
● **Maturing ices** Mature the flavour of ices in the freezer for 24 hours. Soften at room temperature before serving.

USING AN IMPROVISED BOMBE MOULD

Fill centre with soft-fruit sorbet

Hot towel loosens bombe from basin

1 To make an ice-cream bombe without a mould, set a glass pudding basin in a bowl of ice. Pack the base and sides of the basin with firm but slightly softened ice-cream. Fill the centre, and freeze.

2 To turn out the bombe, wrap the basin briefly in a tea towel that has been wrung out in hot water. Run a knife around the inside edge of the basin, then invert the bombe on to a serving plate.

BAKING

Home baking is one of the most rewarding cooking skills. While you are learning basic techniques, follow recipes and weigh ingredients carefully. Once you have gained confidence, you can adapt recipes to your own taste.

MAKING CAKES

There are four basic methods used in making cakes: melting, creaming, rubbing in, and whisking. Whichever method you use, start by preheating the oven and preparing the tins, since you are most likely to get a good rise if the cake is baked as soon as possible after mixing.

LINING TINS
● **Cutting spares** If you often use a particular tin for baking, cut several thicknesses of lining paper at a time, and keep the spares for future use.
● **Protecting the edges** Line a cake tin for a fruit cake with a double layer of lining paper to protect the edge of the cake from excessive heat.
● **Greasing tins** Use oil to grease a cake tin; it is easier to brush on than butter and is less likely to burn or stick.
● **Adding paper** Place a small square of non-stick paper in the base of a greased and floured tin to help turn out.

MAKING RING TINS

Dried beans

Using a food can
Make a ring tin by placing a tall, food can, weighed down with dried beans, in the centre of a round cake tin. The beans will stop the can from moving when the mixture is poured around it.

MAKING HEART SHAPES

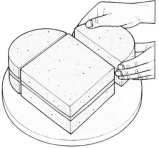

Combining two cakes
Bake a round and a square cake, with the diameter of the circle and the sides of the square the same length. Cut the circle in half, and place one half on each of two adjacent sides of the square.

HEALTHY TIP

Dusting with bran
Grease a cake tin as usual, then, instead of flour, sprinkle a little wheat or oat bran inside it to add fibre as well as flavour to the cake. Tip the tin to coat the base and sides evenly.

TURNING OUT CAKES
● **Allowing standing time**
Leave a sponge cake in the tin for 2–3 minutes to let it contract and firm up before turning it out. Let a fruit cake cool completely before turning out.
● **Loosening sides** Run a knife around the inside of the tin to loosen the sides of a cake.
● **Using a can** To turn a cake out of a loose-bottomed tin, rest the base on a tall can, and push the sides down firmly.
● **Inverting tins** Prevent a sponge from drying out by inverting it on to a cooling rack and placing the tin over it.
● **Using an oven rack** Use an oven shelf as a cooling rack. Put it on a flan ring or can to raise it above the worktop.

TESTING DONENESS

● **Pressing the top** Apply light pressure to the top of a sponge cake with your fingertips. The top should feel firm, and should spring back into shape without leaving an indentation.
● **Checking the edges** Look closely at the edges of a cake. They will have shrunk away slightly from the sides of the tin if the cake has cooked thoroughly.
● **Listening closely** Listen to a cake. A sizzling noise means that it is still cooking.
● **Using a skewer** Test a fruit cake by inserting a skewer into its middle. The skewer will come out clean if the cake is fully cooked.

ADDING FLAVOURINGS AND FILLINGS

A simple sponge or a plain fruit cake can be transformed through the imaginative use of fillings and flavourings. Try enhancing a basic sponge cake with scented leaves or essence, or create a lavish gateau in minutes by adding a dash of liqueur and a rich frosting.

ADDING FLAVOUR

Place lemon-scented geranium leaf in centre of tin

Using a geranium leaf
Before adding sponge cake mixture to a tin for baking, place a lemon-scented geranium leaf in the bottom of the tin. As the mixture cooks, the leaf's delicate scent will permeate the cake.

SANDWICHING CAKES

Filling will hold layers together

Spreading a filling
Before sandwiching two halves of a sponge cake together, spread a filling, such as jam or cream, on to both halves. Press them gently together so that they will remain in position when the cake is cut.

HEALTHY TIP

Making a low-fat filling
For a low-fat filling, mix together 200 g (7 oz) soft cheese made from skimmed milk with 30 ml (2 tbsp) honey, then flavour with finely grated citrus zest. Use as a filling or topping for a sponge or carrot cake as an alternative to a rich cream-cheese frosting.

DISGUISING MISTAKES

Even the most experienced cook can make a mistake when baking. However, most problems can be rectified. If a cake appears burned, for example, it is often only the outer crust that is affected. Remove the crust with a knife, and disguise the top with frosting.

RESCUING SPONGE
● **Correcting curdling** If a sponge cake mixture begins to curdle during mixing, add 15 ml (1 tbsp) flour, then beat the mixture thoroughly.
● **Mending cracks** To repair a cake that has cracked while being turned out, brush the pieces with warmed apricot jam. Reassemble the cake in the tin to cool and set.
● **Concealing cracks** To hide cracks in a roulade or a Swiss roll, pipe cream over them. Sprinkle with icing sugar, cocoa, or grated chocolate.
● **Moistening sponge** Sprinkle a dry sponge cake with fresh orange, or other fruit juice.

USING SUNKEN CAKES

Cut out centre from cooled cake

Cutting out the centre
If a round fruit or sponge cake has an undercooked, sunken centre, make it into a ring cake by cutting the centre out neatly with a sharp knife. Cover the ring with icing or frosting.

MOISTENING DRY CAKES

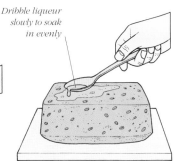

Dribble liqueur slowly to soak in evenly

Adding liqueur
To moisten overcooked or dried-out fruit cake, turn the cake upside down, and pierce it with a skewer several times. Spoon brandy, whisky, or rum over the surface and leave for 24 hours.

DECORATING CAKES

Yου do not need special skills to decorate cakes impressively. The simplest, most basic techniques are often the most effective, so there is no need to spend hours in the kitchen. Cool, dry conditions are best for sugar and icings, so avoid working in steamy kitchens.

APPLYING TOPPINGS

● **Pouring icing** To ice a sponge cake quickly, place it on a wire rack over a baking sheet and pour glacé icing or melted chocolate over the surface in one movement, smoothing around the sides with a knife. Leave to set.

● **Softening almond paste** If almond paste dries out and is hard to roll, warm it in a microwave on Medium for 30 seconds. Knead the paste until it is soft enough to roll.

● **Using fondant** Roll out ready-made fondant icing on a surface lightly dusted with sifted cornflour instead of icing sugar. Cornflour will be easier to brush off the finished cake than icing sugar.

● **Smoothing fondant** To smooth the sides of a cake iced with fondant, roll a straight-sided jar around them. Dust the jar first with cornflour to prevent it from sticking.

DECORATING WITH SUGAR

● **Using a doily** To decorate a plain sponge, place a paper doily on top and sprinkle the cake with icing sugar. Lift the doily off to reveal a lace pattern.

Shake icing sugar through sieve

Using stencils

Cut out paper shapes, and arrange these stencils on top of the cake you wish to decorate. Sprinkle the cake with icing sugar, then remove the shapes to reveal the stencilled design.

USING FLOWERS

● **Washing flowers** Wash delicate, edible flowers with a fine water spray before using. Shake off excess water, and dry on an absorbent paper towel.

Brush gently with egg white

Coating edible flowers

Decorate edible flowers with a thin coating of sugar. First, brush egg white on to the petals with a soft paint brush. Sprinkle the petals lightly with caster sugar, and leave to dry for 24 hours.

COLOURING ICING

Drip colouring into icing

Using a skewer

Control the addition of small amounts of liquid food colouring to icing by using a skewer or a cocktail stick. Dip it into the bottle, and use it like a dropper to drip the colouring into the icing.

FILLING PIPING BAGS

Working with a jug

To fill a piping bag easily and without mess, fit the bag with a nozzle, place it in a jug, and turn the top of the bag over the top of the jug. The bag will be held open while icing is spooned in.

MAKING A PIPING BAG

If you do not have a piping bag to ice a cake, improvise with one of the following:

● **Using a polythene bag** For plain icing, snip a corner off a strong polythene bag without a seam, and insert a nozzle.

● **Making a paper cone** Cut a 20-cm (8-in) square of greaseproof paper, and fold it diagonally to make a triangle. Lift a bottom corner, and curl it around to meet the tip of the triangle at the front. Then curl the other corner around the back to meet the tip. Snip the point off the cone, and pipe through the hole.

BAKING SMALL CAKES AND BISCUITS

Baking small cakes and biscuits is enjoyable as well as practical: techniques are simple, and cooking times are short. Make them to eat yourself or to give away to friends. Small cakes and scones should be eaten as fresh as possible, but biscuits can often be stored for several days.

COOKING MUFFINS

Baking in a microwave
Use straight-sided cups to bake muffins in a microwave, rather than a microwave muffin tin. Brush the cups with oil before adding the mixture. Bake the muffins in small batches.

USING A MICROWAVE
● **Using a flan dish** Use a round, porcelain flan dish to cook flapjacks and traybakes in the microwave. Allow to cool, then cut into wedges.
● **Adding colour** To add colour to microwaved biscuits and cakes, brush them with honey and scatter with toasted nuts.

MAKING SMALL CAKES
● **Using a piping bag** When making a large batch of small sponge cakes, spoon the cake mixture into a piping bag fitted with a large, plain nozzle. Pipe the mixture into cake cases, and bake.
● **Topping with sugar** Create a crunchy topping for plain sponge cakes by sprinkling them lightly with demerara sugar before baking.
● **Creating a surprise** Include a surprise in plain cakes by pressing a small square of chocolate into the centre of the uncooked mixture.

MAKING BISCUITS

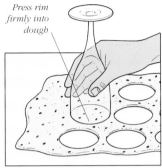

Press rim firmly into dough

Cutting out rounds
Use the rim of an upturned wine glass to cut rounds from rolled-out biscuit dough if you do not have a biscuit cutter. Dip the rim into flour before using it to cut out sticky mixtures.

PREPARING AHEAD
● **Storing biscuit mixture** Roll up firm biscuit mixture and wrap it in foil. Store in the refrigerator for several weeks, baking batches as you need to.
● **Improving flavour** Store ginger nuts in a tin for several days to improve their flavour. Refresh in a hot oven to serve.

SHAPING DELICATE BISCUITS AFTER BAKING
● **Using a jar** Use a fish slice to lift almond tuiles on to the sides of clean jam jars as they come out of the oven. This will allow them to cool quickly and will result in them setting in a curved shape.
● **Rolling on a wooden spoon** Shape cooked brandy-snap mixture into rolls around the handle of a wooden spoon whilst the mixture is still warm. Gently slide the roll off the handle, and cool on a rack. If the mixture sets before it has been shaped, return it to the oven for 30 seconds.

MAKING SCONES
● **Helping scones to rise** To help scones to rise and to soften the gluten in the flour, use buttermilk or soured cream instead of milk, and equal quantities of bicarbonate of soda and cream of tartar instead of baking powder.
● **Rolling scone wedges** Instead of cutting out round scones, roll the dough into one smooth round, and cut into wedges with a sharp knife. Bake, then pull apart to serve.
● **Adding savoury flavour** To give plain scone dough a savoury flavour, sift 5 ml (1 tsp) of celery salt with the flour, or stir in some herbs.

SHAPING STICKY DOUGH
● **Wetting hands** To prevent biscuit mixture from sticking to your hands, wet them in cold water before handling it.
● **Chilling dough** If biscuit dough is too sticky to handle, wrap it in clingfilm, and chill for 30 minutes. If it is still sticky, work in some flour.

Mould mixture over top of orange

Shaping over an orange
To shape delicate biscuits or mould brandy-snap mixture into baskets, arrange each portion of biscuit mixture gently over an orange as soon as it comes out of the oven. Leave them to set.

MAKING BASIC BREADS

Baking your own bread is easy, satisfying, and takes surprisingly little time. Use a food processor to take the hard work out of kneading, and reduce rising times by using fast-action yeast. Alternatively, let dough rise overnight in the refrigerator so that it is ready to bake the next day.

USING YEAST

● **Substituting dried yeast**
When substituting dried yeast for fresh in a recipe, use 10 ml (2 tsp) dried yeast for 15 g (½ oz) fresh yeast.
● **Using fast-action yeast** Add fast-action yeast directly to a dry flour mix, not to liquid, or its action will be delayed.
● **Freezing dough** If you are making dough that is to be frozen before baking, increase the quantity of yeast by about one third, since freezing will kill some of the yeast.
● **Adding potato water** Save the water from boiled potatoes to add to bread mixes. It will feed the yeast, giving a good rise, and add to the flavour.

BAKING LARGE LOAVES

● **Testing for doneness** To make sure that a large loaf is cooked properly, turn it out of the tin, and tap the bottom with your knuckles. If it sounds hollow, the bread is thoroughly cooked. If not, return it to the oven for a few minutes to finish cooking.

Place both doughs in same tin

Combining doughs
If some members of your family like wholemeal bread and others prefer white bread, bake the two kinds of dough end to end in a large loaf tin. Then, you can slice the loaf from either end.

HELPING DOUGH RISE

Make bowl airtight with clingfilm

Covering with clingfilm
To encourage dough to rise, place it in a bowl, and cover with clingfilm that has been brushed with oil. The dampness and warmth created inside the bowl will speed up the rising.

CREATING CRUSTS

● **Baking crusty loaves** For a really crisp crust all over a loaf, turn it out of the tin when it is cooked. Then return it to the oven, placing it directly on the shelf, for a further five minutes to make sure the crust is crisp all over. Cool the loaf on a wire rack before storing.

Making soft crusts
For soft crusts on bread rolls or loaves, dust the tops with flour before baking, and cover with a clean tea towel when cooling. Also, add milk to the dough mix instead of using just water.

BRIGHT IDEA

Baking in a flowerpot
Bake bread in a new, lightly oiled terracotta flowerpot for an unusually shaped loaf. Terracotta gives bread a crisp, golden crust. Heat the pot first for 30 minutes in the oven at 190°C (375°F) or Gas Mark 5.

RISING DOUGHS

● **Adding ascorbic acid** When using fresh yeast, speed up rising times by adding a 25-mg tablet of ascorbic acid for each 1 kg (2 lb 4 oz) flour.
● **Warming flour** To help dough to rise on a cold day, warm the flour first in a bowl in the oven at 110°C (225°F) Gas Mark ¼. Alternatively, put the flour in the microwave on High for 10 seconds.
● **Using a microwave** Place dough in an oiled bowl, brush with oil, and cover with non-stick paper. Stand the bowl in a shallow dish of hot water, and microwave on Low for four minutes. Leave to stand for 20 minutes. Repeat until the dough is doubled.
● **Testing the rise** To test whether dough has risen enough, press it lightly with a floured finger. The dough should spring back without leaving an indentation.

ENHANCING FLAVOUR

Even the most basic breads are transformed by adding extra flavours to the dough. Stir herbs or spices into the dry flour mix to ensure even distribution, or knead in chunky additions, such as olives, just before shaping. Brush tops of loaves or rolls with glaze for last-minute flavour.

ADDING EXTRAS

● **Chopping ingredients** Knead a few chopped olives, herbs, walnuts, or sun-dried tomatoes into plain bread dough for a Mediterranean flavour.

● **Mixing flours** Reduce the strong flavour of buckwheat flour by mixing it half and half with rice flour.

● **Adding spicy glaze** For a spicy, golden crust, brush the tops of loaves with a mixture of oil and curry paste or pesto sauce before baking.

● **Glazing with herbs** For a crisp, savoury crust on bread, dissolve 10 ml (2 tsp) salt in 30 ml (2 tbsp) warm water, and brush over the tops of rolls. Sprinkle with herbs, and bake.

MAKING SAVOURY BREADS

Adding celery salt
Give plain bread a subtle, savoury flavour by substituting celery salt or garlic salt for table salt. If the salt crystals are large, dissolve them first in the liquid that will be used to mix the dough.

MAKING SWEET GLAZES

Using honey
Brush bread loaves or rolls with warmed honey as soon as they are removed from the oven for a glossy, sweet glaze. Alternatively, brush with golden or maple syrup for the same effect.

SHAPING AND DECORATING DOUGH

Bread dough can be shaped before baking, whether in a loaf tin or on a baking sheet. Traditional shapes such as plaits or twists can be adapted for large loaves or small rolls. If you are short of time, decorate dough by scoring a lattice pattern on the surface with a sharp blade.

DECORATING LOAVES

Snip dough with scissors

Snipping with scissors
To decorate a plain loaf quickly, use scissors to cut slashes across the top of the dough before rising or baking. The cuts will open out when the dough rises, making a patterned top.

MAKING ROUND LOAVES

● **Shaping a cottage loaf** Top a ball of dough with a smaller ball. Poke a hole through the centre with your finger to secure them.

Cutting a cross
Cut a deep cross in a plain, round loaf before proving, using a floured, sharp knife. The cuts will open out to form an attractive crown shape when the loaf of bread is baked.

CREATING VARIETY

● **Using seeds** Scatter sesame or poppy seeds over soft rolls after glazing to make an attractive and tasty topping.

● **Marbling dough** Make two batches of dough; one wholemeal, one plain. Pull off small pieces, and then knead together before shaping to give the dough a marbled effect.

● **Sprinkling tins** After greasing loaf tins, sprinkle lightly with cracked wheat or rolled oats before adding bread dough to give the crust a nutty texture.

● **Baking rolls in clusters** Instead of baking rolls separately, pack them closely together in a tin or place on a baking sheet. Serve them to be pulled apart as required.

WORKING WITH PASTRY

Pastry forms the basis of many kinds of dish, whether they are hot or cold, savoury or sweet. Whatever type of pastry you are making, the same rules will apply. Always keep your tools, work surface, and hands cool. Try to handle the pastry lightly and as little as possible.

MAKING SHORTCRUST
● **Cooling hands** If your hands are warm, hold your wrists under a cold tap for a few minutes before handling pastry.
● **Enriching pastry** To make a rich, light-textured pastry, add an egg yolk with the water.
● **Letting pastry rest** Cover shortcrust pastry with clingfilm, and place it in the refrigerator for 30 minutes before rolling it out. This will prevent it from shrinking when it is baked.
● **Making quick pastry** To mix a quick dough, sift 100 g (3½ oz) flour and a pinch of salt into a bowl. Stir in 40 ml (2½ tbsp) oil, 15 ml (1 tbsp) iced water, and a squeeze of lemon juice. Mix to a dough with a fork.

HELPING PASTRY RISE
● **Using water** Before using a baking sheet for baking choux, flaky, or puff pastry dough, sprinkle it lightly with water instead of greasing it. The water will evaporate in the heat of the oven, and the steam will help the pastry to rise.

AVOIDING SOGGY PASTRY

● **Using a baking sheet** Bake a pie on a baking sheet, the heat of which will help cook the pastry base. Preheat the baking sheet in the oven while the oven is heating up.
● **Using metal tins** Use a metal tin for baking a pie or tart. Metal will conduct heat quickly to the pastry.
● **Sealing with egg white** Brush the base of a flan case with egg white to seal it and prevent leakage before adding a liquid filling.

USING TRIMMINGS

Grate pastry straight from freezer

Making a pastry topping
Coarsely grate frozen pastry over fruits as a topping, and then bake until golden. Wrap leftover pastry trimmings in a polythene bag, and freeze so that they can be used in future for this purpose.

USING FROZEN PASTRY
● **Preparing** Make and shape choux pastry ready for use. Freeze it until needed, then thaw before baking.
● **Thawing** Thaw frozen pastry by placing it in a microwave on Defrost; 200 g (7 oz) of pastry will need 2½–3 minutes.

PREVENTING PROBLEMS
● **Ensuring an even rise** Brush only the top surface of puff or flaky pastry when glazing with beaten egg or milk, avoiding any cut or fluted edges. The pastry will then rise evenly.
● **Avoiding leakage** When adding a filling of beaten eggs to a ready-made pastry case, heat the case in the oven first, so that the filling starts to set as soon as it touches the pastry.
● **Preventing overbrowning** When baking a meat pie, allow the pastry to brown and rise first, then reduce the oven temperature to finish cooking.

HEALTHY TIP

Adding fibre
Instead of using plain flour to roll out pastry dough, sprinkle the worktop with rolled oats, wheatgerm, or bran. Roll out as usual for a finished pastry that has added texture and contains beneficial dietary fibre.

MAKING SWEET PASTRY
● **Adding sugar and egg** Mix a sweet shortcrust pastry for fruit pies by adding 50 g (1¾ oz) of caster sugar and one egg yolk to every 100 g (3½ oz) of flour. Bake at a lower temperature (190°C/375°F or Gas Mark 5) than ordinary shortcrust pastry.

Adding ingredients
To add flavour and texture to shortcrust or choux pastry, stir finely chopped nuts such as walnuts or ground almonds into the flour. Alternatively, add spices or finely chopped herbs.

SHAPING PASTRY DECORATIVELY

There is a variety of ways in which you can use pastry as a decorative trim. Shortcrust pastry is the most versatile, since it holds its shape during cooking. Cut leftover pastry into decorative shapes, and bake them separately to keep in store for use as a quick garnish.

MAKING LATTICE TOPS
● **Using trimmings** Cut rolled-out pastry trimmings into long, thin strips. Arrange them over a tart filling to form a lattice.

Space slits evenly

Cutting slits
To make an easy lattice top for a pie, roll out a round of pastry to fit the top of the pie, then cut short slits parallel to each other. Stretch the pastry gently to open the slits and create a lattice top.

DECORATING EDGES
● **Cutting shapes** Roll out pastry trimmings, and cut into small leaves, hearts, or flowers. Overlap around the edges of a pie or tart before baking.
● **Making a plait** Roll spare pastry into long, thin strips, and plait these together. Arrange them around dampened pastry edges, and tuck in the joins.
● **Marking with a fork** To seal the edges of a double-crust pie quickly and easily, flatten the edges together with the floured prongs of a fork.
● **Pinching edges** Seal the edges of a double-crust pie by pressing them between your finger and thumb at an angle. This will create a rope effect.

BRIGHT IDEA

Using a pastry label
Use pastry trimmings to cut out a shaped, edible label to decorate a pie and indicate its contents. Alternatively, cut out letters from the pastry to spell out the name of the pie's contents. Brush with beaten egg before sticking on.

USING FILO PASTRY

Filo is a delicate pastry that needs gentle handling. Nevertheless, it is easy to use for pies, tartlets, and filled pastries. Work quickly, and cover any sheets you are not working on to prevent them from drying out, since filo pastry will become difficult to handle if it dries.

WORKING WITH FILO
● **Brushing with oil** Use olive or nut oil to brush filo before baking savoury pastries. Use butter or a light-flavoured oil for baking sweet pastries.
● **Brushing with egg** For those on a low-fat diet, brush filo lightly with egg white instead of oil. This will give the pastry a crisp texture when baked.
● **Baking in a microwave** Brush filled filo parcels with butter, and cook in a browning dish in a microwave on High until the pastry is crisp. Turn the parcels over halfway through the cooking period.
● **Making spring rolls** Use filo pastry to make spring rolls. Seal with egg white, and deep-fry in hot oil for 2–3 minutes.

KEEPING LEFTOVER FILO
● **Storing for later** Wrap unused filo pastry from a packet in clingfilm, and refrigerate. Use the pastry within 3–4 days.

Keep pastry moist with damp towel

Preventing drying
Work with one sheet of filo at a time, and prevent the rest from drying out by covering with a lightly dampened tea towel. To leave filo pastry for long periods, cover it with clingfilm first.

USING LEFTOVER FILO
● **Using damaged sheets** Use up dried out or broken sheets of filo by inserting them between whole sheets of the pastry.

Cup pastry in hand to shape

Making "moneybags"
To use up small pieces of filo pastry, brush with oil, stack together, and place a spoonful of fruits in the centre. Gather and pinch the pastry, leaving a ruffled edge. Bake until golden.

PRESERVING

I N THE PAST, PRESERVING WAS AN ESSENTIAL PART of a cook's calendar to ensure that storecupboards were well stocked all year round. This is no longer necessary, but preserving is a skill worth having and has rewarding end results.

PREPARING TO PRESERVE

The basic principle of preserving is to take food at the peak of freshness and maintain its nutritive value at that stage. Little specialist equipment is necessary, but it is worthwhile spending some time preparing equipment for use to ensure that your preserves are a success.

USING EQUIPMENT
● **Choosing pan material** For making acid preserves such as chutneys and pickles, use a stainless steel preserving pan, since aluminium or copper may react with the acid.
● **Choosing the right-sized pan** Use a large pan for making jam to allow room for expansion. The pan should be half full when all the sugar is added.
● **Warming a thermometer** To prevent a thermometer from cracking, warm it in hot water before placing in hot preserve.
● **Hooking a spoon** To prevent a wooden spoon from sliding into a pan, attach a wooden clothes peg to the handle at right angles to it. Hook the peg over the side of the pan.

WEIGHING INGREDIENTS

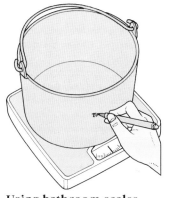

Using bathroom scales
To weigh a large amount of ingredients easily, use bathroom scales. First, note the exact weight of the pan. Then weigh the ingredients in the pan, and deduct the weight of the pan.

PREVENTING SCUM

Applying glycerine
Brush the inner sides of a preserving pan with glycerine before making jams and jellies. This will prevent scum from forming on the surface of the preserve during cooking.

PREPARING JARS
Jars placed upright

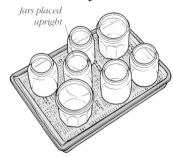

Preventing cracking
To prevent jars from cracking when filled with hot preserve, first wash them thoroughly. Stand them on a baking sheet covered with newspaper, and place in a warm oven for 10 minutes.

STERILIZING LIDS

Plunging into boiling water
Sterilize the metal lids of the preserving jars by placing them in boiling water for six minutes. Remove the lids with food tongs to protect your hands, and drain on absorbent paper towels.

CONSIDERING OPTIONS
● **Using a microwave** If you want to cook jams, jellies, or chutney preserves in a microwave, plan to make only a small amount at a time. To allow for expansion of the ingredients during cooking, use a heatproof bowl that is three times larger in volume than the quantity of preserve you are making in each batch.
● **Pressure-cooking** Reduce the cooking times recommended in recipes for jams and jellies by making them in a pressure cooker. You will also need to use only about half the liquid specified in the recipe.

MAKING JAMS AND JELLIES

A successful jam or jelly is characterized by a firm, clear set, a bright colour, and a good fruit flavour. Use fresh, undamaged produce, ideally mixing ripe with unripe fruits. Pectin is the setting agent found naturally in fruits, and unripe fruits contain the highest pectin levels.

STRAINING JELLIES

Ladle fruit pulp into jelly bag

Using an upturned stool

To use a jelly bag to strain jelly, turn a small stool upside down, place a bowl on its base in the centre, and tie the jelly bag to the legs of the stool. Fill with fruit pulp, and leave to drain.

PREVENTING PROBLEMS

● **Preventing mildew** Pick fruits for preserves when conditions are dry, since moisture on the fruits may cause mildew.
● **Using sugar** Cook fruits for jam until tender before adding sugar, which may toughen the skins. Always warm sugar first so that it will dissolve quickly and help to give a clear set.
● **Removing scum** Skim jams and jellies to remove scum for a clear set. The last traces can be removed with a paper towel.
● **Distributing fruits** If jam or marmalade contains pieces of fruits or peel, leave to cool slightly before potting. This will prevent the pieces from rising to the surface.
● **Covering jam** Place jam jar covers on immediately after potting to discourage bacteria.

SELECTING FRUITS

Apples and blackberries

Some fruits have a tendency to set much better than others.

● **Good** Gooseberries, blackcurrants, redcurrants, apples, damsons.
● **Average** Raspberries, plums, greengages, apricots.
● **Poor** Pears, strawberries, cherries, blackberries, rhubarb.
● **Good combinations** Apple and blackberry; redcurrant and strawberry; pear and damson.

BOTTLING FRUITS

Successful bottling is dependent on efficient sterilization. Modern vacuum bottles extend the lives of preserves, and are available either with clip-on or screw-band closures for a good seal. Bottled preserves make delightful presents, decorated with ribbons and pretty gift tags.

PACKING JARS

Arranging slices

Make jars of bottled fruits look attractive by arranging slices of fruits such as orange, star fruit, or kiwi fruit against the sides before filling. Pack firmly, avoiding gaps, since fruits rise when cooked.

PREVENTING SPLITTING

Prick skin with cocktail stick

Pricking fruits

To prevent fruit skins from bursting, prick whole fruits such as cherries, damsons, and plums before packing them into bottles. This will also aid the absorption of syrup by the fruits.

DEALING WITH LIDS

● **Testing the seal** To make sure that the seal on a bottling jar is good after bottling, remove the screw cover, and lift the jar by its lid. If the lid stays in place, the seal is good.
● **Loosening bands** Once bottled fruits have completely cooled, and the jar is properly sealed, slightly loosen the bands on screw-on closures so that they do not become stuck.
● **Releasing a lid** To loosen a lid that is firmly stuck on a jar with a screw-band closure, stand the jar in hot water for a few minutes, then lever off the lid carefully with a knife.

MAKING CHUTNEYS AND PICKLES

Preserving fruits and vegetables in sugar and vinegar is a traditional cooking method that improves their flavours during storage. A good chutney is smooth in texture and mellow in flavour. This is achieved through lengthy, slow cooking and maturation in the preserving jar.

USING SPICES

● **Substituting whole spices** If you wish to substitute whole spices for ground when following a chutney recipe, you should double the quantity.

Strike spices with rolling pin

Bruising spices

If you are using whole spices such as cloves or cinnamon to flavour chutneys or pickles, bruise them lightly to release their flavours. Wrap them in muslin, then add to the other ingredients.

USING SALT

● **Choosing the right salt** Buy rock or sea salt for pickling or dry salting, since table salt contains additives that modify the flavours of ingredients.

Sprinkle salt over vegetables

Retaining crispness

Make sure vegetables stay crisp by using dry salt instead of brine for salting before pickling. Sprinkle vegetables with salt, and leave overnight to draw out the juices. Rinse and dry before use.

PRESERVING LEMONS

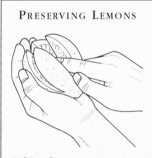

Salting lemon quarters

Cut six lemons into quarters, not quite cutting them through at one end. Rub rock or sea salt into the cut surfaces, and pack the lemons into a preserving jar. Add the juice of one lemon and 15 ml (1 tbsp) salt. Top up the jar with boiling water, and seal. Leave to stand for 2–3 weeks before using the lemons and the liquid in casseroles, soups, and salads.

COOKING CHUTNEYS

● **Reducing liquid** To make sure that a chutney thickens to a good consistency, always cook it uncovered so that the excess liquid evaporates.

Testing before bottling

To check whether a chutney is cooked and ready for bottling, pull a wooden spoon through it, across the base of the pan. If it parts easily and there is no running liquid, it is cooked.

TRADITIONAL TIP

Testing a brine solution

To check whether a brine solution is concentrated enough for salting foods before pickling, lower a fresh egg into the solution. If the egg floats, the concentration of salt is about right. Make sure that you add about 50 g (1¾ oz) salt for every 600 ml (1 pint) water.

ADJUSTING RECIPES

● **Enriching colour** Use brown sugar to give a rich colour to chutneys with a short cooking time. Use white sugar to darken chutneys only if the recipe has a prolonged cooking time.

● **Lightening colour** For a pale colour and mild flavour, use white vinegar in chutneys, pickles, and relishes. Also, add the sugar only after the basic ingredients have reduced.

● **Reducing sugar** If you want to reduce the amount of sugar used in a chutney recipe, then add dried fruits such as dates, raisins, or sultanas instead.

● **Keeping onions soft** Soften onions before pickling by cooking them in a little water for a few minutes before adding vinegar, which has a slightly hardening effect on them.

DRYING FOODS

Drying is a traditional preservation method originating from the observed effects of the sun and wind on fish, fruits, and vegetables. These natural preserving processes can be imitated in the kitchen to dry particular foods by controlling temperature and ventilation.

DRYING HERBS

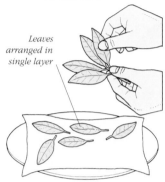

Leaves arranged in single layer

Using a microwave
Arrange fresh herb leaves on an absorbent paper towel, and place in a microwave with a glass of water. Cook on High for about 30 seconds, and repeat until the leaves have dried thoroughly.

VARYING METHODS
● **Hanging bundles** Tie bundles of fresh summer herbs such as parsley, mint, sage, and thyme in mixed bunches. Before hanging them up to dry for the winter, cover with muslin to keep them free from dust.
● **Stringing spices** Thread cotton string through fresh chillies so that they can be hung up for drying.
● **Drying in an oven** To dry mushrooms, first remove the stalks, since these tend to toughen. Thread the mushrooms on to bamboo skewers, and arrange on the shelf racks of an oven on the coolest setting until the mushrooms are crisp and dry. Store in a dry place.

PREVENTING PROBLEMS
● **Avoiding browning** To stop apples from browning during drying, soak in salted water for a few minutes. Use 5 ml (1 tsp) salt to 500 ml (18 fl oz) water.

Place slices on paper towels

Lining racks
When drying fruits or slices of fruit for decorative purposes, lay sheets of paper towel or muslin between the fruits and the drying rack to prevent the ridges from leaving marks on the fruits.

CURING AND SMOKING FOODS

Curing is a method of preserving food by impregnating it in dry salt or a salt solution. Curing is now done mainly to add flavour. Many meats are cured before smoking, both to ensure good preservation and to add flavour. Most fish can be preserved simply by smoking.

PREPARING FOODS
● **Cheese** Remove any rind or wax from hard cheeses such as Cheddar or Emmental before home smoking. Cut the cheese into 2.5-cm (1-in) thick chunks, and smoke at 16°C (60°F) for 2–4 hours.
● **Nuts** Blanch whole nuts such as almonds or hazelnuts, and then spread them in a single layer on a fine wire mesh before smoking.
● **Poultry** When smoking a whole bird such as a chicken or turkey, cover the breast with streaky bacon or pork fat to prevent over-drying.
● **Meat and fish** Instead of salt-curing meat and fish, soak in a marinade for several hours to add a salty flavour.

STORING IN WOOD ASH
● **Keeping cured meat** Wrap salt-cured meat in muslin, and roll in wood ash to deter insects. Hang in a cool place.

REMOVING SALT
● **Soaking** Remove excess salt from food that has been cured for longer than one week by soaking in cold, fresh water.

MAKING YOUR OWN GRAVADLAX

Lay fresh dill on fish

1 Lay a fillet of salmon skin-side down in a wide dish, and rub with oil. Cover with a layer of salt and sugar, then top with roughly chopped dill and crushed peppercorns.

2 Cover with another fillet of salmon, skin side up. Wrap with clingfilm, and place in the refrigerator for 12 hours, turning the fish over half-way through. Serve thinly sliced.

FREEZING

Successful freezing maintains foods at peak freshness, with the minimum loss of vitamins, colour, or texture. Freezing converts water within the cells that make up food to ice, a process that must be done quickly to prevent damage to the cells.

PREPARING TO FREEZE

Most foods require only simple preparation before freezing. It is essential to blanch vegetables, since this will destroy the enzymes that cause deterioration and preserve colour, flavour, texture, and nutrients. Secure packing is vital for all foods to keep them airtight.

PREFORMING LIQUIDS

Top of polythene bag turned over open carton

Using a cardboard pack
Preform liquid in a polythene bag for easy storage in the freezer. Put the bag upright in an empty, straight-sided cardboard pack. Pour the liquid in, and freeze. Lift out the bag, and seal the top.

PREFORMING CASSEROLES

Use enough foil to cover casserole completely

Making a foil lining
Line a casserole dish with foil, and freeze a casserole in it. Lift out of the dish, and overwrap for storing in the freezer. To cook the casserole, unwrap, and return to the dish to defrost and cook.

BLANCHING TIMES

The following blanching times are for average-sized pieces of common vegetables.

- Asparagus: 2–4 minutes.
- Aubergines: 4 minutes.
- Brussels sprouts, broccoli: 3–4 minutes.
- Cabbage: (shredded), red or green 1½ minutes.
- Carrots: 3–5 minutes.
- Cauliflower, celery, peppers: 3 minutes.
- Courgettes: 1 minute.
- French beans: 2–3 minutes.
- Mangetout: 2–3 minutes.
- Marrow: 3 minutes.
- Onions, parsnips, spinach: 2 minutes.
- Peas: 1–2 minutes.
- Sweetcorn: 4–8 minutes.
- Turnips: 2½ minutes.

USING FRESH PRODUCE

- **Cooling quickly** Plunge foods into iced water after blanching. Drain well before freezing.
- **Retaining colour** Dip cut fruits such as apples into lemon juice or ascorbic acid before freezing to retain colour and supplement vitamin content.
- **Using excess fruits** If you have a glut of fresh fruits, stew with sugar, and freeze in pie dishes lined with aluminium foil. When the fruits are firm, remove from the dishes, and overwrap before storing. Use frozen packs as ready-made pie fillings in the future.

OPEN-FREEZING FOODS

Keeping pieces separate
To keep delicate fruits or vegetable pieces separate while frozen, open-freeze them on baking sheets until firm, then pack them into containers or polythene bags for storing.

PREVENTING PROBLEMS

- **Open-freezing cakes** Freeze frosted or decorated cakes until solid before wrapping so that the tops are not squashed.
- **Preventing damage** Protect the top of a pie or delicate dessert by putting an upturned foil pie plate over it. Secure the plate to the dish with tape.
- **Avoiding drying** If food does not fill a container, pack the space with crumpled paper to stop the food from drying out.
- **Omitting garlic** Leave garlic out of food to be frozen – it can taste musty when frozen. Add garlic to food after thawing.

STORING AND LABELLING

Keep your freezer well organized, and rotate foods as you would in a storecupboard, so that you use foods within their recommended storage times. Reuse suitable food containers for freezing, but always make sure that they are thoroughly clean before filling them.

PACKAGING FOOD

● **Repacking meats** When freezing prepacked meats, always remove the packaging, and rewrap. Cut off the label, then tape it on to the new packaging to save relabelling.
● **Using lids** To pack home-made burgers easily so that they do not stick together, and for easy removal, save plastic coffee can lids, and place each burger on a lid for stacking.
● **Recycling containers** Collect plastic containers with snap-on lids for use in the freezer. Some plastics become brittle at low temperatures, so if you are not sure, line containers with polythene bags.

STORING COOKED FRUITS

Mould paper so it presses down on fruits

Using crumpled paper
When freezing food with liquids such as fruits in syrup, prevent the pieces of food from rising above the surface of the liquid by pressing a sheet of crumpled non-stick paper over the food.

LABELLING CONTAINERS

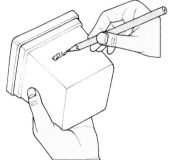

Marking a container
For easy labelling of foods in polythene containers, write the details on the container with a wax-based pencil. This will write easily on polythene, and the writing will not rub off.

PREPARING FREEZER STAND-BYS

A freezer offers a wonderful opportunity for keeping time-saving supplies handy. Freeze containers of garnishes and decorations for use when time is short before a dinner party. Freeze leftovers for those days when you need a meal with the minimum amount of preparation.

SAVING TIME

● **Making extra meals** Freeze ready-cooked meals on foil plates. Arrange the food on the plates, ensuring that meats are covered with gravy or sauce, then cover with clingfilm or foil, seal, and freeze.
● **Making butter balls** Prepare butter balls or curls in advance for entertaining, drop into iced water, then drain and pack into boxes to freeze. Remove and thaw at room temperature about an hour before use.
● **Slicing citrus fruits** Freeze slices of lemon or lime in polythene bags. Add the frozen slices to drinks.
● **Scooping in advance** Before a dinner party, scoop ice-cream or sorbet on to paper-lined trays. Refreeze, ready to serve.

FREEZING CHOCOLATE

● **Protecting with paper** When freezing delicate chocolate shapes, protect the shapes by placing sheets of absorbent paper towels between the layers that are to be stacked.

Using a cutter
Spread melted chocolate on to a cold surface, leave to set, and use a small cutter to cut into shapes. Layer in a box with non-stick paper. Use from frozen to decorate cakes and desserts.

STORING USEFUL BASICS

● **Keeping milk** Freeze spare cartons of milk. Thaw in the refrigerator for two days or at room temperature for six hours.
● **Freezing leftovers** Store leftovers in portion sizes, so that you can take out exactly the number you need.
● **Freezing tomatoes** Freeze whole tomatoes in polythene bags. They can be added directly to casseroles or soups.
● **Keeping spare pastry** Roll out pastry trimmings, and cut into shapes such as leaves or hearts. Freeze in containers, and use straight from the freezer to decorate pies before baking.
● **Using ice trays** Make extra sauce or gravy, and freeze in ice-cube trays, then thaw just the amount you need.

DRINKS

THE MAIN ADVANTAGE OF CREATING both hot and cold drinks at home is that you can concoct special flavours and blends. The possibilities are endless, from non-alcoholic, flavoured fruit drinks to highly spiced, mulled party punches.

FRUIT AND VEGETABLE JUICES

Fruit and vegetable juices are hard to beat for nutrients and fresh flavour. If you enjoy fresh juices, an electric juicer is a worthwhile investment. Otherwise, keep a variety of ready-made juices in store to mix and match flavours and create refreshing drinks at any time of day.

ENHANCING FLAVOURS

Add flower water to plain juice

Adding flower water
Make the flavour of a plain fruit juice more interesting by adding a few drops of orange flower water or rosewater. Stir the juice thoroughly before serving.

PRESSING JUICES
● **Pressing apples** If you are making apple juice in an electric juicer, add a handful of red fruits such as strawberries or raspberries to give the juice a rosy glow and add flavour.
● **Using pulp** Instead of discarding the high-fibre pulp that is left behind after pressing juice, use it in your cooking to add flavour. Add carrot or celery pulp to soups or bread, and include apple or peach pulp in fruit cake recipes.
● **Maintaining colour** Add a squeeze of fresh lemon juice when pressing apples or pears. This will prevent their juices from turning brown.

MAKING SWIZZLE STICKS

Stir juice with spring onion to impart flavour

Using spring onions
Use spring onions as edible swizzle sticks. Trim root ends and the tops of the leaves – leaving some green for colour – just before serving to release flavour.

ADDING INTEREST
● **Using garlic** To pep up the flavour of vegetable juice, rub a cut clove of garlic around the inside of a glass or jug before adding the juice, or add a pinch of garlic or celery salt.
● **Chopping herbs** Improve the flavour and colour of plain vegetable juices by adding chopped fresh herbs. Try basil, parsley, or lovage in tomato juice, and use tarragon or coriander in carrot juice.
● **Adding fruit and fizz** To make a refreshing summer drink, add chunks of fresh fruits to fresh fruit juice, half-fill tall tumblers, and top up the juice with soda or sparkling mineral water.

CHILLING DRINKS

Add frozen grapes

Adding frozen fruits
Instead of using ice to chill juices, freeze fresh fruits such as grapes or lemon slices. Add these to drinks just before serving to chill and decorate.

HEALTHY TIP

Making nut-milk shakes
For a nutritious, milk-free shake, place a handful of blanched almonds or cashews in a blender with a few strawberries or a banana. Add water to cover, and purée.

SPICED DRINKS

Mulled wines and spice-infused drinks are suitable for many occasions, whether as festive party punches or soothing bedtime drinks. Spices such as ginger, cinnamon, and cloves give a depth of flavour to even the simplest hot punch, with or without the addition of alcohol.

VARYING FLAVOURS
● **Using star anise** Add pieces of whole star anise to mulled wine for a rich, spicy flavour.
● **Flavouring coffee** Make an invigorating winter coffee blend by adding ground spices to ground coffee, or grinding whole spices such as allspice, ginger, nutmeg, or cinnamon with fresh coffee beans.
● **Mixing juices** Combine equal quantities of cranberry juice and ginger ale, and mull the mixture gently with cloves or cinnamon to make a delicious non-alcoholic punch.
● **Using savoury spice** Sprinkle a few toasted cumin seeds on top of the yoghurt-based drinks that often accompany curries.

USING FRUITS

Studding with cloves
To add a spicy flavour and decorate a hot party punch, press whole cloves into the skins of several dessert apples, then float the fruits in the punch while heating and serving.

SPICING HOT CHOCOLATE

Stir with cinnamon stick

Using a cinnamon stick
Add a mild hint of spice to hot chocolate or cocoa by adding a cinnamon stick. Alternatively, add a pinch of ground cinnamon to the chocolate or cocoa powder during preparation.

TEAS AND TISANES

Tea is an ancient drink that, depending on the particular choice of ingredients added, can be served as a soothing healer or as a refreshing, stimulating reviver. Most teas are usually served hot, but iced tea can be a very welcome cooler on a hot summer's day.

USING HERBS
● **Adding mint** To use fresh mint in iced tea, place a few sprigs in a large jug, bruise them with a wooden spoon, then add tea. Pour into glasses, and garnish with mint sprigs.
● **Soothing headaches** Try sipping rosemary tisane to relieve a tense headache. Put a few fresh rosemary sprigs in a pot, pour over boiling water, and infuse for 4–5 minutes.
● **Using alternatives** If herbal teas are not to your taste, try infusing herbs with ordinary black tea, adding sugar to taste.
● **Flavouring green tea** Plunge mint sprigs into freshly made, Chinese gunpowder green tea for a refreshing green tea in the Moroccan style.

ENHANCING FLAVOUR

Spoon herbs into pot with tea

Using everyday teas
Bring an interesting flavour to a pot of ordinary leaf tea by adding a few dried herbs, such as dried camomile flowers, while the tea is brewing. Serve plain, or with lemon and sugar if preferred.

USING FRUITS & FLOWERS
● **Adding zest** To make a delicate, fruit-scented tea, add a thinly pared strip of citrus zest to a pot of Indian tea.
● **Making flower teas** Mix a few dried, scented rose petals or jasmine flowers with dry tea leaves, so that the delicate scent mingles with the tea.
● **Creating an exotic flavour** Make a fruit-scented tea by pressing a little juice from a freshly cut mango into tea.
● **Making tea punch** Combine iced tea with chilled fruit juice for a thirst-quenching summer drink. Pineapple or apple juice complements black tea.
● **Adding vanilla** Add a vanilla pod to the tea caddy to infuse a rich flavour during storage.

ENTERTAINING

THROWING A SUCCESSFUL PARTY can be satisfying as well as enjoyable. There are no guaranteed methods of ensuring success, but whether the occasion is formal or informal, large or small, good organization and careful advance planning will certainly help. You need to select an appropriate menu, invite a good mixture of guests, and create a pleasant atmosphere in which they feel comfortable. At the end of the party, you will be able to wave goodbye to happy guests with a great feeling of satisfaction and the knowledge that they – and you – thoroughly enjoyed the occasion.

PLANNING A TIMETABLE

When you are catering for a large number of guests, it is worth planning the occasion well in advance to save yourself time and effort nearer the day. Prepare detailed checklists and timetables, taking all tasks into consideration. This will make the occasion easier to tackle.

PLANNING IN ADVANCE		
COUNTDOWN	FORWARD PLANNING	ACTION NEEDED
4 WEEKS OR MORE BEFORE	Choose venue, theme of occasion, and menu; draw up guest list.	Book venue; send out invitations; arrange hire or loan of equipment.
2-3 WEEKS BEFORE	Make shopping lists; plan cooking schedule, and list other jobs.	Order flowers and drinks; prepare dishes that will freeze.
1 WEEK BEFORE	Monitor guest acceptances and apologies; work out table plans.	Order food; write name and menu cards; wash table linen; clean silver.
3 DAYS BEFORE	Check china and cutlery; finalize numbers of guests and equipment.	Cook food to be reheated or served cold; wash china/glasses.
1 DAY BEFORE	Update cooking schedule; check list of other tasks to be done.	Buy food for last-minute preparation; prepare vegetables/salads; set tables.
PARTY MORNING	Make list of jobs to be done by helpers and hired staff.	Buy fresh bread; arrange flowers and bar; set tables; prepare hot food.
1 HOUR BEFORE	Tick off tasks as they are completed; allow time for relaxation.	Finish off hot food in oven; put out canapés and cocktail snacks.

PLANNING MENUS

The dishes you choose in a party menu must depend not just on personal taste, but on the season, the occasion, and on limitations such as time and budget. Try to appeal to the eye as well as the appetite, keeping the menu simple, and choose tried-and-tested recipes.

SELECTING RECIPES

● **Choosing a main course** Unless you have a favourite starter or dessert that you wish to use, plan the main course first, then choose a starter and dessert to complement it.
● **Keeping courses simple** Help yourself by choosing a simple, cold starter that can be prepared in advance.

BALANCING MENUS

● **Varying courses** Create an overall balance of colour, texture, and flavour in the menu. Avoid choosing courses that are similar, for example all egg- or cheese-based.
● **Offsetting rich dishes** Balance a rich or spicy main course with a plain starter and a light, refreshing dessert.

PREVENTING PROBLEMS

● **Planning alternatives** In case you are unable to get hold of a particular ingredient, have an alternative dish in mind.
● **Checking diets** Check in advance whether guests have special dietary requirements.
● **Limiting courses** Unless you have extra help, keep to three courses to minimize work.

ESTIMATING QUANTITIES

It is a strange fact that the more people you cater for, the less food you need to allow per head, especially for buffets. If you are catering for 100 people, allow full quantities for about 85. Appetites vary from person to person, but allow half portions for children or elderly guests.

ASSESSING FOOD QUANTITIES			
BUFFET FOODS	**10 PORTIONS**	**20 PORTIONS**	**40 PORTIONS**
Soups, hot or cold	1.75 litres (3 pints)	4 litres (7 pints)	8 litres (14 pints)
Cold, sliced meats off the bone	900 g (2 lb)	1.75 kg (3 lb 14 oz)	3.5 kg (7 lb 11 oz)
Boneless meat for casseroles, etc.	1 kg (2 lb 3 oz)	2.25 kg (5 lb)	4.5 kg (9 lb 15 oz)
Roast meat on the bone, hot or cold	1.75 kg (3 lb 14 oz)	3 kg (6 lb 10 oz)	6.5 kg (14 lb 5 oz)
Poultry on the bone (oven-ready weight)	3.5 kg (7 lb 11 oz)	7 kg (15 lb 7 oz)	14 kg (30 lb 14 oz)
Fish, filleted (in cooked dishes)	1.25 kg (2 lb 12 oz)	2.25 kg (5 lb)	4.5 kg (9 lb 15 oz)
Rice or pasta (uncooked weight)	500 g (1 lb 1 oz)	700 g (1 lb 9 oz)	1.25 kg (2 lb 12 oz)
Vegetables (uncooked weight)	1.5 kg (3 lb 5 oz)	3 kg (6 lb 10 oz)	5.5 kg (12 lb 2 oz)
Fresh fruits or fruit salad	1.5 kg (3 lb 5 oz)	2.75 kg (6 lb 1 oz)	5.5 kg (12 lb 2 oz)
Ice-cream	1.5 litres (2¾ pints)	2.5 litres (4½ pints)	5 litres (8¾ pints)
Cheese for a cheeseboard	350 g (12 oz)	900 g (2 lb)	1.25 kg (2 lb 12 oz)
Biscuits for cheese	500 g (1 lb 1 oz)	750 g (1 lb 10 oz)	1 kg (2 lb 3 oz)

TABLE SETTINGS AND DECORATIONS

AN ATTRACTIVE TABLE SETTING ENHANCES A MEAL, whether it is a formal dinner or an informal party. Use your imagination, or look in books and magazines for inspiration, to create an attractive table setting suitable for the occasion.

PREPARING TABLECLOTHS

As well as serving a decorative purpose, a tablecloth protects the surface of the table. White linen or cotton damask tablecloths are conventionally used for formal occasions, but you may prefer to choose a cloth to match the setting or to follow the theme of the occasion.

PROTECTING TABLES

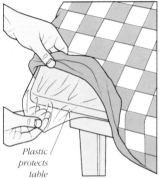

Plastic protects table

Covering with plastic
Prevent spills from damaging a polished table top by placing a layer of clingfilm or polythene over it before laying the main tablecloth. Alternatively, use a plastic tablecloth.

WEIGHTING CLOTHS

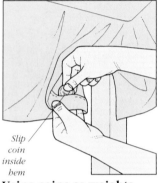

Slip coin inside hem

Using coins as weights
Weight a tablecloth to be used outdoors by unpicking a few stitches around the hem and slipping coins or curtain weights inside. Alternatively, you can tack weights on to the cloth.

PREVENTING FLAPPING

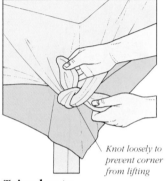

Knot loosely to prevent corner from lifting

Tying knots
Knot the corners of a cloth when eating outdoors to prevent them from flapping. Place the cloth over one of a contrasting shade or slip a posy of dried flowers into each knot for decoration.

FINDING ALTERNATIVES
● **Using sheets** If you do not have enough tablecloths for a large party, improvise by using sheets or lengths of muslin.
● **Using several cloths** If you have only small tablecloths, use a plain sheet as an undercloth, and lay several small, pretty tablecloths diagonally on top to cover a large table.
● **Using a blanket** If you do not have an undercloth, use a thick blanket underneath a tablecloth to prevent the top of the table from being marked.
● **Substituting rugs** For a party with an Arabian or Oriental theme, lay brightly coloured kelims or rugs over large tables.

DECORATING PLAIN TABLECLOTHS

Making herb posies
Make small posies of fresh herbs, such as rosemary or thyme, to attach to a plain tablecloth. Tie the posies with ribbon, and pin them to the cloth in each corner, or at intervals along the edges.

● **Decorating with stencils** Use stencils and fabric paints to decorate a plain cloth. Stencil a border around each place setting.
● **Spray-painting** Brighten up plain fabric or paper cloths with spray-paints in colourful, abstract designs for children's parties.
● **Scattering petals** Scatter rose petals or other edible flowers over a cloth for a romantic touch.
● **Adding sparkle** At a festive event, sprinkle gold or silver stars over the tablecloth.
● **Using wallpaper borders** Decorate the edges of a plain cloth with a pretty wallpaper border, securing it around the edges with double-sided tape.

SETTING TABLES

The same basic principles apply to setting any table, whether for an informal or a formal meal, although the menu dictates which cutlery is used. To avoid overcrowding the table at the start of a meal, additional cutlery can be brought to the table with the appropriate courses.

LAYING A TABLE FOR DINNER

Large goblet for red wine

Dessert spoon laid above fork

Water glass

Small wine glass for white wine

Butter knife

Plate set for first course

Napkin placed on side plate

Forks to left of plate in order of use

Knives and spoon to right of plate, knife blades towards plate

Laying a setting
However many courses there are, lay the cutlery in the order it will be used, working from the outside inwards. To save space, you can place both the dessert spoon and fork at the top of the setting. Arrange glasses at the top, right-hand corner, with the main wine glass placed above the tip of the main knife.

CHOOSING GLASSWARE

If you have taken care with your choice of drinks, you will want to choose glassware equally carefully to complement the drinks and the table setting. When calculating how many glasses you need for entertaining on a large scale, allow an additional 10 per cent for breakages.

CHOOSING WINE GLASSES

Choosing the right shape
To enjoy the bouquet of either white or red wine, serve it in glasses that are narrower at the rim than in the body. This shape enhances a wine's bouquet.

USING GLASSWARE
● **Removing labels** To remove sticky labels from new glasses, rub with lighter fuel.
● **Removing water marks** If glasses are dulled by water marks, restore their sparkle by soaking in water with a little malt vinegar. Rinse thoroughly in cold water, drain, and dry.
● **Washing crystal** Wash fine, lead crystal glasses by hand in warm water and detergent. Rinse in clear water, and dry while warm. Washing lead crystal in a dishwasher will dull the surface of the glasses.
● **Serving champagne** Serve champagne in slender flutes, which show off the bubbles and colour of the wine.

CHOOSING JUGS

Sturdy handle allows good grip when pouring

Fruit and ice remain in jug and continue to flavour and cool

Pouring fruit punch
Serve fruit punches and iced drinks from a glass jug that has a pinched pouring lip or a filter to prevent slices of fruits or ice cubes from falling into the glass.

121

CHOOSING TABLEWARE

The careful selection of tableware is essential to the visual success of a dinner party and to show off the food at its best. Choose simple yet striking colours and shapes when deciding which china, cutlery, and linen to use. Arrange them so that they do not detract from the food.

MIXING & MATCHING TABLEWARE

Contrasting side plate

Underplate contrasts with dinner plate

Patterned napkin

Mixing colours
If you do not have enough matching tableware to cater for all your guests, then mix and match what you have, combining colours and styles to dramatic effect. Layer contrasting colours on top of one another.

USING LARGE PLATTERS

FINDING ALTERNATIVES TO CROCKERY

● **Using disposable platters**
Buy large, disposable foil platters for buffet foods. To make them look decorative, line with salad leaves before arranging the food on top.

● **Using wicker containers** For an unusual presentation, serve bread and canapés in wicker containers. Line baskets with napkins for bread, and trays with large leaves for canapés.

Arranging ingredients
If you do not have a plate that fits the size of a quiche or flan exactly, choose a large platter. Place the quiche in the centre, and fill the space around it with a mixed salad or pretty garnish.

MAKING CENTREPIECES

Even on an informal occasion, a colourful centrepiece of flowers or fruits will bring an extra-special touch to the table. Make sure that the size and shape of a centrepiece allows your guests to see one another across the dining table. Stabilize vases with stones or marbles.

USING FRUITS

Carve pattern with sharp knife

ARRANGING FRUITY, FLORAL DISPLAYS

Apple wedge

Fruit holds stem in place

Citrus slice adds colour and prevents other fruits from browning

Making a melon basket
Make a dessert centrepiece for serving fruit salad by making a melon basket. Cut a slice from the melon, and scoop out the flesh. Carve the melon skin to decorate, then fill with fruit salad.

Using fruits
Arrange flowers for a buffet-table centrepiece in a glass dish packed with pieces of fresh fruit. The fruits feed the flowers, keeping them fresh.

DECORATING PLACE SETTINGS

Whatever the occasion – whether formal or informal – imaginative place settings will help to make guests feel welcome and break the ice as they sit down to eat. Always keep decorations simple and fresh, and use edible flowers if they will be in contact with the food.

CREATING AN INDIVIDUAL DISPLAY

Decorate underplate with flowers before serving food

Using flowers
To give a place setting a fresh, seasonal touch, arrange edible flowers or fresh herbs around a dinner plate on a wide underplate. Spray the flowers gently with water to keep them fresh for as long as possible.

GIVING EDIBLE FAVOURS

Gathered edges of net form a pretty frill

Tying net bundles
Make edible favours for guests to take home as mementos. Place sugared almonds and chocolates on small circles of fine net. Then gather up the net, and tie each bundle with ribbon.

DECORATING PLATES & TABLEMATS
● **Stencilling underplates** Decorate large underplates by stencilling around their rims. Using non-toxic paints, spray holly leaves, hearts, stars, or a band of gold or silver colour.

● **Decorating tablemats** For a themed adults' or children's party, cut out paper shapes of hearts or cartoon characters to decorate plain tablemats. Secure in place with glue.

SETTING THE SCENE
● **Making a pastry garland** For a romantic occasion, shape shortcrust pastry or biscuit dough into small hearts. Pierce a hole in each with a skewer, and bake. Thread the hearts together with ribbon to make a garland around each plate.
● **Decorating chairs** To trim chairs for a wedding, use wired florist's ribbon to fashion extravagant bows, and attach one to the back of each guest's chair. Alternatively, tie on small posies of fresh flowers to match the bride's bouquet.
● **Adding roses** Place a single red rose across each place setting as a romantic gift for each guest at a wedding or ruby anniversary celebration.
● **Lighting candles** Just before the guests are seated, place a red apple with a long taper candle stuck in it at each setting. Lower the lights when all the candles are lit.

USING FRUITS & SPICES
● **Making spice bundles** Gather together small bundles of warm, winter spices such as cinnamon sticks and ginger root with a few bay leaves. Tie together with ribbons as festive gifts for your guests.

Use toothpick to make holes in skin

Decorating citrus fruits
Make spice-scented pomanders as gifts to decorate each table setting. Stud small oranges or limes with cloves, then tie a patterned ribbon around each, and finish with a decorative bow.

USING FINGER FOODS
● **Making edible treats** For a summer party, thread two or three fresh strawberries each on to wooden skewers with a mint leaf between the fruits. Place a skewer on each plate for a pre-dinner appetite teaser.

Tuck herb sprigs between bread sticks

Decorating with herbs
Decorate a country-style table setting by tying each napkin loosely around two or three bread sticks. Add a few sprigs of fresh rosemary or bay leaves for a delicate scent.

123

MAKING MENU CARDS

Menu cards are most commonly used for formal dinners, but there is no reason why they cannot be used for any occasion. Follow the same theme that was used on the invitations. Guests may like to keep the menu cards as a fun memento of a special occasion.

COVERING MENUS

Tying with cord
To make a handwritten menu look more formal, place it on top of a large piece of coloured card. Attach the card and menu together with furnishing cord, and finish with a neat bow.

DECORATING CARDS

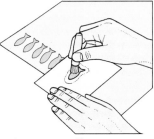

Using a stencil
Stencil a border on to a menu card using a food motif that reflects the menu. Cut a stencil from stiff card in the shape of your choice, then use a stiff brush to apply the paint evenly.

DESIGNING INFORMALLY

● **Using marker pens** For festive occasions or special anniversaries, use silver or gold marker pens to write out menus and decorate the edges of simple menu cards.

● **Writing on plates** For an informal party, buy plain paper plates, and write menus on them with coloured felt-tip pens. If you have children, they can decorate the menus.

● **Making a collage** Make plain menu cards look festive by cutting up old greetings cards and sticking the images around the edges of the menu cards.

DESIGNING PLACE CARDS

Name cards and seating plans can serve a useful purpose even on small, informal occasions. A successful seating plan will place guests so that they enjoy one another's company, avoid confusion as guests sit down at the start of a meal, and help shy guests to break the ice.

CREATING MARKERS

● **Using fruits** Spray fruits such as apples, pears, or lemons with gold paint, leave to dry, then attach gold name tags for festive settings.

● **Baking gingerbread men** Make and bake gingerbread men, and tuck them into small envelopes with a guest's name attached to each biscuit.

● **Piping icing** Cut biscuit dough into decorative shapes, bake and cool them, then pipe a guest's name and a decorative motif on to each biscuit with coloured icing.

● **Painting eggs** For a spring party, paint eggs with guests' names incorporated into the design. Place in pretty egg cups, one at each setting.

● **Saving time** Buy gift tags to use as festive name cards if you are short of time.

USING THEMES

● **Making masks** For a themed costume party, buy plain party masks, and decorate them yourself in a way that reflects the theme. Individualize the masks by incorporating a guest's name into each design.

MODELLING FIGURES

● **Using dough** Mix water and flour to make a paste, shape into figures, and bake in a cool oven for two hours until dry. Inscribe a guest's name on each figure, decorate it with acrylic paint, and then varnish.

MAKING A POP-UP PLACE CARD

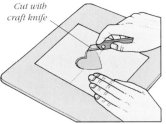

Cut with craft knife

1 Draw a shape in the centre of a sheet of thin card, and colour if desired. Mark a fine line to indicate where the fold will be. Cut carefully around the shape above the fold line.

2 Fold the card along the marked line. The upper part of the shape will extend above the fold. Inscribe the guest's name on it, and then position the card on the table.

FOLDING NAPKINS

Folded table napkins can enhance a table setting on a special occasion, and knowledge of a few simple folds is all that you require. The best fabrics to use for folding are starched linen and cotton, which hold their shape well. Even paper napkins can be folded successfully.

FOLDING SIMPLE NAPKIN FANS

Pleat evenly

Tie pleats together with ribbon

Hold centre pleats of napkin

1 To make a simple napkin fan, first starch and iron a fabric napkin, or use a good-quality paper napkin. Starting from one side, fold the napkin into evenly spaced accordion pleats all the way across.

2 Continue until the whole napkin is pleated, and press the pleats firmly in place. Fold the pleated napkin in half. Tie a small, decorative ribbon bow around the base of the pleats, above the folded end.

3 Place the napkin on a dinner plate, hold the two centre pleats together, and open out the pleats to either side to form a fan shape. A napkin fan can also be placed upright in a wine glass.

CREATING NAPKIN RINGS

Napkin rings add a finishing touch to rolled or folded napkins, and there are many ways of creating decorative devices to hold napkins prettily as part of a table setting. Keep them simple, so that they enhance rather than detract from the food and the other table decorations.

FOLLOWING THEMES

● **Creating lavish effects** Buy opulent curtain braids and tassels to wrap around napkins for a sophisticated celebration.
● **Weaving raffia** For a rustic, harvest, or country theme, weave strips of raffia or straw into napkin rings. Tuck dried flowers into the ring.
● **Using ribbons** Tie simple coloured ribbons around napkins to follow a colour theme, or buy special, festive ribbons to suit the occasion.
● **Celebrating anniversaries** Wind strings of imitation pearls or other costume jewellery around table napkins for an anniversary celebration.
● **Threading shells** Make a marine-themed napkin ring by threading small shells on to fine wire, then twisting the ends together to make a ring.

USING FRESH HERBS

● **Attaching herb sprigs** To bring a pleasant scent to the dinner table and decorate simple, rolled napkins, tuck sprigs of herbs or herb flowers into plain napkin rings.

Tying with chives
Use freshly cut chive fronds to tie around a plain, rolled napkin. Cut the chives so that they are as long as possible. The longer the fronds, the easier it will be to tie them. Trim the ends to neaten.

USING FOOD AND FLOWERS

● **Making garlands** Make garland napkin rings to match bridal flowers. Bend a piece of florist's wire into a ring, and bind it with ribbon. Cut sprays of flowers such as mimosa or freesia, and bind them around each ring with fine wire.
● **Using leaves** Select flat-shaped leaves from plants such as iris, and tie around a simply folded napkin in a loose knot.
● **Threading sweets** Thread colourful liquorice sweets on to thick cotton, and tie to make edible napkin rings.
● **Baking bread rings** Instead of bread rolls, shape dough into rings, glaze with egg, and sprinkle with poppy or sesame seeds. Bake until golden, and slip one on to each napkin before serving.

DRINKS PARTIES

Drinks parties can be formal or informal, offering a simple glass of sherry or a choice of cocktails, depending on the particular occasion. If you are inviting more than 20 guests, consider hiring a barperson to serve drinks.

MAKING AND SERVING CANAPÉS

Food is essential at any drinks party, but there is no need to spend hours preparing elaborate dishes. Simple canapés or dips are all that is needed. Offer your guests a choice of finger foods and other savouries that can be eaten with one hand, in one or two bites.

SKEWERING CANAPÉS

Thread small pieces on to cocktail stick

Making tricolore sticks
Thread cubes of feta cheese on to cocktail sticks between squares of raw green and red peppers to make tricolore sticks. If you prefer, cook the peppers first under the grill, and skin them.

SERVING CANAPÉS WITH STYLE

Using a mirror
Arrange bite-sized finger foods on to a mirror tile instead of a plate for an unusual presentation at a formal drinks party. Leave space between each canapé to achieve the best effect.

Use pastry brush to glaze

Making a dough platter
Roll out shortcrust pastry or bread dough in a round shape. Edge with shaped leftover dough, place on a baking sheet, glaze with lightly beaten egg, and bake until golden. Use to serve canapés.

QUICK AND EASY CANAPÉS

● **Piped celery** Pipe soft, herb-flavoured cream cheese into the hollows of celery sticks.
● **Paté-filled mushrooms** Remove the stalks from small cup mushrooms, and pipe paté into the hollows left by the stalks.
● **Blue-cheese grapes** Mix equal amounts of blue cheese and butter. Cut large black or green grapes in half, and sandwich back together with the mix.
● **Mini-scones** Make mini-sized savoury scones, and bake until golden. Cool, and top with cream cheese and an olive.
● **Chicken-liver toasts** Sauté chicken livers quickly in a little butter and sherry. Cut into bite-sized pieces, and spoon on to small, French bread toasts.

● **Nachos bites** Spoon a little spicy guacamole or hummus on to tortilla chips, and sprinkle with paprika to garnish.
● **Bacon twists** Twist thin slices of smoked streaky bacon with strips of puff pastry. Bake at 200°C (400°F) or Gas Mark 6 for about 15 minutes, or until firm and golden brown.
● **Salami cones** Wrap thin slices of salami carefully around melon sticks, and secure each one by piercing with a cocktail stick.
● **Almond olives** Stuff pitted olives with whole, salted, or smoked almonds.
● **Ham with kiwis** Wrap thinly sliced smoked ham around wedges of peeled kiwi fruit, and secure each with a cocktail stick.

PREVENTING PROBLEMS
● **Preventing soggy pastry** To serve vol-au-vents and other pastries with moist fillings, bake the pastry cases in advance, but add the fillings only one hour before serving.
● **Making bite-sized foods** Make canapés small enough to be easily held in the hand and to be eaten in one mouthful to prevent mess.
● **Serving in stages** Serve hot and cold canapés in small batches over a period of about an hour, instead of serving them all at the same time.
● **Clearing space** Make space so that guests can put down their drinks and not juggle food and drinks. Clear away empty glasses and food debris.

MAKING CRUDITÉS AND DIPS

Crudités and dips make excellent food for serving at informal drinks parties, since they are simple to make and can be prepared in advance. Serve plenty of crudités and savoury crisps for dipping, and make the dippers small enough to be eaten in one mouthful.

PREPARING & PRESENTING CRUDITÉS

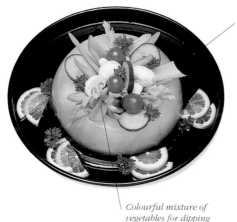

Deep serving dish allows ice to melt without spilling

Colourful mixture of vegetables for dipping

Making an ice ring
Keep vegetables fresh by serving them in an ice ring. Fill a large ring mould with water, and freeze. Turn out on to a deep serving dish, and arrange vegetables in the centre. Garnish around the ice ring to complete the effect.

SIMPLE DIPS

● **Tuna** Drain a can of tuna, and mash with plain yoghurt. Add chopped dill to taste.
● **Devilled sauce** Mix tomato ketchup with a small amount of Worcestershire sauce.
● **Pesto** Stir pesto sauce into Greek-style yoghurt.
● **Blue cheese** Mash equal amounts of blue Stilton and soft cream cheese, softening with a little milk if necessary.
● **Avocado** Mash avocado with a little mayonnaise, and add lemon juice to taste.

MAKING AND SERVING DRINKS

Offer drinks to guests as they arrive. Make sure that there is a good selection of soft drinks as well as alcoholic drinks. If you are serving only one or two different drinks, pour them out in advance, and place them on trays to serve. Mix cocktails in jugs for easy serving.

CHILLING & SERVING

● **Chilling bottles** If you are short of refrigerator space for chilling bottles, fill the bath with ice, and store the bottles in it until you need them.
● **Freezing fruit juice** To prevent drinks from being watered down by plain ice cubes, freeze fruit juice into cubes as an alternative.
● **Rinsing glasses** Rinse all traces of detergent from glasses before pouring champagne, since detergent destroys the bubbles.
● **Serving soft drinks** Always include fresh fruit juices and mineral waters among soft drinks for non-drinkers.
● **Making punch** Serve a mixed punch at a large party. This is particularly suitable for large numbers, and can be less expensive than serving a wide selection of wines and spirits.

PREPARING & PRESENTING DRINKS

Cucumber garnish

Strawberry stirrer adds flavour

Fizz created by dissolved, brandy-soaked sugar cube

Rim frosted with food colouring and caster sugar

Twist of peel adds flavour

Napkin placed under iced drink absorbs moisture

Adding finishing touches
It is worth taking care to serve drinks well, and some of the most effective ideas are quick and simple to achieve. If you want to add a garnish to a cocktail, make sure that you choose a large enough glass so that the drink will not overflow.

BUFFETS

Preparing a self-service, buffet-style meal is the easiest way to cater for a large number of people, since it allows you to provide for a range of different tastes, ages, and appetites, as long as you organize the food well in advance.

ARRANGING A BUFFET TABLE

For an appealing buffet, try to add variety to the appearance of dishes by varying their shapes and heights. Select food, tableware, utensils, and accessories such as napkins so that colours, textures, and shapes complement or contrast with each other in an imaginative way.

PLANNING THE LAYOUT OF A BUFFET TABLE

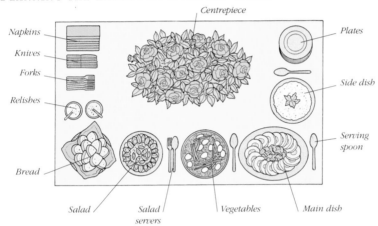

Centrepiece

Napkins

Knives

Forks

Relishes

Bread

Plates

Side dish

Serving spoon

Salad *Salad servers* *Vegetables* *Main dish*

Arranging dishes
When arranging the dishes on a buffet table, start with the plates, then side dishes, followed by the main dish, and finally vegetables and salads, with serving utensils alongside. Breads, any relishes, cutlery, and napkins are usually positioned at the end of the selection. Place decorations in the middle of the table.

ORGANIZING BUFFETS
● **Positioning a buffet table**
Leave room behind a buffet table so that you have easy access for replacing dishes.
● **Taping wires** If you place the buffet table in the centre of a room, make sure that all electrical wires are taped down safely to the floor.
● **Grouping chairs** Make sure that there are enough chairs, and position them together in groups of three or more so that guests can sit and chat.
● **Setting drinks aside** Place drinks, glasses, and cups on a separate table to avoid congestion at the buffet table.
● **Leaving space on the table** Leave space between dishes on the buffet table so that guests can put down glasses or plates when serving themselves.

KEEPING FOODS COLD
● **Making a cold plate** Fill a dish with water, and freeze. Put it in a plastic bag, then place a plate on top to keep food cold.

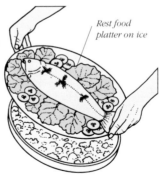

Rest food platter on ice

Using crushed ice
Remove chilled foods from the refrigerator just before serving. To keep food cold on the table, fill a wide dish with crushed ice, and nestle a serving dish into it.

CALCULATING QUANTITIES

Use this checklist to work out buffet quantities for basic foods. A more detailed guide (p. 118) will help you calculate main- and side-dish quantities.

● **Bread** A large, thinly sliced loaf has 18–20 slices. One French stick serves 10 people.
● **Butter** 25 g (1 oz) butter will cover seven slices of bread.
● **Green salad** A large Webbs lettuce will serve 10 people, a large Cos will serve eight, and a Butterhead, four.
● **Celebration cake** A 2.25-kg (5-lb) cake can be cut into approximately 50 slices.
● **Wine** A 70-cl bottle fills six glasses; a 1-litre bottle, nine.
● **Ice** 10 kg (20 lb) ice cools two cases (24 bottles) of wine.

PRESENTING FOOD

Take care with the presentation of food for a buffet table in order to show off the food at its very best. If you are catering for a large number of guests, replenish serving dishes and clear away empty plates regularly so that the table always looks attractive for your guests.

USING LARGE PLATTERS
● **Stacking sandwiches** Cut sandwiches into quarters, and place them with the points upwards to show the fillings.

Fill centre with grated carrot

Arranging a salad
Instead of tossing salad in a bowl, arrange ingredients in a colourful pattern on a large, wide platter. Spoon dressing, if desired, over the salad before serving.

DISPLAYING FRUITS

Making a fruit pyramid
Cut the flesh from a large pineapple, leaving the central core and leaves. Fix on to a cake stand. Build up seasonal fruits around the core into a pyramid.

BRIGHT IDEA

Making a cake stand
If you do not have a cake stand for a buffet table, use a large plate or platter. Stand it on an upturned sugar bowl or soufflé dish. Make sure that the plate is absolutely central. Secure the two firmly with putty adhesive.

SERVING DRINKS

If guests are to help themselves to drinks at a buffet party, punch is ideal, since it is easy to serve. Offering a punch is also a good way to make alcohol go further. Warm hot punches on a low heat if you wish to prevent the alcohol from boiling off, and serve in heatproof glasses.

SERVING COLD DRINKS
● **Making a punch bowl** You can use any large, glass bowl as a punch bowl. Decorate the edges with frosted sugar or fruit slices, and drape edible flowers around the sides. Tie ribbon to the ladle handle to serve.
● **Keeping punch chilled** To keep a fruit punch cold, and to serve it in an unusual way, cut the top off a large watermelon. Scoop out the flesh, and freeze the shell for 2–3 hours. Add the punch, and serve from the shell.
● **Flavouring ice cubes** To chill and flavour fruit cups, freeze strawberries, maraschino cherries, or mint into ice cubes.

SERVING COCKTAILS

Replace lid when straw is in place

Using melon shells
For an unusual way of serving a fruit cocktail, cut a slice from the top of a small melon, and scoop out the flesh. Before filling, cut a hole in one side of the lid for a straw to fit through.

SERVING HOT PUNCHES
● **Mulling wine** To keep mulled wine or a hot punch warm, make the drink in an electric slow-cooker crockpot placed on the buffet table.
● **Floating apples** For a festive winter punch, float a few sweet, dessert apples and spices in a hot wine or ale punch. The apples will poach gently, and after an hour or so will make a delicious dessert.
● **Doubling up cups** If you are serving hot punch in disposable paper or plastic cups, test the cups first to check that they are heatproof. Double up cups to make them comfortable to hold.

DINNER PARTIES

A DINNER PARTY IS AN EXCUSE to show off cooking skills that you may not necessarily use in everyday cooking. Plan carefully, and prepare as much as possible in advance so that you are able to enjoy time with your guests.

PRESENTING FOOD

Good presentation of food needs only basic decorating skills and simple but effective garnishes. Elaborate presentation of food can be reserved for formal occasions, but always make sure that the way in which the food appears enhances rather than overshadows your cooking.

MOULDING VEGETABLES

Using a pastry cutter
To serve cut vegetables, place a round pastry cutter on each plate, and spoon in the cooked vegetables, packing them firmly. Lift off the cutter, leaving the vegetables moulded to shape.

ARRANGING FOOD
● **Adding height** Pile stir-fried dishes high in the centre of a plate so that the helping looks attractive and generous.
● **Fanning slices** To arrange sliced food decoratively, such as an avocado or a chicken breast, slice the food, and lift it whole on to a plate with a fish slice. Then fan out the slices evenly.
● **Tieing bundles** Use a chive "ribbon", or thin strips of green leek blanched for 30 seconds, to tie vegetable sticks or baby vegetables together in small bundles.

SHAPING CHOCOLATE

Making chocolate baskets
Spread melted chocolate evenly over 18-cm (7-in) circles of non-stick paper to within 2.5 cm (1 in) of the edges. Mould over upturned cups, leave to set, and peel off the paper. Use for serving desserts.

SERVING CREAMS AND SAUCES

Join up drops of cream with cocktail stick

Feathering cream
Flood a plate with chocolate sauce or fruit purée, then carefully spoon drops of double cream on to it at regular intervals. Draw the tip of a cocktail stick through each drop to make a chain of feathered heart shapes.

Spoon sauce carefully to create pattern

Designing a pattern
Serve two sauces of similar consistency but contrasting colours together to create an impact. Create a simple but effective pattern by swirling one around the other, for example, on each side of a plate.

● **Making shapes** Spoon a little sauce into a small piping bag, and pipe the outline of the shape you want on a plate. Carefully spoon the rest of the sauce to fill in the shape.
● **Setting purées** Dissolve 5 ml (1 tsp) gelatine in every 200 ml (7 fl oz) hot fruit purée, then pour the purée while still hot on to a serving plate. Chill the purée until set, then arrange the dessert however you wish.
● **Creating a marbled effect** Marble dark and white chocolate sauces by stirring them together very lightly immediately before serving.
● **Enhancing gravy** Sprinkle fine strips of citrus zest, such as lemon or lime, into plain gravy to accompany grilled meat.

ADDING FINISHING TOUCHES

Garnishes add an attractive finishing touch to a dish, particularly if you are cooking for a special occasion. Remember, however, that it is the dish that is important: garnishes should complement, not compete with, the ingredients. Prepare elaborate garnishes in advance.

ENHANCING GARNISHES

● **Shaping with a canelle knife** Before slicing a cucumber as a garnish, run a canelle knife or the prongs of a fork down its sides at intervals. The slices will then have a fluted edge.

● **Dipping in parsley** Add colour to lemon or tomato wedges by dipping their edges into finely chopped parsley after cutting. Alternatively, dip the edges of tomatoes into finely grated Parmesan cheese.

● **Deep-frying parsley** To prevent parsley sprigs from becoming limp, deep-fry them first in hot oil until they are bright green and crisp. Drain on a piece of paper towel.

GARNISHING WITH FRUITS

● **Preparing strawberry fans** To decorate summer desserts, leave the leafy tops on fresh strawberries, and use a sharp knife to cut thin slices through the fruits, leaving the slices attached at the stem end. Hold each stem, and lightly press the slices into a fan shape.

Use sharp knife for accurate cutting

Cutting apple leaves
Cut a series of long, V-shaped notches in the side of a dessert apple, each notch slightly bigger than the one before. Remove the pieces from the apple, and push each piece along on top of the one below to form a leaf shape.

PREPARING VEGETABLE GARNISHES

Slice horizontally to produce hearts

Making carrot hearts
For a romantic dinner garnish, shape a peeled carrot by cutting a groove down one side. Cut the opposite side to a point, so that cross-sections form heart shapes. Slice for individual hearts.

Cut leaves into thin ribbons

Making onion tassels
Trim spring onions, and cut short lengths from the leaf ends. Cut slits lengthways, extending halfway along each piece from the leaf end. Place in iced water until the sliced leaf ends curl.

GARNISHING QUICKLY

● **Using trimmed leaves** Keep the central leaves from a head of celery, and scatter them over savoury dishes to add colour.

● **Scattering nuts** Keep ready-toasted, flaked almonds in a jar for scattering over hot and cold savoury or sweet dishes as an instant garnish.

● **Sprinkling sugar** As a quick, effective topping for hot or cold desserts, shake sieved icing sugar lightly over the surface of the dish.

● **Using zest** Make a last-minute garnish for savoury and sweet dishes by using a zester to grate fine strips of zest from citrus fruits. Scatter the zest over the food before serving.

● **Grating coconut** Use a vegetable peeler to grate curls of fresh coconut over savoury dishes or desserts. Remove the flesh from the shell, but retain the brown skin. Grate across the skin and the flesh to keep the skin on the curls.

SAVING TIME

● **Preparing ahead** When entertaining, make garnishes such as lemon twists, spring onion tassels, and tomato wedges in advance. Place on a plate, and add to the food at a later stage. Cover with clingfilm, and they will keep fresh for up to four hours.

EDIBLE FLOWERS

The following flowers are edible, and are therefore good for decorative purposes. The large flowers of some vegetables, such as courgettes, and the flowers of some herbs are also edible. If you cannot identify a flower, do not eat it.

Apple blossom	Lily
Borage	Marigold
Clover	Nasturtium
Daisy	Orange
Dandelion	Pansy
Elderflower	Primrose
Geranium	Rose
Lavender	Violet

SERVING WINE

Alcoholic drinks stimulate the appetite and enhance the flavour of food, so they can add to the enjoyment of any meal, however simple the food or the setting. If you are unsure about choosing wines, consult a good wine merchant, who will let you taste a selection before you buy.

MATCHING WINE WITH FOOD

There are no strict rules about which wine to serve with which dish, but the following guidelines are useful.

● **Order of drinking** White wine is generally preferred before red, young before mature, and dry before sweet.
● **Appetizers or canapés** Serve crisp white wines, sparkling wines, or fino sherry.
● **Fish dishes** Serve dry white wines such as Muscadet, or young, light reds.
● **Pasta and cheese dishes** Serve robust wines such as Bardolino (red).
● **Creamy dishes** Choose slightly acid wines such as Sauvignon Blanc (white).

PREPARING WINE
● **Chilling wines** To chill white wines, refrigerate for a maximum of two hours, or bury the bottles in crushed ice for 30 minutes before serving.
● **Accelerating chilling** Put wine in the freezer to cool quickly, leaving only for about five minutes. Set a timer so that you remember to remove it.
● **Loosening wires** To save time, loosen the wires of champagne corks while the bottles are chilling so that the corks are ready to pop.
● **Warming red wines** Pour red wine into a slightly warm decanter to warm quickly, instead of heating the wine directly. Uncork young red wine about an hour before serving to develop the flavour.

TRADITIONAL TIP

Decanting wine
Decant bottle-aged wine or port to remove sediment. To do this easily, insert an unbleached coffee filter into the neck of a glass jug, and pour the wine gently into it.

SERVING NON-ALCOHOLIC DRINKS

Whatever the occasion, offer your guests a selection of non-alcoholic drinks. Always have mineral water available for both drinkers and non-drinkers as well as fruit juices and cordials. Some people may prefer wine "lookalikes" such as grape juice or alcohol-free wines.

ADDING FLAVOUR
● **Stimulating the appetite** Add a thin slice of fresh lemon or lime to each glass of mineral water to sharpen the appetite.
● **Accompanying spicy food** Serve a refreshing, lassi-style yoghurt drink with spicy food, such as an Indian curry, instead of wine or beer. Place 300 ml (½ pint) plain yoghurt in a blender with 600 ml (1 pint) water, 2.5 ml (½ tsp) salt, and a sprig of fresh mint. Blend until smooth, then serve in tall, chilled glasses.
● **Adding celery sticks** Use a small, trimmed piece of celery as a swizzle stick for stirring tomato or vegetable juice.

MAKING MILK SHAKES

Shake until frothy before pouring

Using a screw-top jar
If you do not have a blender with which to make a milk shake, mix fruit purée with milk in a large screw-top jar, such as a coffee jar, and shake. Alternatively, whisk the mixture with a balloon whisk.

ALCOHOL-FREE COCKTAILS

● **Cranberry spritzer** Stir equal parts cranberry juice, white grape juice, and sparkling mineral water.
● **Raspberry mint fizz** Pour 50 ml (2 fl oz) raspberry syrup into a tall glass. Add a handful of crushed mint leaves and ice. Top up with soda water.
● **Shirley Temple** Blend two parts pineapple juice with one part passion fruit juice until smooth. Top with fizzy lemonade for a bubbly froth.
● **Peppermint cream** Shake peppermint cordial with cream and a little crushed ice.

CATERING FOR SPECIAL OCCASIONS

A wedding, birthday, or other celebration is an excuse to prepare elaborate food, but clever presentation and original use of colour can also contribute to a memorable meal. Use your imagination to carry the theme of an event through to the table decorations and the food.

MAKING UNUSUAL CAKES

EXTENDING COLOUR THEMES TO FOOD

Duck with orange

Tomato and pepper salad

Selecting golden food
For a golden-themed celebration, serve yellow and orange foods such as carrots, yellow peppers, saffron rice, and fruits such as oranges and peaches.

Peach served with brandy snaps

Creating different shapes
For an unconventional celebration cake, fill small choux buns with cream or crème pâtissière, then pile into a pyramid shape. Tuck roses or mint leaves in the gaps, and sprinkle with icing sugar.

USING FLOWERS
● **Making a cake stand** Instead of using a formal, silver cake stand for a wedding or a christening cake, choose a firm wooden box that is slightly larger than the base of the cake, and cover it with a lace cloth. Pin on silk or fresh flowers and ribbons to decorate.
● **Flavouring with flowers** Add a few drops of orange flower water or rosewater to whipped fresh cream, and stir gently. Spoon into pretty bowls, and scatter with fresh orange blossom or rose petals. Serve with desserts instead of plain whipped cream.
● **Floating candles** To make an unusual, evening table decoration, half fill a large, wide glass bowl with water. Float small candles and lavish fresh blooms, such as camellias, on the water.

● **Creating a tricolore dinner** Mix red, green, and white foods to carry an Italian theme through the meal. For example, use red and green peppers, or tomatoes and basil, with white cheeses.

CREATING MOULDED ICE DECORATIONS
● **Making ice sculptures** Use an elaborate jelly mould to freeze an ice sculpture for a celebration buffet table. Turn out, and use as a centrepiece for crudités or fresh fruits.

● **Using dark foods** For an elegant dinner, create a stunning, almost black theme by using black plates and dark foods such as beetroot, purple basil, black rice, black grapes, and blackberries.

● **Using boiled water** When making ice sculptures and bowls, first boil the water. This will result in clearer ice than if unboiled water is used. Cool completely before freezing.

MOULDING A DECORATIVE ICE BOWL

Tape bowls to ensure evenly shaped ice

1 Make an ice bowl in which to serve ices. Place a small, freezer-proof bowl inside a larger bowl, and fix the bowls in position with tape. Fill the space in between with water.

Use knife point to push flowers into position

2 Push some edible flowers into the water, and freeze. Fill the small bowl with warm water, and lift out. Dip the outer bowl in warm water, and turn out.

PARTY MANAGEMENT

THERE ARE NO SECRETS TO THROWING the perfect party, but careful planning in advance is the best insurance you can have against disasters. Once a party is organized, allow yourself some time to relax before your guests arrive.

LOOKING AFTER GUESTS

Whatever the occasion, the most important thing to remember is that the guests come first. Give some thought to creating a warm atmosphere that will make guests comfortable as soon as they arrive, and spend time with them instead of disappearing into the kitchen.

PROVIDING FINGER BOWLS

Add lemon slices to refresh hands

Napkins for wiping hands

Placing finger bowls
If you are serving foods that are to be eaten with the fingers, such as asparagus spears or shellfish, provide each guest with a finger bowl if they are sitting down to eat, or spread finger bowls liberally around the room for a buffet.

● **Scenting water** Add a few drops of orange flower water, rosewater, or lemon juice to the water, or scatter rose petals or jasmine flowers to leave a pleasant scent on the fingers.

● **Warming water** If you are serving sticky or fatty foods, such as spare ribs, warm the water to hand-hot for finger bowls, and put them out just before you serve the food.

PLAN OF ACTION

Remember these points before and during a party.

● **Checking insurance** Check with an insurance broker in case you need special insurance for a large event.
● **Preparing ahead** Do as much as possible in advance to make sure that you are free to welcome guests.
● **Circulating among guests** Introduce guests to each other, and "rescue" anyone who is left on their own.
● **Drinking alcohol** Do not encourage guests to drink large quantities of alcohol.

WELCOMING GUESTS
● **Creating atmosphere** Depending on the occasion, tie a garland of fresh flowers, a lantern, or a bunch of balloons on a gatepost or a door to set the scene as guests approach the house.
● **Adjusting lighting** Before your guests arrive for a party, dim the house lights or light some candles around the rooms. Make sure that the light is soft but not too low, so that guests can see their food as well as each other.
● **Checking bathrooms** Check bathrooms and cloakrooms to make sure that they are clean, with soaps and towels put out for guests to use. Leave lights on if they are difficult to locate.

CREATING A FRAGRANT ATMOSPHERE

Place ingredients in small bowls

Making pot pourri
Instead of making a heavily flower-scented pot pourri, make a food-based mixture. Combine bay leaves, thinly pared or dried citrus zest, cinnamon sticks, rosemary sprigs, juniper or allspice berries, and star anise. Sprinkle with vanilla or almond essence.

● **Reviving pot pourri** Freshen up pot pourri that has lost its scent by spreading it on to a baking sheet, and sprinkling it with water or scented oil. Place in a hot oven for five minutes to draw out the fragrances.

● **Positioning bowls** Place bowls of pot pourri in the warmest areas of the room, such as on a mantelpiece, on a shelf above a table lamp, or around candles. The warmth will enhance the fragrances.

COPING WITH EMERGENCIES

Howeffer carefully you plan and prepare for entertaining, it is a good idea to be well prepared for emergencies. Whether someone experiences a medical problem or there is simply a spillage, remain calm so that you can deal with the situation quickly and effectively.

CLEANING SPILLS

● **Preventing permanent stains** If red wine is spilled on to a carpet, splash it with soda water. Pat with paper towels to soak up the excess liquid, and treat with carpet shampoo.

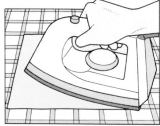

Removing candle wax
If candle wax drips on to a tablecloth, rub it with an ice cube, and chip off the wax. Cover with absorbent paper, and press with a warm iron. Dab with methylated spirit to remove any residue before washing.

PREVENTING PROBLEMS

● **Informing neighbours** If you are throwing a party, let the neighbours know, or invite them along, so that noise will not be a source of irritation.
● **Spot-cleaning** Have to hand a bottle of spot-cleaner or dry-cleaning fluid for dealing with minor spills as they occur.
● **Noting useful numbers** At a children's party, make sure that you have each parent's telephone number, and keep the number of the nearest hospital by the telephone.
● **Avoiding spoiled food** If cooking food such as a soufflé, the timing of which is critical, ensure that it will not be ready before it is due to be eaten.
● **Checking allergies** Be aware of any special dietary needs of guests, and ask parents if their children have food allergies.

COPING WITH DRINKERS

● **Preventing drink-driving** If a guest has drunk too much to drive, insist that a sober guest drives them home, or ring for a taxi. Alternatively, suggest they stay overnight.

SAFETY

If someone is choking, follow this first-aid technique:

1 Remove food or false teeth from the mouth. Encourage the victim to cough.

2 Place victim's head lower than the chest, and slap hard between shoulder blades.

3 Stand behind the person, and put your clenched fist – thumb inwards – underneath the breastbone. Hold the fist with the other hand, and pull firmly upwards and inwards.

CLEARING UP

Clearing up after a party need not spoil the fun. If you work in a sensible, organized manner, the task will be simple and quick. A dishwasher will help, but if you do not have one enlist as many people as possible to help with the washing up, drying, and putting away.

WORKING ORDER

Work in a logical order so that clearing up runs smoothly.

● **Clearing away** Load glasses, cutlery, crockery, ashtrays, and other items on to trays and carry them to the kitchen.
● **Removing food waste** Remove food debris from plates and serving dishes.
● **Soaking utensils** Soak crockery, glasses, and cutlery in a sink of soapy water.
● **Washing up** Wash up in the sink, or load the dishwasher.
● **Tidying up** Rinse, drain, and dry items, then put them away.

DRYING GLASSWARE

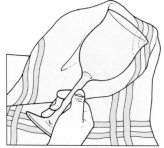

Avoiding damage
Cup the bowl of a stemmed glass in a tea towel when drying it, rotating the glass gently without twisting. Alternatively, rinse in clear water, and drain on a towel.

SAVING TIME & EFFORT

● **Heating water** Make sure that there is plenty of hot water for washing up.
● **Clearing the sink** Ensure that the sink or dishwasher is empty before starting to clear up.
● **Soaking cutlery** Prepare buckets of hot, soapy water, and drop cutlery into them to soak as it is cleared away.
● **Stocking up** Check that you have plenty of refuse sacks, disposable cloths, detergent, and paper towels in stock.
● **Emptying ash** Empty the contents of ashtrays into an old biscuit tin for safe disposal.

CHILDREN'S PARTIES

Good planning is the secret of success for children's parties and will make them fun for you as well as for the young guests. Start well in advance to organize food, space, and activities, and to enlist help from other parents on the day.

PREPARING FUN FOOD

Children's party food should be colourful, fun, and good to eat. Keep it simple and healthy, easy to hold in the hand, and in small mouthfuls. Encourage the children to eat more than just sweet foods by making savouries in fun shapes and colours to tempt fussy appetites.

MAKING NOVELTY CAKES

- **Using Swiss roll** Cover a ready-made Swiss roll with coloured, ready-to-roll fondant icing that is longer than the roll. Pinch the icing at each end so that it resembles a cracker. Decorate with coloured sweets.
- **Cutting bricks** For a young child's party, make individual cakes by cutting a sponge cake into blocks and covering with fondant. Pipe a child's initial on each piece, and pile up the cakes like play bricks.
- **Making a clock** Pipe a clock on a birthday cake, with the "time" showing the child's age.

DECORATING BISCUITS

Baking window biscuits
Roll out firm biscuit dough, and cut into shapes, then remove centres with a small cutter. Fill the holes with crushed, clear, boiled sweets. Bake until firm.

USING FRUIT NOVELTIES

Fill with ice-cream

Carving satsuma lanterns
Sculpt satsumas to look like Hallowe'en lanterns. Slice off the tops, scoop out the flesh, and carve faces into the skins. Fill, and replace the tops to serve.

FEEDING TODDLERS

- **Making traffic lights** Set layers of green, orange, and red jelly in clear tumblers. Let each layer set before adding the next.

Pipe melted chocolate for face and tail

Creating meringue mice
Make oval meringues, and bake at the coolest oven setting for 1½ hours. Stick halved chocolate buttons gently into the meringue for ears, and pipe other details.

SERVING HOT FOODS

- **Saving time** To make quick, individual pizzas, top crumpets or plain muffins with savoury toppings, and grill until golden.

Frankfurters resting against mashed-potato pyramid

Making a wigwam
Mould mashed potatoes into a pointed heap on a plate. Pile frankfurters or sausages around the outside of the potatoes to form a decorative wigwam shape.

FEEDING TEENAGERS

- **Choosing a theme** Try a Tex-Mex theme for a teenage party. Serve food such as tacos with fillings, salsas, chilli con carne, and guacamole.
- **Making mini-kebabs** Thread chunks of salami, cheese, cherry tomatoes, and button mushrooms on to bamboo skewers to serve with dips.
- **Filling pitta breads** Serve burgers in picnic-sized pitta breads. They will be easier and less messy to eat in the pitta than in burger buns.
- **Making iced bananas** Push lollipop sticks into peeled bananas, and freeze for 30 minutes. Dip in melted chocolate, and roll quickly in desiccated coconut. Serve while still slightly frozen.

MAKING PARTY DRINKS

Inventing children's drinks for parties can be fun, and you can be especially creative with the trimmings. Wherever possible, try to use healthy, nutritious ingredients, such as fresh fruit juices instead of fizzy, high-sugar drinks, and use fresh fruits for decoration or in ice cubes.

DECORATING DRINKS

● **Adding ice-cream** Put scoops of ice-cream into fruit juice or fizzy drinks just before serving. Half-fill glasses with the drink, add ice-cream, and serve.
● **Making lollipops** Freeze fruit juice on lollipop sticks to make drinks on sticks.
● **Decorating milk shakes** Sprinkle fruity milk shakes with grated chocolate or hundreds and thousands.
● **Freezing juices** Fill separate ice cube trays with apple, cranberry, and orange juices, and freeze overnight. Put mixed cubes into tall glasses, top up with clear lemonade, and decorate with fresh fruits.

DECORATING GLASSES

Use brightly coloured stickers

Using stick-on shapes
Instead of buying decorated party glasses, attach stick-on shapes to the outside of plain tumblers or plastic cups. Remove all the stickers before washing up.

ADDING EXTRAS

Making "magic" drinks
Delight children with this special effect. Freeze chocolate chips for 30 minutes, then add a handful to glasses of fizzy lemonade. The chips will bounce up and down.

USING FOOD FOR PARTY GAMES

Incorporate fun foods into party games. Plan energetic games, preferably outdoors, before the children eat. Hunting for edible treasure is popular. Use novelty foods for this or for quiet activities after the meal. If the weather is bad, try egg decorating with food marker pens.

MAKING EDIBLE GAMES

● **Icing domino biscuits** Pipe dots of white icing or cream cheese on to rectangular chocolate biscuits to make dominoes. Let the children play with the domino biscuits and then eat them when they have finished the game.

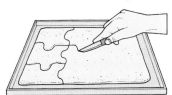

Baking a biscuit jigsaw
Roll out plain, firm biscuit dough. Cut jigsaw shapes in it. Bake and cool, then decorate with coloured icing or food colours. Let the children fit the shapes together before they eat the biscuits.

ENTERTAINING TODDLERS

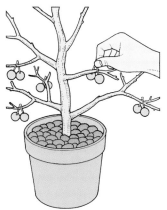

Making fruit trees
Encourage small children to eat fruit by making a "tree" for the table. Fill a plant pot with stones, and insert a small branch into it. Hang cherries, or tie other fruits to the branches, for children to pick.

PLAYING OUTDOORS

● **Apple bobbing** Float some apples in a large bowl or bucket of water. Ask each to try to bite an apple without using his or her hands. The first child to do so wins the game.
● **Egg-and-spoon racing** Hold a race with each child carrying a hard-boiled egg in a spoon. The winner is the first to finish without dropping the egg.
● **Passing the orange** Form two teams. Put an orange under the chin of each team leader. The winning team is the first to pass the orange along the team line without using their hands.
● **Playing noughts and crosses** Bake bread dough into large 0s and Xs. Mark a grid on an old sheet, and lay it down. Let the children place the shapes.

BARBECUES

H OWEVER BASIC THE EQUIPMENT AND SIMPLE THE FOOD, barbecues are often more fun and the food better-tasting than meals cooked indoors. With planning, they can set you free from the kitchen, and fresh air will sharpen the appetite.

SETTING UP BARBECUES

T here are many well-designed, sophisticated barbecues on the market today that are very easy to light, control, and clean. It is not essential, however, to spend a lot of money on barbecue equipment. You can improvise quite successfully using only basic equipment.

BUILDING A SIMPLE BARBECUE

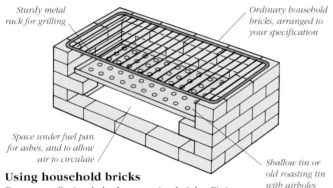

Sturdy metal rack for grilling

Ordinary household bricks, arranged to your specification

Space under fuel pan for ashes, and to allow air to circulate

Shallow tin or old roasting tin with airholes

Using household bricks

Erect a small, simple barbecue using bricks. Fit it with a metal grill rack and a pan in which to place the fuel. If the barbecue is to be permanent, then line the inside with fireproof bricks.

PREPARING FIRES

● **Using foil** Line the base of a barbecue with foil before adding fuel to reflect heat and to make cleaning easy.
● **Lighting fuel** If you find charcoal briquettes difficult to light, buy a bag of easy-light charcoal. It is clean and safe to use, since you need not handle the charcoal. Just place the specially designed bag of fuel in position, and light it.
● **Burning wood** Choose hardwoods from a sustainable source. Woods such as apple, oak, or cherry will burn slowly without spitting or smoking.

PREPARING TO COOK

● **Adding flavour** Instead of buying expensive bags of hickory or oak chips for a flavoured, smoky taste, scatter sprigs or twigs of juniper, rosemary, thyme, or fennel over the fire just before cooking. Soak them in water first to make them last.
● **Greasing racks** Keep trimmed meat fat for rubbing over a barbecue rack before placing food on it to prevent food from sticking. Alternatively, brush the rack with oil.
● **Heating up** Wait for the flames to die down before starting to cook. Charcoal takes at least 25–30 minutes to heat up, and gas barbecues take 10 minutes. Coals should be ash-grey in colour.

PREVENTING PROBLEMS

● **Avoiding flare-ups** To prevent a fire from flaring up, do not add too much oil to marinades, and trim excess fat from meat.
● **Controlling a fire** Keep a bucket of sand and a water spray nearby in case a fire flares up out of control.

SAFETY

● **Site** Choose a firm, level surface away from buildings and out of the wind.
● **Children and pets** Keep them away from the fire.
● **Protection** Use long-handled tools and insulated gloves.
● **Fire control** Let the fire heat naturally. Never add petrol.
● **First aid** Keep a first-aid kit handy in case of accidents.

MONEY-SAVING TIP

Using a biscuit tin

To make a small, impromptu picnic barbecue, punch holes around the sides of an old biscuit tin. Fill the tin with barbecue fuel, and place a metal grill rack or a piece of chicken wire on top to hold the food for grilling.

CHAR-GRILLING FOODS

Cooking foods on an open grill directly over charcoal will give them a unique, smoky flavour, and using robust marinades, herbs, and spices will give additional impact. Plan the order of char-grilling carefully so that foods receive the precise amount of cooking that they need.

COOKING EVENLY

● **Precooking foods** Make sure that meat and poultry are well cooked by precooking in the microwave. Transfer them immediately to the barbecue.
● **Parboiling potatoes** Parboil new potatoes for five minutes, then thread them on to metal skewers. Brush with oil, and grill for 8–10 minutes.
● **Using heat zones** Use the cooler, outer edges around the grill to avoid overcooking food that needs gentle heat such as vegetables or fruits.
● **Controlling heat** If your barbecue has no heat control, raise and lower the grill rack to control the heat. Sear meats such as steaks about 4–5 cm (1½–2 in) above the coals, then raise the rack to finish cooking on a lower heat.

ADDING FLAVOUR

● **Spicing vegetables** Toss vegetables such as corn on the cob in butter or oil, and sprinkle with Cajun or curry spice.

Spread pesto with pastry brush

Glazing food with pesto
Brush low-fat food such as turkey or chicken breasts with pesto to add flavour and to keep the flesh moist during cooking. Pesto will also impart a rich, Mediterranean flavour to the dish.

QUICK VEGETARIAN DISHES

● **Char-grilled vegetables** Brush halved aubergines, peppers, courgettes, and onions with oil, and grill until golden and tender.
● **Aubergine rolls** Slice an aubergine lengthways, brush with oil, and grill until tender. Wrap around sticks of feta cheese and basil leaves, then grill lightly.
● **Garlic bruscetta** Grill whole bulbs of garlic until tender. Brush slices of bread with olive oil, and grill. Squeeze the garlic on to the bread, and sprinkle with basil.
● **Tofu kebabs** Thread cubes of tofu on to kebab skewers with cherry tomatoes, mushrooms, and courgettes. Brush with oil, and grill.

WRAPPING FOODS

Some foods benefit from a little protection to prevent them from drying out or breaking up in the fierce heat of a barbecue. To seal in juices and keep foods moist, use natural wrappings such as vine leaves, corn husks, or banana leaves, or wrap foods in foil, and cook gently.

USING VINE LEAVES

Overlap vine leaves, enclosing food completely

Wrapping fish
Use vine leaves to wrap delicate foods such as fish to prevent them from drying out or breaking up during cooking. If you are using fresh vine leaves, blanch first for one minute to soften.

USING CORN HUSKS

Wrapping chicken
Retain unwanted husks from corn on the cob, and use them to wrap chicken breasts stuffed with dried apricots. Use several layers of husk to keep the chicken moist during cooking.

TRYING NEW IDEAS

● **Using bacon** Slice large sausages lengthways, and spread with mustard or pickle. Wrap in streaky bacon, secure with cocktail sticks, and cook.
● **Making calzone** Use pizza dough to enclose pizza-style toppings. Fold the dough in half, then pinch the edges together to seal them. Brush with oil before grilling.
● **Making fruit parcels** Wrap fruits in foil with a dash of liqueur and a knob of butter.
● **Cooking in skins** Grill whole bananas, turning occasionally, for 6–8 minutes. Slit the skins, and serve with maple syrup.

PICNICS

PICNICKING IS IN MANY RESPECTS THE IDEAL WAY to enjoy good food and company. It enables you to eat in a favourite beauty spot or at an outdoor event. Whatever the occasion, keep picnics simple for maximum fun and minimum fuss.

MAKING PICNIC FOOD

The type of picnic you are planning will determine your selection of food. For a walking trip, food will need to be packed into a small space, and must be eaten in the hand. If you are travelling by car, you will be able to pack more sophisticated foods and equipment.

MAKING SANDWICHES
● **Freezing in advance** Make sandwiches for a picnic in advance, and freeze them. Fillings containing hard-boiled eggs, mayonnaise, or salad are not suitable for freezing.
● **Making crab bites** For bite-sized sandwiches, stamp out shapes from bread using a biscuit cutter. Then pipe with cream cheese from a tube, and wrap around crab sticks. Secure the bites with cocktail sticks, and pack into boxes.
● **Mixing breads** Add interest to sandwiches by using wholemeal and white bread together with a filling between.

ADDING VARIETY

Damp towel prevents bread from cracking

Rolling pinwheels
Cut the crusts from thinly sliced bread, and spread with butter. Place on a dampened tea towel, spread with filling, and roll up inside the towel. Then slice to create pinwheel shapes.

USING WHOLE LOAVES

Wrap tightly in foil

Filling a baguette
Instead of packing individual, filled rolls for a picnic, split a long baguette lengthwise. Drizzle the surface with olive oil, add a savoury filling, and wrap. Slice into portions at the picnic site.

TRANSPORTING DESSERTS

Dip sliced fruit into purée

Serving a fruit dip
Purée fresh fruits, such as strawberries or mangoes, with honey to taste. Pour into a small plastic container, and transport to the picnic site inside a larger container together with sliced fruits for dipping into the purée.

CHOOSING EASY FOODS
● **Serving crudités** Pack a basket of simple, fresh crudités with a tub of garlic mayonnaise for easy eating without plates. Choose vegetables that require little preparation, such as whole baby carrots, baby sweetcorn, radishes, mushrooms, and cooked new potatoes.
● **Packing individual portions** Take individual quiches or pies instead of a large one, so that they can be eaten easily in the hand, and there will be no need to slice into portions.
● **Wrapping potatoes** For cold-weather picnics, wrap baked jacket potatoes in foil. Pack in several layers of newspaper or in an insulated bag to keep them hot during transportation.

BRIGHT IDEA

Stacking desserts
Make individual mousses or crème brûlées in small ramekins, then stack them together with a piece of card between each one. Wrap the whole stack in clingfilm for transportation.

Choosing Equipment

There is no need to buy lots of specialist equipment for picnics, but an insulated cool bag with ice-packs is essential for keeping food cold and fresh, especially in summer. Disposable plates and glasses are lighter and safer to carry than crockery and save on washing up.

Selecting Containers
● **Packing foods** Use square food containers where possible, since they are easier to stack than round ones and therefore take up less space. Round plastic containers often have good seals, so use these for transporting liquids.
● **Choosing food flasks** Use wide-necked food flasks to keep foods such as fruit salad cold. They can also be used to keep casseroles or soups hot.
● **Using boxes** If you do not have a wicker picnic hamper, use a large cardboard box instead. It will hold more and will be easier to pack than a traditional picnic hamper.

Using Camping Stoves

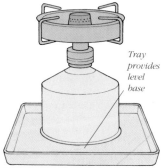

Tray provides level base

Making a firm base
If you take a small portable camping stove on a picnic, make sure that you use it safely. Before lighting, place it on a metal tray on a level piece of ground, well away from plants and trees.

Picnic Checklist

Check that you have packed the following useful items:

● Salt and pepper.
● Paper napkins or towels.
● Corkscrew.
● Sharp knife for cutting bread and other foods.
● Plastic or paper plates, glasses, and cutlery.
● Serving spoons.
● Drinking water.
● Picnic rug or tablecloth.
● Large umbrella.
● Dampened disposable cloth in a polythene bag.
● Insect repellent.
● First-aid kit.
● Refuse bag for clearing up.

Packing Foods

Packing food for a picnic is largely a matter of common sense. With a little careful planning, your food will arrive at the intended picnic site cool, undamaged, and ready to eat. A general rule is to pack heavy or unsquashable items first, and to put more delicate items on top of them.

Transporting Salads
● **Leaving space** Pack salads loosely into rigid containers to prevent crushing, and to allow the ingredients to breathe.

Packing a dressing
To keep the crispness of a leaf salad, toss it with the dressing at the picnic site. Transport the dressing in a screw-top jar packed in the same container as the salad.

Packing Small Items

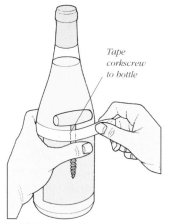

Tape corkscrew to bottle

Packing a corkscrew
To ensure that you remember to take a corkscrew, and to make it easy to find at the picnic site, tape a corkscrew to a bottle of wine using masking tape.

Preventing Problems
● **Using tissue paper** Place tarts with delicate edges in rigid boxes, and surround them with crumpled tissue paper for protection during transportation.
● **Wrapping glasses and china** Carefully wrap drinking glasses or china plates that you are taking on a picnic in bubble wrap to prevent damage.
● **Packing bottled drinks** Lie bottles on their side in ice in a covered cool box to keep them cool and avoid breakage.
● **Packing foods in order** As far as possible, pack foods in the order they will be needed, with desserts at the bottom.
● **Avoiding spills** Leave fizzy drinks to stand for a while after the journey so that they do not over-fizz when opened.

IMPROMPTU ENTERTAINING

THE MOST ENJOYABLE MEALS are often the ones that have not been planned – for example, when guests arrive unexpectedly. You will be able to cope with these occasions easily if you keep certain items in stock and use them creatively.

PREPARING STAND-BY FOODS

Always keep your kitchen storecupboard well stocked, so that if you have to entertain at short notice you will be prepared. Everyday foods can quickly be transformed into impressive dishes with a little imagination. Keep a stock of luxury foods to add last-minute special touches.

STORING IN THE FREEZER
● **Making individual portions** When freezing main dishes or desserts to keep as stand-bys, freeze in one-portion packs so that you can remove just as many servings as you need.
● **Freezing stuffings** Make rich fruit or herb stuffings for meat and poultry, and store them in the freezer to use on special occasions in the future.
● **Making bruscetta** Slice ciabatta bread, and reassemble for freezing. When guests arrive, spread the frozen slices with pesto sauce, sprinkle with grated cheese, and bake until golden. Serve with salad.

FREEZING CREAM

Pipe rosettes in well-spaced rows

Piping rosettes
Store cream rosettes in the freezer, ready to remove for a last-minute decoration. Pipe on to a baking sheet lined with non-stick paper. Freeze until solid, then pack in rigid boxes to store.

FREEZING PANCAKES

Interleaving with paper
When you cook pancakes, make more than you need, and freeze those you do not use. Interleave with non-stick paper, overwrap, and freeze. You will be able to remove as many as you need.

USING BASIC STORES
● **Serving snacks** Keep jars of olives, nuts, and savoury nibbles in the storecupboard to serve with drinks while you are preparing a meal for unexpected guests.
● **Making antipasto** Combine canned or bottled ingredients such as artichoke hearts, sun-dried tomatoes, cannellini beans, sardines, and pimentos to make a quick antipasto. Serve with crusty bread.
● **Creating rice dishes** Mix canned or frozen long-grain rice with a variety of foods such as flaked salmon or tuna and vegetables such as peas or sweetcorn. Heat gently before serving as a main course, or serve cold as a salad.

STORECUPBOARD PUDDINGS

Stuffing pancakes
Thaw frozen pancakes in the microwave, fold into quarters, and fill with canned fruits. Heat until bubbling, and serve with cream or ice-cream.

● **Baked peach snowballs** Fill the hollows of canned peach halves with mincemeat or crumbled macaroon biscuits, cover the peaches completely with meringue, and bake until "snowballs" are golden in colour.

● **Apple fool** Mix together canned apple purée and ready-made, canned custard. Spoon the mixture into serving dishes, and top with toasted nuts.
● **Raspberry rice** Stir frozen raspberries into canned rice pudding, and spoon into dessert glasses to serve.
● **Pears in port** Drain canned pear halves, and arrange the fruits in a shallow dish. Pour over enough port to cover, and chill before serving.
● **Fried pineapple rings** Drain canned pineapple rings, and sauté them gently in butter until they are golden in colour. Sprinkle with brown sugar and a little brandy. Serve hot with cream or ice-cream.

CATERING FOR EXTRA GUESTS

If you find yourself with an extra mouth to feed, and it is too late to go shopping, think quickly and add extras to what you are already cooking. Bulk out casseroles with canned or frozen vegetables, offer bread with each course, and serve fresh fruits as well as a dessert.

ADDING TOPPINGS

● **Topping with cheese** To extend a vegetable dish, pour over a cheese sauce and flaked almonds, then grill.

Shaping a dough topping
Roll out savoury scone dough, and cut into shapes with a biscuit cutter. Arrange the dough shapes over a casserole filling, and bake in a hot oven for 12–15 minutes.

INCREASING QUANTITIES

● **Adding stock** Increase the volume of a soup by adding a well-flavoured stock or a glass of dry white wine. Heat until boiling, and then stir in cream to taste before serving.
● **Adding beans** To bulk out cooked rice, stir in a can of drained kidney beans or chick-peas and a few chopped herbs.
● **Stirring in oats** Add a handful of porridge oats and a can of chopped tomatoes to extend a bolognese sauce.
● **Serving a starter** To make a quick and easy starter to accompany a main meal, serve a sliced tomato and onion salad with crusty bread.
● **Serving accompaniments** Serve stuffing or complementary sauces to extend roast meats.

DOUBLING UP DESSERTS

Alternate fruit fool and cream layers

Layering with cream
If you have made a fruit fool or mousse that is not sufficient to feed extra guests, increase the number of portions by layering the fruit with cream in tall glasses.

ENHANCING BASIC DISHES

If you are faced with making an everyday family meal into something more exciting for visitors, create a sense of occasion by combining ingredients in unusual ways. Pep up casseroles with crispy, herbed croutons, or spoon desserts into pretty glasses instead of plain bowls.

SERVING SOUPS

Combining colours
Make canned soups special by lightly swirling two contrasting colours together. Cream soups work best, and good partners are tomato with asparagus or celery with green pea.

EMBELLISHING DESSERTS

Finish with biscuits for crunchy topping

Layering ingredients
Sprinkle canned fruit with sherry or brandy, and serve with a store-bought dessert such as lemon mousse. Alternate layers of each with crumbled biscuits, and spoon into attractive glasses.

BRIGHT IDEA

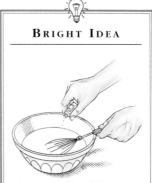

Flavouring longlife cream
Mask the distinctive flavour of longlife cream by whisking in a few drops of vanilla essence or rosewater to taste before adding it to a dessert.

COOKING MEASUREMENTS

SUCCESSFUL COOKING OFTEN DEPENDS UPON ACCURATE MEASUREMENT. If you lack the experience to guess amounts accurately, make sure that you have reliable kitchen scales, a measuring jug, standard measuring spoons, and a good oven.

HANDY CONVERSIONS

Many recipes give measurements in both metric and imperial units. Use whichever system you prefer, but do not mix the two, since they are not interchangeable. Teaspoons and tablespoons are always treated as level measurements and should not be heaped.

REPLACING WEIGHTS
● **Using coins** If you lose small weights from your kitchen scales, use coins instead to avoid buying new weights. Substitute a 20-pence coin for a 5-g weight and a £1-coin for a 10-g weight. For imperial weights, you can use a 2-pence coin as a ¼-oz weight.

SAVING TIME
● **Using spoons** Use level, standard-sized measuring spoons to measure small amounts of ingredients quickly. For easy reference, 45 ml (3 tbsp) flour, 30 ml (2 tbsp) butter, 15 ml (1 tbsp) golden syrup, and 30 ml (2 tbsp) rice are all equal to 25 g (1 oz).

MEASURING LIQUIDS
● **Using everyday items** If you do not have a measuring jug, use other kitchen items to measure liquids. A small yoghurt pot or an average-sized teacup will each hold about 150 ml (¼ pint). An empty 400-g (14-oz) can of tomatoes will hold 425 ml (15 fl oz).

APPROXIMATE METRIC/IMPERIAL EQUIVALENTS

WEIGHT		VOLUME		LENGTH	
METRIC	IMPERIAL	METRIC	IMPERIAL	METRIC	IMPERIAL
15 g	½ oz	1.25 ml	¼ tsp	3 mm	⅛ in
25 g	1 oz	2.5 ml	½ tsp	5 mm	¼ in
50 g	1¾ oz	5 ml	1 tsp	1 cm	½ in
75 g	2¾ oz	10 ml	2 tsp	2 cm	¾ in
100 g	3½ oz	15 ml	1 tbsp/3 tsp	2.5 cm	1 in
125 g	4½ oz	30 ml	2 tbsp/1 fl oz	3 cm	1¼ in
150 g	5½ oz	45 ml	3 tbsp	4 cm	1½ in
175 g	6 oz	50 ml	2 fl oz	5 cm	2 in
200 g	7 oz	100 ml	3½ fl oz	6 cm	2½ in
225 g	8 oz	125 ml	4 fl oz	7 cm	2¾ in
300 g	10½ oz	200 ml	7 fl oz/⅓ pint	8 cm	3¼ in
325 g	11½ oz	250 ml	9 fl oz	9 cm	3½ in
350 g	12 oz	300 ml	10 fl oz/½ pint	10 cm	4 in
400 g	14 oz	400 ml	14 fl oz	12 cm	4½ in
425 g	15 oz	450 ml	16 fl oz	13 cm	5 in
450 g	1 lb	500 ml	18 fl oz	14 cm	5½ in
500 g	1 lb 2 oz	600 ml	1 pint/20 fl oz	15 cm	6 in
750 g	1 lb 10 oz	700 ml	1¼ pints	16 cm	6¼ in
1 kg	2 lb 4 oz	1 litre	1¾ pints	17 cm	6½ in
1.25 kg	2 lb 12 oz	1.2 litres	2 pints	18 cm	7 in
1.5 kg	3 lb 5 oz	1.5 litres	2¾ pints	19 cm	7½ in
2 kg	4 lb 8 oz	2 litres	3½ pints	20 cm	8 in
2.25 kg	5 lb	2.5 litres	4½ pints	22 cm	8½ in
2.5 kg	5 lb 8 oz	3 litres	5¼ pints	23 cm	9 in
2.7 kg	6 lb	3.5 litres	6 pints	25 cm	10 in
3 kg	6 lb 8 oz	4 litres	7 pints	30 cm	12 in

TEMPERATURE CONVERSIONS

Most recipes specify a cooking temperature to ensure the best results. Ovens vary according to type, fuel used, and fluctuations in power, so you may need to make adjustments if a dish is cooking more quickly or slowly than the suggested cooking time in the recipe.

OVEN TEMPERATURE CONVERSIONS			
DESCRIPTION	°C	°F	GAS
COOL	110°C	225°F	¼
	120°C	250°F	½
WARM	140°C	275°F	1
	150°C	300°F	2
MODERATE	170°C	325°F	3
	180°C	350°F	4
FAIRLY HOT	190°C	375°F	5
	200°C	400°F	6
HOT	220°C	425°F	7
	230°C	450°F	8
VERY HOT	240°C	475°F	9

MAXIMIZING OVEN USE
● **Baking dishes together** To bake several dishes that each require different temperatures together, adjust cooking times instead. With the oven on a moderate setting, cook dishes requiring a higher temperature for longer, and those needing a lower temperature for less.

USING A FAN OVEN
● **Adjusting times** Reduce cooking times in a fan-assisted oven by 5–10 minutes per hour, or reduce the oven temperature by 10–20°C (20–50°F), since a fan-assisted oven will cook food faster than a conventional oven. Check the manufacturer's handbook for specific timings.

ROASTING TEMPERATURES

Use these roasting times as a rough guide only, since they will vary according to the cut of meat. Meat on the bone will cook more quickly, since bone conducts heat. Beef, lamb, and duck may be served rare, but other meat must be cooked until the juices run clear.

ROASTING TEMPERATURES AND TIMES					
MEAT TYPE		°C	°F	GAS	APPROXIMATE COOKING TIME
BEEF	rare	200°C	400°F	6	20 minutes per 500 g (1 lb 2 oz) + 20 minutes
	medium	200°C	400°F	6	25 minutes per 500 g (1 lb 2 oz) + 20 minutes
	well done	200°C	400°F	6	30 minutes per 500 g (1 lb 2 oz) + 20 minutes
LAMB		180°C	350°F	4	30 minutes per 500 g (1 lb 2 oz) + 30 minutes
PORK		180°C	350°F	4	35 minutes per 500 g (1 lb 2 oz) + 35 minutes
CHICKEN		180°C	350°F	4	25 minutes per 500 g (1 lb 2 oz) + 25 minutes
TURKEY		190°C	375°F	5	20 minutes per 500 g (1 lb 2 oz) + 20 minutes
DUCK		190°C	375°F	5	30 minutes per 500 g (1 lb 2 oz) + 30 minutes
GOOSE		180°C	350°F	4	30 minutes per 500 g (1 lb 2 oz) + 30 minutes

NUTRITIONAL INFORMATION

A HEALTHY DIET IS IMPORTANT TO EVERYONE, young or old, and not only helps to prevent heart disease, tooth decay, and obesity, but protects against some serious illnesses. Achieving a balanced diet is easy and can be enjoyable.

BALANCING YOUR DIET

The nutritional value of any diet depends upon a good balance of all the essential nutrients. The best way to achieve this is to eat a variety of foods from all the different food groups. Try to eat at least one balanced meal every day, and limit unhealthy snacks.

INCREASING FIBRE
● **Serving wholemeal bread** Switch from white to wholemeal bread, and use less filling and more bread in sandwiches.
● **Varying salads** Mix beans, rice, or pasta into green salads.
● **Eating healthy snacks** Serve wholemeal toast with peanut butter instead of sweet biscuits.

REDUCING SUGAR
● **Cutting down gradually** If you add sugar to drinks, reduce the amount gradually, and you will not notice the difference.
● **Buying fruits** Keep fruits handy to replace sugary snacks.
● **Adding mineral water** Dilute fruit juices with mineral water to reduce natural sugar intake.

REDUCING FAT
● **Using substitutes** Consider using minced turkey in recipes instead of minced beef or lamb, since it is much lower in fat.
● **Spreading butter thinly** If you like butter on bread, soften it first for a few seconds in the microwave so that it will be easy to spread thinly.

RECOMMENDED DAILY INTAKE OF ESSENTIAL FOODS

Choosing food for a balanced diet
To achieve a balanced diet, you should eat the right amounts of the foods that provide protein, vitamins, carbohydrate, fibre, and minerals every day. This pyramid shows the number of servings of each type of food you should eat, and lists a selection of sample servings.

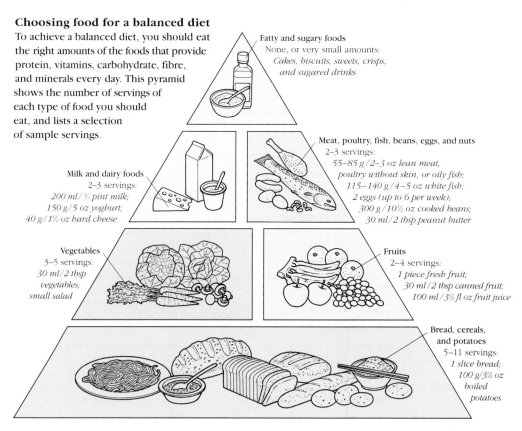

Fatty and sugary foods
None, or very small amounts:
Cakes, biscuits, sweets, crisps, and sugared drinks

Meat, poultry, fish, beans, eggs, and nuts
2–3 servings:
55–85 g/2–3 oz lean meat, poultry without skin, or oily fish; 115–140 g/4–5 oz white fish; 2 eggs (up to 6 per week); 300 g/10½ oz cooked beans; 30 ml/2 tbsp peanut butter

Milk and dairy foods
2–3 servings:
200 ml/⅓ pint milk; 150 g/5 oz yoghurt; 40 g/1½ oz hard cheese

Vegetables
3–5 servings:
30 ml/2 tbsp vegetables; small salad

Fruits
2–4 servings:
1 piece fresh fruit; 30 ml/2 tbsp canned fruit; 100 ml/3½ fl oz fruit juice

Bread, cereals, and potatoes
5–11 servings:
1 slice bread; 100 g/3½ oz boiled potatoes

Eating the Right Nutrients

A well-balanced diet should include all the vitamins and minerals listed below. Many of them cannot be stored in the body, so they need to be included in your diet on a daily basis. Specific dietary requirements vary from person to person, but use this chart as a guide.

IMPORTANT VITAMINS AND MINERALS		
NUTRIENT	GOOD SOURCES	FUNCTIONS IN THE BODY
VITAMIN A	Milk and dairy foods, oily fish and fish-liver oils, liver, butter, margarine, spinach, carrots, dried apricots and yellow fruits, nuts and seeds.	Aids vision in dim light; essential for growth of healthy skin and normal development of tissues, especially those that secrete mucus.
B-GROUP VITAMINS	Fortified breakfast cereals, meat, offal, fish, cheese, bread, yeast extract, eggs, whole cereals.	Encourage release of energy for growth; repair and maintain nervous system; aid muscle and heart function; encourage healthy skin and hair.
VITAMIN C	Citrus fruits and juice, lightly cooked green vegetables such as Brussels sprouts and cabbage, potatoes, all fresh fruits, especially blackcurrants.	Maintains healthy skin, gums, teeth, and blood vessels; essential for iron absorption. Heavy smoking and drinking increase the need for Vitamin C.
VITAMIN D	Oily fish, margarine, eggs, fortified breakfast cereals.	Controls calcium and phosphorus levels in blood; develops strong bones.
VITAMIN E	Vegetable oils, wholemeal cereals, butter, eggs, animal fats, green vegetables, nuts.	Helps body cells to function properly; protects essential fats against oxidization.
IRON	Meat, especially liver and kidneys, bread, flour and other cereals, vegetables.	Vital component of red blood cells, which carry oxygen from lungs to cells.
CALCIUM	Milk, cheese, bread and flour, green vegetables, canned sardines and salmon.	Develops strong bones and teeth; aids muscle development and blood clotting.
PHOSPHORUS	Milk and milk products, bread and other cereals, meat and meat products.	Develops healthy bones and teeth; is essential for release of energy.
MAGNESIUM	Milk, bread and other cereal products, potatoes and other vegetables.	Essential constituent of all cells; is necessary for utilization of energy.
SODIUM	Salt, yeast extract, bacon, sausages, bread, processed foods.	Essential for maintaining water balance and for muscle and nerve activity.
POTASSIUM	Vegetables, meat and milk, fruits and fruit juices.	Works with sodium in the functioning of muscles and nerve cells.
ZINC	Meat and meat products, milk, bread and other cereal products, oysters, sardines.	Needed for development of reproductive organs, healthy teeth, immune system.
TRACE ELEMENTS	*Copper* meat/vegetables; *iodine* seafood/milk; *fluorine* water/seafood; *selenium* meat/fish/cereals; *chromium* widely distributed.	All known to be essential. Research is ongoing to discover specific roles and consequences of dietary deficiencies.

USEFUL COOKING TERMS

THIS GLOSSARY EXPLAINS THE MEANING of common cooking terms that are used but not fully explained in the text of this book. The list includes equipment, ingredients, cooking techniques, dishes, and other culinary terms.

● **Al dente** An Italian term describing cooked pasta that is just firm to the bite.

● **Antipasti** An Italian term for hot or cold hors d'oeuvres.

● **Au gratin** A French term describing a dish topped with a sauce, sprinkled with breadcrumbs or cheese, and grilled or baked until golden.

● **Bain marie** A French term describing a pan or dish half-filled with hot water in which a container of food is cooked. The water is kept heated to just below boiling point.

● **Baking blind** Part-baking a pastry case for a tart or flan. The pastry is weighed down, with baking beans for example, to prevent it from rising and from remaining uncooked beneath a moist filling.

● **Barding** Tying bacon or pork fat over meat or poultry before roasting to keep it moist and eliminate the need for basting.

● **Basting** Brushing or spooning liquid fat or juices over meat or poultry during roasting to prevent it from drying out while cooking.

● **Beignet** A French term describing a sweet fritter lightened with whisked egg whites and often flavoured with ground almonds.

● **Beurre manié** A French term for a paste made by kneading together equal parts of butter and flour. The paste is used to thicken sauces and stews.

● **Blanching** Plunging foods into boiling water for a short time to reduce strong flavours, whiten, preserve colour, destroy bacteria, or parboil.

● **Bouquet garni** A French term describing a small bunch of herbs, tied together or wrapped in muslin, that is added to stews or casseroles for flavour.

● **Braising** Baking or stewing meat, poultry, or vegetables in a small amount of liquid in a covered pot.

● **Brine** A salt and water solution, in which food is immersed for preserving.

● **Brûlée** A French term describing a dish that has been sprinkled with sugar and grilled until a caramelized crust has formed on top.

● **Canapés** A French term describing small, bite-sized appetizers served with drinks.

● **Caramel** A dark, toffee-like substance made by heating sugar or sugar syrup until it turns a rich, golden brown.

● **Casserole** A covered baking dish used for cooking stews in the oven; the name of dishes cooked by this method.

● **Char-grilling** Cooking food, unwrapped, on an open grill directly over charcoal to allow the unique, smoky flavour of the fuel to penetrate the food.

● **Clarifying** Removing impurities from butter or stock by heating the liquid, then skimming or straining it.

● **Compote** A mixture of fruits cooked in a syrup. The mixture is usually served warm.

● **Coulis** A French term describing a liquid purée of a pourable consistency used as a sauce. Usually made of fruit.

● **Creaming** Beating together fat and sugar. Used as the basis of some cake mixtures.

● **Crêpe** A large, thin, French-style pancake that may be either sweet or savoury.

● **Crockpot** An electric casserole that simmers food very slowly over a long period.

● **Croûtons** A French term describing small pieces of fried or toasted bread used for garnishing soups or salads. A croûte is toasted bread on which food is served; en croûte describes baked food wrapped in pastry, while a croustade is a fried bread or pastry case in which hot, savoury mixtures are served.

● **Crudités** Raw vegetables cut into sticks to be dipped into a sauce as an appetizer or an hors d'oeuvre.

● **Crystallize** To form into crystals. This occurs in sugar- or honey-based syrups. The term also describes the coating of fruits or flowers with sugar.

● **Curdling** The separation of a food, usually as a result of the overheating of or the addition of an acid substance to milk- or egg-based sauces.

● **Decanting** Pouring a liquid such as wine or vinegar from its bottle into a clean container, leaving behind the sediment.

● **Deglazing** Diluting sediment or concentrated juices left in a pan after cooking meat by stirring in a liquid such as water, stock, or wine.

● **Dredging** Sprinkling lightly and evenly with flour or sugar. A dredger has holes pierced in the lid for even sprinkling.

● **Dusting** Sprinkling food lightly with flour, sugar, or spices for a light coating.

● **Emulsion** A mixture of two normally insoluble liquids. Droplets of oil, for instance, are suspended in vinegar in a vinaigrette dressing.

● **Flambé** A French term describing a dish that is sprinkled with alcohol and set alight. The alcohol burns off, but its flavour remains.

● **Flameproof** Describes equipment resistant to direct heat and oven heat, which can be used on a hob, under a grill, and in an oven.

● **Folding** Incorporating a light mixture into a heavier one – such as whisked egg whites into a cake mixture – by cutting and mixing lightly with a spoon to keep as much air in the mixture as possible.

● **Fool** A sweetened fruit purée mixed with whipped cream or custard to make a dessert.

● **Freezer burn** Dried out and discoloured patches on food, caused by a long period of exposure to air in the freezer, resulting in dehydration.

● **Frosting** A fluffy icing used to cover cakes; a coating of sugar around the rim of a glass.

● **Glazing** Brushing the surface of a food with a liquid such as beaten egg, milk, or honey to moisten the food or give the surface a glossy appearance.

● **Hulling** Removing the leafy parts from soft fruits such as strawberries or blackberries.

● **Infusing** Extracting the flavours of spices or herbs by soaking them in liquid heated in a covered pan.

● **Julienne strips** Vegetable pieces that have been cut very finely into matchstick slices.

● **Kneading** Working a dough firmly by pressing, stretching, and folding it with the hands.

● **Liaison** A thickening agent such as flour, egg yolk, cream, or beurre manié, that is used for thickening or binding sauces and soups.

● **Macerating** Softening food by soaking in a liquid or syrup.

● **Marinating** Soaking food in a seasoned liquid – usually a blend of oil, wine, and vinegar – to add flavour or to tenderize the texture.

● **Mocha** A combination of coffee and chocolate.

● **Mousse** A lightly set mixture, sweet or savoury, that is usually based on whisked eggs or egg whites.

● **Ovenproof** Describes equipment resistant to oven heat only, not direct heat.

● **Parboiling** Partly cooking food in water or stock.

● **Paring** Peeling or trimming a food, usually vegetables.

● **Peaks** The pinnacles of mounds created in a mixture, such as egg white, that has been whisked to stiffness. Peaks are either "soft", if they curl over, or "stiff", if they stay upright.

● **Pectin** A substance that is found naturally in fruits and vegetables, and is essential for setting jams and jellies. Artificially produced pectin can be bought in bottles.

● **Petits fours** French-style, bite-sized sweetmeats and cakes served with coffee.

● **Pilau/pilaf** A spiced, savoury rice dish, usually including meat, poultry, or fish.

● **Piquant** A French term meaning pleasantly sharp, pungent, or sour in flavour.

● **Pith** The white, fleshy part of citrus rind that lies just beneath the coloured zest.

● **Proving** Leaving dough or a yeasted mixture to rise.

● **Purée** A French term describing food that has been mashed, liquidized, or sieved until completely smooth.

● **Ramekin** A small, straight-sided ovenproof dish.

● **Reducing** Thickening a liquid mixture, such as a soup or sauce, by boiling uncovered to evaporate surplus liquid.

● **Refreshing** Pouring cold water over freshly cooked vegetables to retain colour and prevent further cooking; reviving limp salad ingredients by standing in cold water.

● **Rendering** Melting down solid fats to make dripping.

● **Rising** The expansion of dough or a yeast mixture as a result of the action of the yeast.

● **Roux** A French term describing a mixture of equal amounts of fat and flour that are cooked together as a basis for thickening sauces.

● **Sautéeing** A French term describing the continual tossing of food in shallow fat so that it browns evenly.

● **Scalding** Plunging fruits or vegetables into boiling water to facilitate the peeling of skins; heating a liquid to just below boiling point.

● **Skimming** Removing the surface layer of impurities, scum, or fat from liquids such as stocks and jams while cooking. This is usually done with a flat, slotted spoon.

● **Sweating** Cooking food, usually vegetables, very gently in melted fat to release juices for flavour, but without allowing the food to brown.

● **Syrup** A concentrated solution of sugar and water.

● **Tang** The prong of a knife blade embedded in the handle.

● **Terrine** An earthenware or china dish used for baking or steaming pâtés and potted meats; the name given to food that is cooked in this way.

● **Trussing** Tying or skewering meat or poultry into a neat shape before cooking.

● **Tuiles** A French term for thin, sweet biscuits shaped to resemble curved tiles.

● **Vintage** Wine from a particular year's harvest.

● **Zest** The outer, coloured part of citrus peel, which contains flavour in its oils.

INDEX

ACKNOWLEDGMENTS

AUTHOR'S ACKNOWLEDGMENTS

I would like to thank Jo Richardson, Judy Garlick, and Sarah Hall for their inspiration, patience, and thoroughness during the making of this book. Many thanks are also due to the rest of the Dorling Kindersley team, especially to Helen Benfield, Colette Connolly, Adèle Hayward, and Samantha Gray for all their hard work. Finally, I would like to thank my husband, Don Last, for giving such enduring support and enthusiasm.

PUBLISHER'S ACKNOWLEDGMENTS

Dorling Kindersley would like to thank the following:

Prop loan Elizabeth David Cookshop, Covent Garden, and MFI Furniture Centres Ltd.

Editorial and design assistance Samantha Gray and Adèle Hayward for editorial assistance, Austin Barlow for design assistance; Chris Bernstein for the index; and Debbi Scholes for proofreading.

Artworks by Kuo Kang Chen and John Woodcock, apart from additional artworks by Geoff Denney on pages 10–11, 12–13, 60–61, 77, 128, and 138.

Photographs by Andy Crawford, John Elliot, and Steve Gorton.
Photographic assistants Sarah Ashun and Gary Ombler.
Hand models Penelope Cream, Toby Heran, and Audrey Speitel.